NEW DEVELOPMENTS
IN
EDUCATIONAL ASSESSMENT

BRITISH JOURNAL OF EDUCATIONAL PSYCHOLOGY
MONOGRAPH SERIES No. 3

NEW DEVELOPMENTS

IN

EDUCATIONAL ASSESSMENT

Edited by
H. D. BLACK AND W. B. DOCKRELL

Published for
THE BRITISH JOURNAL OF EDUCATIONAL PSYCHOLOGY
by
SCOTTISH ACADEMIC PRESS
EDINBURGH

First published in Great Britain, 1988
for the British Journal of Educational Psychology
by Scottish Academic Press Limited,
33 Montgomery Street, Edinburgh EH7 5JX

ISBN 0 7073 0546 2

British Library Cataloguing in Publication Data

New Developments in Educational Assessment
(British Journal of Educational Psychology
Monograph Series; No. 3)
1. Education — Evaluation
I. Black, H.D. II. Dockrell, W.B.
III. Series 379.1′54 LA133

ISBN 0-7073-0546-2

Printed by Lindsay & Co. Ltd.
Edinburgh

Contents

INTRODUCTION

In the last five years or so there has been a marked change in emphasis in assessment in Britain, partly as a result of technical developments like criterion-referencing, partly as a result of classroom developments like graded testing and partly in response to new demands like profiling. This monograph contains papers which cover many of these new issues, all of them with an emphasis on the contribution of research.

The first paper is concerned with criterion-referencing. Sally Brown examines critically the notion of criterion-referencing and the role of research in its implementation. She emphasises the relationship between technology and policy decisions, the purposes of education and its control. There are questions about the 'how' of criterion-referencing which are being explored by a number of research teams, but more fundamental are the 'why' questions about what we expect from criterion-referencing which must also be addressed. The public or policy questions are more obvious in external examinations, but the fundamental political issues about what is to be expected of the schools are implicit in the uses of assessment within the schools.

The next group of papers is concerned with the working of external examinations. French and his colleagues are concerned to ensure that the assessments of candidates are fair and consistent. A major problem is the co-ordination of the marks of the many examiners required by the large number of candidates. There is inevitably an element of subjectivity. Marks are examiners' judgments of candidates' performances, which must be handled appropriately. These authors believe that it would be impossible to make an examination of the complexity of GCSE criterion-referenced, and support instead of the notion of 'limen-referencing', and describe the appropriate procedures.

Marion Devine examines the Scottish attempt to introduce grade-related criteria into Standard Grade assessment. The merits of the system, were it feasible, are clear; so are the difficulties which have been encountered. Her own research has been into the application of these criteria in the classroom where the question of comparability which is crucial for external examinations does not arise. Here teachers have found the approach helpful. In the case of external examinations the difficulties have been more obvious than the advantages so far, but Devine concludes that grade-related criteria, while being far from a simple and comprehensive criterion-referenced approach, is a substantial improvement on previous practice, acceptable in its own right.

The next three papers address three topics of increasing importance. David Pennycuick looks at some of the issues arising

vii

from the use of graded testing. Like Brown he sees this development as being embedded in broader issues of curriculum and instruction. As with Devine he concludes from his own research that teachers support graded testing because it benefits pupils more than what it has replaced.

Yates and Hall describe one of the recent modular programmes and the use of criterion-referenced assessment within it. They report their findings of the response within the Further Education Colleges in Scotland to this new approach. As with the other developments there are problems with the new ideas and with their implementation, but they too conclude that the new system is an important advance, offering opportunities for substantial benefits.

The accreditation of work-based learning poses its own problems. Criterion-referencing, however, is not one of them. The 'can do' statements seems the appropriate one for this kind of practical achievement. David Matthews analyses the process and draws attention to the multidimensional nature of performance and to the problems of specifying the situations that the assessed skills will transfer to. In common with the authors of a number of other chapters, he draws attention to the inappropriateness of the traditional psychometric models for what is a subjective decision-making process.

The three papers on the assessment of personal qualities address different issues. John Raven is concerned with the complexity of what he calls competencies, constructs like initiative, and as with Matthews, French and others, the inadequacy of traditional psychometric models. Analogies always have limitations, but his suggestion that chemical rather than physical equations are more apposite is suggestive, revealing the limitations of traditional methods and suggesting an alternative approach.

Records of Achievement are perhaps best thought of as structured and extended references, as French *et al.* suggest in their article. Many of them include statements about the personal qualities of pupils. There are many technical problems in making these assessments, and Bryan Dockrell describes the work of the Scottish team in trying to overcome, or at least mitigate them.

Harry Black uses the views of pupils to highlight the problems from new assessment and reporting procedures that are not fully understood by both pupils and parents. There were striking differences in the responses from the different case-study schools which seemed to be attributable to factors other than the actual reporting system used. Young people need to be actively involved in the assessment and reporting system if its value is to be fully realised.

The final two papers are concerned more directly with policy-making than the others. Patricia Broadfoot poses a number of fundamental questions about the implications and often unintended consequences of what are seen to be technical advances. In many of the other papers these implicit policy issues are recognised and addressed, by Pennycuick for example, but Broadfoot brings them together and looks at the whole pattern of recent developments. She, too, recognises the opportunities as well as the problems.

In the final paper Bryan Dockrell points out that technical excellence is no guarantee that research will guide policy or practice. He questions the value of national surveys as a source of information for policy, and advocates instead studies with a specific focus designed to throw light on specific issues.

Perhaps the most interesting feature of this collection is that 10 years ago the invitation we put out to contributors would have yielded very different responses. Criterion-referenced assessment was then a twinkle in the eye of a few British educationists who suspected that it had greater pedagogic potential than existing approaches. Assessment for diagnostic purposes was something teachers did with 'remedial' groups. Grade-related external examination systems, graded tests, modular assessments, work-based accreditation, profiling and records of achievement were not on the agenda, or if they were, they were not 'mainstream' issues.

In essence, then, what we have seen is the British assessment scene's coming of age. The prevailing assumption is that assessment should be offering what is required to satisfy the needs of education and not simply supplying what existing psychometric models dictate. If that means that the education tail has come to wag the assessment dog, progress has probably been made.

CRITERION-REFERENCED ASSESSMENT: WHAT ROLE FOR RESEARCH?

SALLY BROWN
Scottish Council for Research in Education

Introduction

Research on criterion-referenced assessment has been going on for more than a quarter of a century in North America, and has received considerable attention over the last decade on this side of the Atlantic. To the uninitiated (and many of the initiated) the field can seem something of a morass, and some have expressed the view that research has not provided the panacea for educational problems which this approach to assessment seemed to promise in the early years.

In response to such a view, I would wish to say three things. First, like many other educational ideas, criterion-referencing may have promised, or been interpreted as promising, much more than it could deliver. Secondly, by its very nature criterion-referenced assessment is intimately linked to a particular curriculum or to specific opportunities to learn; development of the assessment procedures, therefore, must be the responsibility of those who are closest to the curriculum and learning rather than of researchers. There is no way research can provide a comprehensive set of assessments to be selected 'off the shelf' to serve all the purposes which teachers and others may have. Thirdly, there are some things which research *can* be expected to address very effectively in relation to criterion-referencing, and research efforts should be concentrated on those rather than on specific development work which is better left to those who are closer to the assessments.

It is the third of these points towards which this paper is directed. The aim is to make a start on mapping out the kinds of things which research can, and cannot, be expected to accomplish. It first considers the matter of what is to count as 'research', and then attempts to identify and exemplify the kinds of questions which research can most usefully address. Illustrations are drawn from the assessment of pupils of secondary school age in Scotland and the (more sensitive) assessment of teachers.

Research to Inform Decisions

Research on criterion-referenced assessment, in common with the rest of research in education, is about *extending knowledge*. In the kind of research I am considering in this paper, that knowledge is

1

expected to be *relevant* to the educational issues which are of current concern in assessment, and the intention is to design research projects so they produce information which can be *used*.

The research can involve a variety of processes such as data gathering, analysis, development, evaluation, and clarification; these processes provide a means of generating information for decision-making. The kinds of decisions to which the information from the research will be relevant may be those of policy (making it or implementing it) or of practice (e.g. decisions about the formulation of assessment schemes or about the way to deal with classroom problems associated with the implementation of such schemes). In general, it will not be researchers themselves who make these decisions except in so far as they have other roles as teachers, administrators, curriculum developers, examiners or advisers.

This is not to say that decisions of policy and practice will be based solely on information available from research. A host of other political, administrative and practical factors are taken into account and this may well mean that decisions or actions taken often seem to fly in the face of research evidence. It may be the case that there was some other factor which, at the time, was over-whelmingly important to the decision-maker. More importantly perhaps, it has to be accepted that the knowledge which research creates often takes a substantial period of time to be understood and internalised by those who make the decisions; researchers have to be patient and judge the effect they have on policy thinking and practice over a period of years. And, most crucially, research is not (or should not be) designed to give the policy maker and practitioner the 'right answer'; it is best suited to a role of articulating the different decisions, or courses of action, which can be taken, and of developing an understanding of the implications of choosing among these alternatives. In other words, research does not tell anyone *what* they should do; its function is to explain why things are the way they are and what the consequences of deciding to change things in particular ways are likely to be.

If the findings of research are to be of value to anyone apart from the researchers themselves in their own specific contexts, then the knowledge generated by the enquiry has to be in some sense generalisable. This does not imply that it has to be generalisable in a probabilistic sense, and that the research must be restricted to large scale studies with a positivist approach, representative samples, experimental or survey designs and high powered statistics. But it does mean that if samples are small, or case study approaches are used, then the information conveyed by the research has to include enough detail of contextual and other variables to enable others to judge how similar is their own situation to that of the researcher. If that judgment can be made, then the extent to which one can generalise from the researcher's findings to other contexts can be inferred. This kind of 'naturalistic' generalisation, often from one single context to the next, does not have the quantifiable 'level of significance' of the probabilistic generalisation to back it up. It will always have the status of a testable hypothesis of the kind: 'In the researcher's context things seemed to work in this way with those consequences. I hypothesise, therefore, that in my context, which is in some ways similar and some not, "X" will be the same as, and "Y" will be different from, the researcher's findings.'

To summarise then, the researcher will not be in a position to offer 'the right answer' to a practical problem, or 'the correct' policy decision. What she or he can do is to enable the practitioner to have a better understanding of (i) the possibilities for 'action' that are available, and (ii) what is involved in choosing to resolve a problem, or formulate a policy, in a particular way. Perhaps the most important task for the researcher is to hold in question those things which practitioners may take for granted, and then make the practitioners aware of what they are taking for granted.

Broad Research Questions on Criterion-referenced Assessment

Within the general framework of what research can be expected to do, there is a wide range of questions which work on criterion-referenced assessment could address. The following identify four of the broad areas which the research might be expected to inform:

1. What is meant by criterion-referenced assessment and what purposes can it fulfil? Information arising from concern with this question will be relevant to decisions about whether or not to proceed with criterion-referenced assessment.

2. Where a decision is made to implement criterion-referenced assessment (or to explore the possibilities of implementation), how are criteria to be chosen, justified and elucidated? This question is relevant to decisions about what is to be assessed.

3. Where it is clear that there is some agreement on what is to be assessed, how is that assessment to be made and reported? Decisions about assessment procedures and systems depend on information of this kind.

4. What factors are likely to inhibit or encourage the introduction of any given set of procedures or system for criterion-referenced assessment? This relates to decisions about the implementation of procedures or systems for criterion-referenced assessment.

There is a variety of ways in which researchers can generate information relevant to these four broad questions. The rest of the paper is concerned with illustrating some of those processes.

Criterion-referenced Assessment: Meaning and Purposes

It may be important for the researcher to provide, at an early stage in any criterion-referencing initiative, a clarification of what 'criterion-referenced assessment' means to different groups or in particular contexts. This enables people to establish a shared understanding of what they are talking about *before* the disagreements arise. If that shared understanding is not established early on, then the debate will be caught up in innumerable trivial arguments.

What is not trivial, however, is the difference in expectations which people with different interpretations of CRA will have of such an approach. For example, anyone who adopts the following (my preferred) meaning of CRA

> 'Criterion-referenced assessment provides an evaluative description of the qualities which are to be assessed (e.g. an account of what pupils know or can do) without reference to the performance of others.'

will have quite different expectations from someone whose interpretation includes a requirement that *criterion levels* of achievement are defined. The former places few constraints on how the assessment will be formulated: narratives, numbers, grades, or other forms will be acceptable in so far as they are appropriate to the quality which is being assessed. The latter interpretation, however, implies that the description has to be in the form of something like grade-levels, and that the achievements can be described in some sort of step-wise progression. It is this kind of assumption which underpins the Scottish Standard Grade developments in which grade-related criteria are identified for a series of levels. The National Certificate at 16+ in Scotland takes a rather different approach which many of its proponents refer to as 'genuine criterion-referencing'. This adopts a dichotomous procedure for each 'module' of work; a decision has to be made about whether the student 'has' or 'has not' achieved the learning outcomes. Statisticians and computers love variables which have only '1' and '0' as alternatives. Researchers, however, do not have the luxury of so easily accepting one interpretation of CRA as the 'best' or most 'genuine'; their role is to hold the interpretations in question and persuade the practitioners to examine the assumptions they are making.

The debate about CRA has inevitably included a scrutiny of current assessment systems and questions about norm-referenced assessment. A good deal of pointless argument about whether, for example, the Scottish Certificate of Education (SCE) Ordinary (O) and Higher (H) Grade certificates are norm-referenced has ensued. Once again, there are different meanings ascribed to norm-referencing. If one accepts the following (my preferred) interpretation

'Norm-referenced assessment gives no information about what has been achieved or peformed but only about how the achievement or performance compares with that of other people.'

then obviously the SCE 'O' and 'H' grades are norm-referenced. There is little that the general public can infer from, say, a B in history other than that in some undefined overall way this candidate has done better than those with Cs and worse than those with As. On the other hand, if norm-referencing is interpreted as a system which requires the assessments to be fitted to a normal curve, then SCE 'O' and 'H' grades are clearly not norm-referenced.

As well as doing all it can to make sure we know *what* we are talking about, research has an obligation to make explicit and question the assumptions, philosophies and political orientations implicit in our practices. For example, it is doubtful whether anyone (well maybe the lunatic Right) would publicly claim that schooling should be about sorting pupils out and labelling them for the social roles they have in society. Much more likely are we to hear that schooling must be about fostering learning and providing opportunities for a range of experiences. But look at the certification system which, despite all the work of the last decade, is still being pursued for 14 to 16 year olds in Scotland. Which of these two functions of schooling does it more closely reflect with the retention of single grades and reluctance to move to something like school-based records of achievement? Do recent moves to consider the introduction of short courses to the evolving SCE Standard Grade certificate imply a relaxation which allows better descriptions of what pupils have had the opportunity to achieve in school? Or do they herald a more rigid control of adolescent society through the conversion of the school curriculum to centrally determined modules? The onus is on researchers to raise the awareness of policy makers and practitioners about their own assumptions, and about the implications of what they decide and what they do.

Over the last decade researchers have addressed many of these issues in relation to assessment of pupils. They have also provided logical analyses of the kinds of functions which criterion-referenced assessment can fulfil (e.g. reporting achievements, diagnosis, selection, course evaluation, pupil motivation) and compared these with those fulfilled by other forms of assessment such as norm-referencing. Before leaving the matter of analysing the purposes of CRA, however, perhaps we should briefly shift the focus to the sensitive subject of the assessment of teachers. There is much clarification which needs to be done before decisions on teacher appraisal can be made and that clarification might well be carried out by researchers. It is surely a criterion-referenced system which would be considered, but what would that mean and what purposes could it fulfil? To promote good teaching? To reward good teaching? To weed out poor teachers? To diagnose teachers' areas of weakness? To share expertise among teachers? To enable teachers to be accountable to the public? Such arguments must be critically analysed as must be questions of who decides on the criteria, who does the assessment and what are the criteria against which the teaching might be judged.

These last questions provide the link to my second broad area of research concerns: the criteria for assessment.

Criteria for Assessment

Those who make the decisions about what is assessed have effective control over what those who are assessed learn and/or how they spend their time. There will always be a diversity of views on where power of this kind should lie, and the nature of those views may vary as society develops its thinking about the concept of democracy. Because, at any given time, it cannot be assumed that there is a consensus on who has the right to make such decisions, there is scope for preliminary research to be undertaken before the identification of the criteria for assessment. Such research would aim to provide a clarification of who could, and who different groups think should, decide what constitutes achievement in a particular area of knowledge (like mathematics), or what is involved in a particular kind of activity (like teaching).

In practice, that type of analysis is seldom undertaken. The usual pattern is for some group to be assigned the task of making the decisions. In Scotland that group is often a Working Party with representation from the Scottish Examination Board, the Scottish Education Department, teachers and local authority advisers. More rarely, the task is given to curriculum/assessment development teams or to researchers. Whatever the nature of the group, its members will have to make assumptions and employ some kind of logic as they conceptualise the relevant area of knowledge or activity. From the perspective of those who may have to implement schemes of criteria it is important that they are aware of these assumptions and the logic which the team has invoked. Since such features are often not made explicit, research may well be undertaken to analyse what it is that has been taken for granted in the various versions of the conceptualisation process which may be available, to clarify the criteria which are implicit in the different conceptual schemes and to provide an account of the implications of choosing a particular scheme and set of criteria.

There is, of course, no *one* way of conceptualising any given area of knowledge, but some ways will seem 'better' than others in specific circumstancs. Decisions about what kinds of structures will be adopted will rest on many factors. The decision to adopt a modular structure for everything in the National Certificate at 16 + , for example, may have been made on good grounds; but those grounds were not based on evidence that modules were the best way to reflect the nature of all the different kinds of knowledge included in the 16 to 18 programme. No structure could be so universally applicable. The SCE Standard grade, for pupils from 14 to 16, requires a particular form of graded assessment which enables a common pattern across subjects for certification purposes. Since the structure of knowledge in different areas of the curriculum can vary very greatly, it is inevitable that some subject areas will be ill-served by this imposed common pattern.

Researchers engaged in the analysis and clarification of criteria in specific areas find themselves in a variety of circumstances with regard to the conceptualisation of that area. A project at Stirling University on the Assessment of Communicative Skills in Foreign Languages for 14 to 16 year olds, for example, found itself in a position where there was extensive concern that a communicative approach be adopted, but little shared understanding of what counted as communicative competence. At the time the research started the working party for Standard Grade had only just begun its deliberations and so had generated no model of communicative competence. A preliminary exploration of teachers' views found little in the way of common concepts and the relevant literature from other countries was sparse. The researchers, therefore, took a lead and worked with a framework (attributed to Canale — a Canadian) in which there are four components: grammatical competence (mastery of the language system), sociolinguistic competence (appropriateness of utterances in the social context), discourse competence (coherence of conversation) and strategic competence (strategies to deal with linguistic or communication problems).

This framework has been shown to reflect the characteristics of genuine communication and to provide a basis for assessing oral performance against communicative criteria. What is not so clear (and this is part of the project's investigations) is the extent to which it reflects the oral work that currently goes on in classrooms,

B

and whether teachers would subscribe to it and structure their
teaching accordingly if they knew about it.

A second project which took a lead was Jordanhill College's
Techniques for Assessment of Practical Skills in science at
Standard Grade Foundation level (TAPS). Their conceptualisation
took an objectives approach (familiar to science teachers) to the
assessment of 'practical skills' (unfamiliar to science teachers).
TAPS developed a framework of objectives categorised in six
groups: observation, recording, measurement, manipulation,
procedural and following instructions. The framework formed the
basis of the Foundation certificate assessments of practical skills
and had a considerable influence on subsequent developments in
science throughout the country. It was taken up because it was a
well thought out scheme and teachers needed it. It is not, of course,
the only way of looking at practical skills and some people may
want to use other conceptualisations. What is interesting is that
another project at Aberdeen College, which looked at assessment
of 'knowledge and understanding' in science and also worked from
a base of objectives, found teachers much less ready to follow the
researchers' lead in adopting a conceptual framework. That may
well have occurred because teachers were already familiar with
assessment in this area and had their own implicit frameworks of
criteria. The final two elements of Foundation science, 'handling
information' and 'problem solving', pose the question of whether
conceptual frameworks for their criteria should also be based on
objectives models; such models can constrain and may have
doubtful validity in terms of the ways teachers think about these
elements.

Sometimes researchers enter the picture at a rather later stage
when the major decisions about the framework of criteria have
been made. So, for example, in Standard Grade Foundation
English those practitioners involved in the Government's extended
feasibility studies determined that English should consist of four
modes: writing, reading, talking and listening. In these
circumstances there are important research questions to be
addressed in analysing and illuminating the implications of the
assumptions which have been made, and in exploring the
possibilities for development work within the conceptual
framework.

One could, for example, pursue the implications of
distinguishing two receptive modes (reading and listening) from
two productive modes (writing and talking) when achievements in
the former can only be assessed through performance in the latter.
Or one might explore the effects of the substantial variations *within*
modes (e.g. 'writing' conceived as conveying information,
deploying ideas, arguing, evaluating, describing personal experi-

ences, expressing feelings, employing specific literary forms), in comparison with the commonalities *across* modes (e.g. much of the 'writing' could equally well be manifest as 'talk').

On the development front, researchers can take a small part of the conceptual framework and explore the possibilities (e.g. an Edinburgh University project on talk, in the sense of the transmission of information, and on writing at Stirling University). What research cannot do, is to resolve problems arising from basic assumptions which are made in the conceptualisation and which are fundamentally in conflict. For example, there is a clear disjunction between a system of assessment which is product-oriented and concerned with judgments about the individual, and aims for learning which are concerned with group processes such as co-operation and discussion. Research is not about solving the insoluble.

What about the assessment of teaching? Researchers have a responsibility to analyse and illuminate the decisions which might be taken and the explicit or implicit assumptions on which they rest. In the first place, what sort of activity is teaching? Is it seen as a social role governed by a set of conventions about appropriate behaviour? A display of personal characteristics such as warmth, extroversion and social dominance? A skilled craft? A technology based on theory? A complex synthesis of several of these? None of these? There are, of course, those who see teaching as a political activity in which teachers attempt to impose on pupils their view of society and concept of reality.

And who is competent to decide the criteria against which teachers are to be assessed? Is it the case that if teaching is viewed as a theory-based technology then 'experts' (e.g. from colleges of education) should make these judgments? If the public service function of schools is emphasised, then is it a matter for elected representatives? If teaching comprises shared professional expertise, then should the profession itself make the judgment? If teaching is about personal understanding and commitment, then does the responsibility lie with individual teachers? The fact is we know little about what good experienced teachers do in the classroom, and research on this should be a priority in anybody's book.

Assessment Procedures and Systems

Work on CRA is often involved in the development, testing or appraisal of procedures for the assessment of specific achievements, qualities or experiences. From a research perspective, it is important that such work is not simply a matter of somehow (anyhow) developing and using assessment procedures which look as if they will do. It has to involve a systematic enquiry into the validity of the procedures in relation to

(i) whether the procedures assess those things they are supposed to assess (content and construct validity)

(ii) whether those assessed have had the opportunity to learn, develop and demonstrate the qualities on which they are assessed

(iii) whether the assessments are reliable.

If the criteria for assessment have been properly clarified, the development or selection of assessment procedures is usually straightforward. For example, a project at Aberdeen College of Education on assessment in reading was particularly careful to make clear the purposes of the assessment (diagnostic or formative) and the nature of the achievements to be assessed. One of the schemes related to pupils' use of a dictionary. It was clear from the identification of the criteria that pupils were expected to *search* in their dictionaries, to *comprehend* what they found and then *do* something with what they found. The different levels of achievement in these three elements were reflected directly in the assessments tasks. Thus any given task could involve elements of searching, comprehension and doing, and the difficulty of each element could be adjusted to match directly the criteria for assessment.

The use of the dictionary is a particularly straightforward example, especially since the purpose of the assessment in this instance was primarily formative and diagnostic. The universe of ways of making the assessments is relatively small and there are likely to be high levels of agreement on their validity. In other circumstances, researchers may have to analyse much more complex systems with major constraints imposed on them. The system incorporated in the National Certificate at 16+, for example, requires a dichotomous form of decision to be made on whether or not a student has mastered the learning outcomes of a given module. When the module is on something like 'Caring', clarification of the criteria for achievement may prove difficult. As a last resort, procedures for assessment of mastery may be assigned to 'the teachers' professional skill'. In that case, and before invoking any of the technical approaches to the exploration of reliability and validity, the researcher is likely to have to address the following kinds of questions:

— What concepts of 'caring' are implicit in the judgments the teacher(s) makes in assessing the student?

— To what extent do these conceptualisations reflect the intended criteria for 'caring'?

— If there is a range of interpretations or concepts of 'caring', should the assessments be covering that range or only a sub-set of the concepts?

— To what extent are these assessment procedures which directly assess 'caring performance'? Is it necessary to resort to high-inference measures? If so, is there a battery of such measures which can help to provide a comprehensive assessment?

In general, therefore, the problems of the development and nature of assessment techniques follow directly from the conceptualisation of what is to be assessed. If that concept is clear, then the generation of the assessment procedures will be straight-forward. Indeed, it is likely that there will be techniques available which are already well tried. If the concept is not clear, then the formulation of new procedures will be necessary and probably difficult. Furthermore, it may be that lower standards of validity and reliability will have to be accepted. The researcher has a responsibility to make practitioners aware that this is the case, and to raise their consciousness about the different interpretations which can be put on the assessment of such qualities. The more precisely defined the quality, the more likely there is to be a single assessment approach universally regarded as appropriate and valid. 'Caring' is unlikely to fall into that category.

The matter of summarising assessments is problematic. Researchers may well have a role in the identification of the different kinds of principles which might be used to summarise assessments into some form of report, and in an analysis of the assumptions underlying, or the implications of choosing, any particular principle.

One approach to CRA is to assert that no attempts to summarise or aggregate assessments should be made. The whole point of criterion-referencing, the argument goes, is to report on all the different things that pupils or students have achieved. To carry that argument on to 'certificate' reports seems not to take account of the real world. While one feature of a CRA report must be that it conveys information about achievements, in a way that traditional single grades never did, it is also necessary that the report be sufficiently succinct for readers to attend to it and understand its meaning. Researchers, such as those involved in the Criterion Referenced Certification Project at Jordanhill College, have a responsibility to explore alternative ways of summarising the assessments, and the implications of choosing among these alternatives.

But what about summarising assessments of teaching? This introduces new matters for consideration. For example, when *pupils* are assessed it is up to the assessor to create the conditions under which they can display the competence on which they are assessed. The necessarily small sample of teaching chosen for the assessment of a *teacher,* however, may not provide an opportunity to display all (or any) of the competences being appraised. Furthermore, the teacher and the assessor may have different ideas about the conditions under which it is appropriate to use those competences. The design of any kind of assessment procedure or system will inevitably depend on the value decisions made about the extent to which a professional teacher has any say in what he or she is to be assessed on and how the different elements of any assessment are summarised.

Clearly there is great scope for researchers to unravel the logic and values inherent in any approach to the appraisal of teachers. But there are also possibilities for empirical research. The assessment procedures may be planned as requests for ratings of teachings from those in authority such as headteachers, advisers or HMIs. Is there reason to believe, as earlier research has indicated, that such people assess highly those teachers whose views and practices most closely match their own? If that were the case, what would be the implications of invoking such a system? What would be the effects of a system which involved no observation of the practice of teaching? Can an 'outsider' observe those aspects of a teacher's classroom practice which are most crucial in influencing that teacher's effectiveness?

The introduction of any new or reformed procedures for assessment will have human and other resource implications. Innovating agencies could well look to researchers to estimate these implications of alternative approaches to implementation in terms of finance, materials and new skills required for teachers or other assessors. In practice, this is seldom done. Decisions are made on the basis of such things as the money available and political pressures, and alternative approaches are seldom fully considered. Research is sometimes used to analyse the factors influencing implementation of the assessment scheme, but this is *after* the implementation has taken place.

Factors Influencing Implementation

The manner in which any new approach is introduced can ensure the success or wrecking of valuable innovations. The factors which influence that are important and research has had a lot to say about them.

For example, Moray House College's project on Assessment in Home Economics has shown how ineffective is the development of assessment materials which are then simply handed to the teachers, in comparison with the stimulation of, and support for, teachers to generate their own materials. Aberdeen College's research on Assessment in Health Studies demonstrated the deleterious effect on intiatives, shown by one school in developing assessments, when the control of the innovations was switched from the pilot schools to the centre (the Scottish Education Department and the Scottish Examination Board). The Scottish Vocational Preparation Unit's work on Social and Vocational Skills made clear how the nature of the course (in this case process-based) can conflict with external requirements for certification (produced-oriented).

To be of help to innovators in making implementation decisions a researcher might consider approaches which:

— explore how those who would be expected to carry out the assessments interpret, value, understand and are able to undertake those tasks;
— investigate how those who are to be assessed regard, are likely to respond to, or co-operate with, the assessment procedures;
— analyse the constraints which may be imposed by other factors (e.g. a requirement that all assessments be made in relation to a set number of grades, or a reluctance to provide the necessary resources for the assessment innovations).

Some research, such as the work by the Scottish Council for Research in Education (SCRE) on the National Certificate, has looked at students' views on new assessment procedures. On the whole, however, those assessed in schools and colleges are expected to accept the system as it is. If there are protests we hear little about them. Can we expect such a passive response from teachers if they are to be appraised? We know a lot from research (e.g. SCRE's work on English over the years, and Edinburgh University's research on 'O' grade examinations) about the limits of our competence in assessing pupils. What about the competence of the appraisers of teachers? An understanding of the teachers' perspective of teacher appraisal, and of the power and validity of different ways of implementing such appraisal, is crucial if an innovation is not to be overwhelmed with chaos and conflict. The value of an independent research perspective on such matters is immense.

In Conclusion

This is clearly not an exhaustive list of questions which research on criterion-referenced assessment might address, nor is it meant as some sort of required minimum for all research projects on

THE ROLE OF DESCRIPTIVE AND NORMATIVE TECHNIQUES IN EXAMINATION ASSESSMENT

S. French
Department of Mathematics, University of Manchester
J. B. Slater
SWURCC, University of Bath
M. Vassiloglou
Computing Centre, University of Salford
A. S. Willmott
University of Oxford Delegacy of Local Examinations

Introduction

In this paper we shall focus on the English GCE, CSE and GCSE examinations. These are subject-based and administered by many public examination boards. These examination boards do their best to ensure that all work is marked fairly and consistently with due credit being given for good work. They also seek to award final subject grades which are sufficiently detached from particular syllabi, examination papers, examiners, etc., so as to stand as having meaning to those receiving and using them. Our purpose in this paper is not to consider the ways in which particular boards try to achieve this in particular subjects, rather it is to explore more general considerations, which are common in some measure to all boards' examinations in all subjects.

The ways in which the boards approach their task of examining students differ, reflecting different attitudes to the task in hand and different preferences for particular stages in the examining process. Therefore, in a strict sense, there can be no such thing as a 'typical examination procedure', although for a point of focus for our discussions we shall introduce an idealised abstraction which builds upon our general experiences in a number of boards. It should be realised, of course, that any particular procedure used by any given board to award any given subject may depart from this abstraction in many ways.

We begin by discussing the purpose of public examinations and then describe the procedures involved in our abstraction of a typical examination. Next, we introduce and define the terms *descriptive* and *normative measurement*. In the remaining sections we return to our description of the conduct of a typical examination and examine in greater detail the interpretation of the procedures, particularly the quantitative procedures, undertaken during the assessment process.

15

At the outset we should make two points clear. First, at many places in our discussion we shall appear critical of many assessment practices; and, indeed, we are critical, but our criticisms are primarily directed at current assessment theory. We do not believe the public examination boards to be without blemish but we do believe that they undertake the task entrusted to them remarkably well. It is with the theory of assessment as commonly portrayed in the literature that we disagree. Practice, thankfully in this instance, does not always follow theory. Second, we would emphasise that our remarks are entirely our own and do not represent the views of the various boards with which we have connections.

Our discussion draws heavily upon our longer paper (French *et al.*, 1987) and is supported by remarks in several of our other papers (French, 1985, 1986a, b; French and Vassiloglou, 1986; Vassiloglou, 1982, 1986).

The Purpose and Conduct of Public Examinations

The purpose of an examination might be to assess the current knowledge, achievement and skills of candidates; it might be to assess some measure of their innate, untutored ability; it might be to predict some aspect of their future performance; it might be to serve some pedagogic purpose; or, of course, it might be some combination of all these objectives. In this paper we have the paradigm of a GCE/CSE examination very firmly in mind. We are not intending that the discussion should cover entrance, selection or 'mock' examinations. We believe that the purpose of GCE/CSE examinations is to assess current knowledge, achievement and skills. In support of this, if any be needed, we would cite the emphasis placed upon the assessment of positive achievement in the GCSE. Undoubtedly, a candidate's performance is limited by innate ability, but that ability is not the primary objective of the assessment. Equally, GCE/CSE grades are used by employers, college admission officers, and many others as data on which to base predictions; again this is not the primary purpose of the assessment. It is, perhaps, sad but probably true that the main pedagogic role of these examinations is that of carrot-and-stick.

We would also suggest that the intention is to assess the candidates on the basis of their performances at the time of assessment. Day-to-day variability in candidate performance cannot be allowed for. It is the performance that exists that is assessed, not that which might be inferred to exist. In this sense it is the candidates' performances that are assessed, not the candidates themselves; and we should speak of assessing performances, not candidates. However, we shall be lax in places.

Given that the purpose of examinations is to assess a candidate's performance, it might be supposed that we should view the marks assigned to a candidate's work during the assessment process as quantified measures of aspects of performance, and, similarly, that we should view the eventual grades as a classification of overall performance. We do not. We do not believe that examinations measure a candidate's performance in the same sense of 'measure' as, say, a thermometer measures temperature. We hold this view despite the theories of educational assessment current in much of the literature (see, for example, Noll *et al.*, 1979).

We believe that the marks are a quantification of the examiners' judgment of the performance. They encode or measure something about the examiners — their judgment of the performance — rather than something directly about the candidate. Similarly, the eventual grade awarded is a highly summarised statement of the examiners' judgment. In a sense, we see the role of public examinations as providing a detached academic reference on the candidate's achievement. The current movement towards Records of Achievement (DES, 1984) is to our minds, a recognition of this role. A Record of Achievement is, in one sense, simply a reference, academic and otherwise, on a candidate, constructed on a standard format with the degrees of detachment of each comment (examination-board-written, teacher-written or candidate-written) made clear. There are, of course, many other more important pedagogic aspects of Records of Achievement (OCEA, 1985), but, for our purposes here, it is sufficient to note that of providing a reference on the candidate.

Thus, we do not believe that there is some objective entity within each candidate's mind or exemplified by each candidate's scripts that can unambiguously be called his/her current ability, achievement or performance. To suggest that there be is analogous to a return to the philosophies of the anatomists of the middle ages who dug about in the brain (and the rest of the body!) looking for that part in which wisdom and the soul resided. Had they found it, they would undoubtedly have measured its length and weighed it. In a similar manner, it seems to us, many modern theories of educational assessment seek to use the scalpel of psychometrics to tease out and measure a candidate's ability. We do not believe that anything exists to be so measured. The quality of a candidate's performance does not exist within the candidate or within his/her work. It is a mental construct of an observer of that performance: it exists only within the perception of the examiner. Moreover, it is not something that springs into being the moment the examiner sees the candidate's work. It is formed gradually and undergoes many revisions as the examiner studies the candidate's script. We believe that the purpose of many of the quantitative and other procedures used in examination assessment is to help the examiner form his perception and his judgment of the candidates' performances in a manner that is fair and consistent to all candidates.

Accordingly, for the rest of this paper, we shall use the term *current performance* or simply *performance* as a shorthand for 'perceived current knowledge, achievement and skills demonstrated during the examination'.

We hold our views to be in accord with much of current practice, but we accept that they would find little company in much of the current literature, although there are similar themes to be found in Christie and Forrest (1981).

Enough of purpose: How are public examinations conducted? What procedures are involved? In what order do they occur? We shall describe an abstraction of a typical examination. For the sake of brevity, we shall only consider the case in which the papers are entirely set and assessed by examiners within the examination board. We shall not consider internal assessment; we shall address some of the issues raised by this possibility in a future paper.

An obvious point to take as the start of the assessment process in an examination is the design of papers and marking schemes. However, it should be realised that these are not designed in vacuo; earlier decisions concerning the syllabus and assessment objectives have their influence. The chief examiners, usually guided by a panel of revisers, design the question papers and marking schemes at the same time. Parts of questions are designed to allow the candidates to demonstrate their achievement in respect of different assessment objectives. Marks are allocated to each part according to the importance, or 'weight', of the associated objective. Questions are constructed from part questions and papers are constructed from questions in such a way that, in the examiners' judgment, the examination as a whole samples the syllabus in a balanced fashion.

In general, examinations are hierarchical structures, with the subject dividing into papers, the papers into sections, the sections into questions, etc. Several such hierarchies can also be combined to form, for instance, part of Records of Achievement. This view emphasises that the relation between a component and those components that comprise it is essentially the same at all levels in the tree. Throughout this paper, we shall refer to the parts of an examination as components in order to emphasise the fact that our discussion refers equally to all the levels of the hierarchy. In this context a mark profile will be the marks obtained on a set of components by a candidate. The particular set of components involved in a mark profile will depend on the use to which the profile is to be put.

Next, the candidates sit the examination.

For the vast majority of examinations there are simply too many candidates for it to be possible for a single examiner to mark all the scripts. Thus, teams of markers are used. The use of teams of markers immediately brings with it the problem known as *co-ordination* (or *standardisation*: but note that this does not imply any connection with the ideas of standardised testing — there is an unfortunate conflict of terminology here). The chief examiners have to satisfy themselves that the markers are interpreting the marking schemes in the manner intended.

There are several procedures employed in the process of co-ordination, the most important being *co-ordination meetings*. These occur as soon as each marker has been able to look at a number of scripts. The relevant chief examiner meets with the markers and discusses how the marking scheme is working in practice. Modifications to the scheme may be made in the light of experience, but, most importantly, the markers come to an agreement with the chief examiner on its interpretation. The chief examiner also double-marks a sample of each marker's scripts and discusses with each marker individually any discrepancies. The markers now mark their complete allocation of scripts. To check the markers' interpretations further, the chief examiners may double-mark further samples of scripts and they may also look at statistical summaries of each marker's distribution of marks on his/her allocation. Co-ordination is a dynamic process through which a high level of consensus amongst the markers can be achieved. This consensus emerges primarily as a result of the markers' increasing understanding of the chief examiner's intentions. However, the dynamic nature of co-ordination makes it also likely for the chief examiner to be influenced by the process.

At this point, the chief examiners will have a feel for how their assessment instruments performed. None the less, to confirm and broaden their insight, they are likely to look at statistical summaries and analyses of the various individual mark distributions. In addition, they may also study joint distributions — how do the marks covary between components? They may also read all the scripts submitted on all papers by a sample of candidates.

When they believe that they understand how their examination as a whole performed, they turn their attention to the *aggregation* of each candidate's marks into an overall mark. Usually, this involves simply adding marks together or, perhaps, taking a weighted sum. However, other aggregation procedures are used or have been suggested: see French (1985) for a survey.

The final task facing the chief examiners is that of awarding candidates grades. *Awarding grades* is a two-phase procedure; the second phase, *borderlining*, is often considered quite distinct, but it is an integral part of the procedure. First, the chief examiners decide on the requirements for a grade: e.g. candidates whose marks fall within such and such a range should provisionally be awarded such and such a grade. However, emphasis should be placed upon the provisional nature of this decision, because the second phase considers those candidates who might thereby be misgraded — a better term would be 'misjudged'. The scripts of candidates falling close to any boundaries are re-read and their grades reviewed. Moreover, other candidates may be reviewed if their profile of marks exhibits an odd mark pattern, i.e., if they seem atypical in any sense. Candidates may also be reviewed if the markers noted something interesting about them at the earlier stage of marking the papers. Finally, candidates who were ill or otherwise adversely affected by circumstance are reviewed. Throughout the process, the chief examiners are supported by statistical and other information, much as they were in the case of aggregation. Only when they are satisfied with the borderline review is the process complete.

   The above is little more than a thumbnail sketch of the assessment procedures involved in public examinations, but it will serve to set our later discussion in context. See Christie and Forrest (1981) and Mathews (1985) who give further information on assessment procedures.

Descriptive and Normative Measurement

Suppose that an observer is studying a system. In descriptive measurement numbers are used to represent qualitative properties of the system under study. The observer's role in assigning these numbers is minimal; essentially, they are read off scales attached to measuring instruments. The position of a pointer on a scale is determined by the physical system. No matter how hard the observer thinks about the system, the pointer cannot be willed to move. Thus, the numbers involved in descriptive measurement are determined by the physical system (subject to arbitrary choices of unit, etc.). They are beyond the observer's control, although they might be misread. As a consequence, whenever such descriptive measurements are used in a mathematical or statistical analysis, any parameters involved are fitted to immutable data.

   By contrast, the observer's role in normative measurement is more active. Here, numbers are used to construct and encode the observer's subjective feelings about the system under study. Any 'scale' is a mental one and the position of the pointer upon it is under his or her direct control. If the observer so wishes, judgments can be changed without the system changing; and, indeed, the purpose of normative measurement is in part to help make such changes of judgment in the direction of consistency with some behavioural axioms which are felt to be desirable. Therefore, when mathematical models are fitted to normatively measured data, not only are the parameters moulded to the data, but also the data are moulded to the parameters. The latter occurs as the observer revises his or her judgments in the direction of consistency with the axioms. However, note that, in doing this, the observer is not saying that the model is more valid than the judgments. Rather, the model in question is first adopted because the behavioural axioms that underpin it seem to embody the consistency that he or she would like to see reflected in his or her judgments. In fitting the model, attention is drawn to any inconsistency between particular instances of judgments and the behavioural axioms that are felt desirable. Judgments are revised because of this inconsistency, and not simply because they do not fit the model. Alternatively, a revised set of axioms may be adopted. The process is then iterated until the observer is satisfied.

As an example, consider how an examiner might mark these candidates' answers (A, B and C) to a particular question. Initially, he or she might judge A and B to be of equal quality and so attach equal marks. Subsequently, C might be read and its quality judged to lie between A and B. It is clear that the marks given to A and/or B could be adjusted so that there is an intermediate mark available for C, assuming that the mark scale is fine enough to permit such discrimination. Alternatively, the marker could reflect on the quality of C and decide that, after all, it is equal to that of A and B.

The marking process is calling to the examiners' attention the behavioural axiom that a piece of work should not be judged intermediate in quality between two pieces of work that are judged to be equal in quality; and he/she revises his/her judgments accordingly.

The distinction between descriptive and normative measurement is discussed in greater detail in, *inter alia*, French (1986c), Phillips (1984), Pitz and Sachs (1984), Vassiloglou (1986). We shall not dwell on this distinction further, save to emphasise that there is a clear distinction to be made: to apply descriptive measurement techniques in a situation in which normative ones are needed — or vice versa — can lead to quite inappropriate, meaningless, numerical procedures — and does.

The Grading Process

We have indicated several of the assessment procedures involved in public examinations. In the following sections we discuss these procedures in greater detail. We begin with the process of grading. This may seem perverse; but to discuss the earlier procedures satisfactorily we need to be clear about how their results will be used.

Thus we shall suppose that the chief examiners have before them a ranking of the candidates provided by the ordering of their overall aggregate marks such that the higher a candidate is within this ranking the better they have provisionally judged the quality of his/her overall performance. The task before them is to partition the candidates into grades. In the current debate on the reform of the public examination system there is the tacit assumption that currently grades are norm-referenced. Furthermore, there seems to be a widespread belief that this should be changed: grades should be criteria-referenced.

The terms *norm-referenced* and *criterion-referenced*, and the concepts that they describe, were imported into the educational assessment literature from psychometrics. Unfortunately, while psychometric tests might be so categorised, it seems to us that public examinations can neither be norm- nor criterion-referenced in the strict sense. We give arguments in support of this belief in French *et al.* (1987).

When the GCSE was announced, the intention of some seemed to be that it should be a criterion-referenced examination in the strict sense. The concept of strict criterion-referencing has roots in psychological mental testing. There, the aim is to record whether a person could or could not perform a particular, tightly defined, simple task. It is important to note that interest in psychometrics focuses on simple, easily specified tasks and, moreover, that the number of tasks is small. The abilities and achievements required of GCSE and GCE candidates are neither simply specified nor few in number. They are complex and very varied. This complexity and variety means that to specify the criteria defining the grades in a criterion-referenced examination — assuming that this can be done — would require tens of pages. Such a document would be impossible to use during an examination: no marker could be continually consulting something of that length. Marking schemes that become longer than a few pages are almost impossible to use. However, most members of the working parties had appreciated the impracticability of such examinations long before the GCSE was announced. Few have ever thought that strict criterion-referencing was a practical possibility in the context of the British examination system. Thus the intention is now that grading at GCSE should be criteria-related (SEC Working Party Reports, 1985). This is a much softer notion than that of strict criterion-referencing, implying, we understand, a greater role for the examiners' judgment and interpretation. Perhaps the best way to explain this is to discuss the notion of limen-referencing, which was introduced by Christie and Forrest (1981).

Christie and Forrest argued that there has always been the intention that grades should correspond to certain standards of performance. Those standards, however, have never been formalised and written down as precise criteria. In the British system, the standards exist, by and large, in the minds of the examining profession, not on paper. The system is based upon consensus. Various mechanisms, such as external examinerships, cross-moderation, and the apprenticeship of one examiner under another, ensure that there is general agreement amongst the body of examiners about the standards represented by a given grade. Thus, to a large extent the body of examiners form the repository of educational standards. As a society, we charge our examiners with the task of assessing educational achievement by comparison with consensus standards of performance. Christie and Forrest term the comparison of a particular candidate's performance with these consensus standards *limen-referencing*.

A way of making operational the notion of limen-referencing is to suggest that each examiner has in his mind for each grade a typical, but perhaps hypothetical, candidate whose performance represents the qualities or standards of that grade. Perhaps better is to suggest that the examiner has in mind several typical candidates for each grade, since several different spreads of abilities may be judged equivalent.

In a particular examination, the examiners will look at their provisional ranking of candidates and make comparisons with the performances expected of these hypothetical candidates in order to partition the ranking into provisional grades. The examiners do not make these judgments in vacuo; they use many techniques to support their judgments. First, the examination papers and marking schemes were designed with certain standards in mind and so the examiners will have some idea of what aggregate mark should represent the dividing line between two grades. Second, they may read some scripts from the previous year's examination to refresh their memory of the standards of performance to expect. Third, they may consider what proportion of candidates will be awarded each grade. This is not an attempt at norm-referencing, but a large sample check on their grading, based upon the assumption that the distribution of abilities in a population of candidates will not change much over time.

With all the candidates provisionally graded, the second phase, borderlining, now takes place. The purpose of this phase is to consider more carefully those candidates who might have been misgraded or misjudged by the partitioning of the candidates according to simple rules. In terms of limen-referencing, this means that these candidates' scripts are reread and their performances compared directly with the consensus standards.

Within this limen-referencing view of examinations, the reforms underway in the GCSE can be interpreted as follows. The working parties who have been labouring hard to write grade-related criteria have, *inter alia*, been trying to make much more explicit the consensus standards that hitherto have existed mainly in the minds of examiners. This has several advantages, the two most important being to make the standards much clearer to the non-examining public and to make the degree of consensus amongst examiners much closer. However, it should be noted that we are not arguing that the grade criteria being proposed are criteria in the sense of criterion-referencing. They are simply careful, clear, but not perfectly precise statements of standards. They are descriptions of 'typical candidates' i.e. grade descriptions.

Aggregation

The purpose of aggregating candidates' marks is to place candidates into a rank order. It is well to note that any numerical procedure which combines each candidate's profile of marks into a single number will achieve this. The question is, of course, whether the aggregation procedure leads to an appropriate rank order. A question which is begged in turn is that of what contributes an appropriate rank order.

We have already argued that marks and grades do not measure and classify anything directly about the candidates; rather they report examiners' judgments of the candidates' performances. This distinction has serious implications for the choice of aggregation method. If we believed there to be an unambiguous, objective ordering of the candidates according to the current performances, then we would have little choice but to argue that the profiles of marks were simple multivariate data on the performances and that, with appropriate descriptive statistical techniques (test theory, generalisability theory, etc.) we might discover and report this ordering. In French (1985) there is a survey and critique of the statistical methods of aggregation that have been proposed on the basis of such an argument. However, we do not believe that the candidates are in any way ordered objectively. This follows naturally from our rejection of the existence of any objective entity which we might call ability of a candidate or the quality of performance.

Certainly, we would accept that, in the majority of cases, when two or more examiners were asked to compare the 'overall performance' of a pair of candidates, they would agree on who did the better in their judgment in the light of the syllabus and assessment aims. However, in accepting this, we are not accepting the existence of an objective ordering of the candidates. There is no natural ordering external to the examiners that they recognise when they compare candidates' performances. Rather, we believe that there is consensus amongst the examiners in their judgmental ordering of the candidates' performances, just as we believe that there is consensus amongst them in the standards that they apply through limen-referencing during the grading process.

By using the term 'judgmental ordering' we are implying that the examiners play an active role in producing the ordering of the candidates. No relevant ordering exists without the examiners' judgment.

Moreover, we would argue that every chief examiner expresses his/her judgmental ordering subjectively and individually. The consensus of their judgments arises through a variety of complex interactions. Firstly, chief examiners are themselves part of the teaching profession, a large proportion of which is involved in the preparation of candidates and often in the marking of scripts. Thus, chief examiners' judgments are inevitably conditioned by a common educational and professional background. Secondly, the whole process of teaching and examining takes place within the framework of a curriculum, which acts as a common basis and reference point. Finally, consensus is undoubtedly improved by the various mechanisms referred to previously, such as external examinerships, cross-moderation, the apprenticeship period spent by each chief examiner and, especially, the GCSE grade criteria. Perfect consensus, however, is not guaranteed. Indeed examiners do differ in their judgments of the relative merits of some pairs of candidates; although in such cases they usually agree that their judgments are difficult ones to make, becuse the candidates' performances are disparate in detail but little different overall. None the less, general consensus amongst examiners does exist; isolated disagreements are usually resolved by the chair's decision. If it did not exist, examining would be difficult, if not impossible.

Having acknowledged the existence of general consensus, we shall focus attention on judgments of the chief examiner responsible for a particular examination. We shall assume that the judgments he/she expresses reflect the general consensus.

We can now answer the question of what is the appropriate rank order that the aggregation procedure is meant to produce? The appropriate rank order is one that puts the candidates into order of improving overall performance according to the chief examiner's judgment. Why, therefore, are aggregation procedures needed? Why not let the chief examiner read the candidates' scripts and shuffle them into the appropriate rank order? Indeed, why need he/she rank the candidates at all? Why not ask him/her to read each script, compare it with the consensus standards of performance implicit in limen-referencing and grade it accordingly. There are two reasons, both deriving from one simple fact. There are too many candidates.

Firstly, the sheer volume of candidates means that there is not enough time for the examiner to judge all the scripts holistically. We have already noted that this means that each candidate's performance needs to be summarised as a profile of marks early in the assessment process. Similarly, pressure of time requires that the provisional ranking of the candidates is produced by an aggregation procedure that can be applied to the mark profiles. (As we noted, in the borderlining process the chief examiner does consult scripts as a basis for his/her judgments.)

Secondly, society and candidates have a right to expect that judgments are made of them in a fair and consistent manner. It is well known from many psychological studies that holistic judgment can be flawed with many inconsistencies, particularly when there are many comparisons to be made (see, e.g. Fischer, 1979; Hogarth, 1980; Kahneman *et al.*, 1982 and Slovic and Lichtenstein, 1971). The very process of going through the intermediate stage of aggregating marks and forming a ranking instead of directly grading scripts brings much consistency into the assessment. Also without a much finer provisional ranking of the candidates' performances than the rather coarse ranking given by their ultimate grades, it is difficult to identify those candidates most at risk of being misgraded and hence those candidates to whom the chief examiners' attention should be directed during the borderline review.

Of course the above presupposes that there is agreement about what is meant by 'consistent' judgment. The papers of French (1981, 1985) and Vassiloglou (1985) discuss this in detail and suggest possible principles of consistency — behavourial axioms — that might be appropriate to judgments of examiners. Accepting that such principles can be identified, one of the purposes of the aggregation procedure is to guide the chief examiner towards the ideal of consistent judgment. Thus, referring to our earlier discussion of normative measurement, we would argue that the techniques used to construct the aggregation procedure should derive from normative measurement.

Suppose that the chief examiner has reached the point in the awarding process at which he/she wishes to produce the provisional ranking of the candidates according to his/her judgment of their overall performance. He/she has, for each candidate, a profile of marks.

We shall assume that the examiner faces up to the task with several general principles in mind. Perhaps he/she wishes to give some emphasis to a good performance on component 1; i.e. component 1 should have a 'high weighting', whatever that might mean. Alternatively, his/her intention might be to treat all the components symmetrically. Perhaps he/she feels that candidates who perform roughly equally well on all the components should have some advantage over those who perform disparately. The examiner may wish his/her judgments to be independent in the sense discussed in French (1981). Such general principles will usually be indicated in the assessment aims in the syllabus and have been discussed by the examiner and the appropriate subject committee within the examining board long before the examination was sat. However, having such principles in mind does not necessarily mean that the examiner can judge the overall performance of the candidates. He/she must decide how to apply these principles to the particular performances on the particular papers that were sat. The purpose of normative measurement is to help him/her make this decision fairly and consistently. In a sense, it provides the examiner with a framework for thought. (Berkeley and Humphreys, 1982; French, 1986, Chapter 9; Phillips, 1984.)

As illustrated in French (1981, 1985) and Vassiloglou (1984), the general principles that the examiner wishes to embody in his/her judgments prescribe limits on the form of the appropriate aggregation procedure, but leave some details of the procedure unspecified. For instance, if independence holds across all components, then the aggregation procedure should scale the component marks and then add the scaled marks together. However, the precise form of the scaling functions, which could be nonlinear, is not determined. To help the examiner discover precisely which aggregation procedure within these limits reflects his/her judgments of overall performance, the examiner would be asked to compare the performances represented by carefully chosen pairs of profiles of marks. The pairs would be chosen so that the examiner's responses quickly determine the aggregation procedure. Once the aggregation procedure has been determined, it may be applied to the mark profiles of all candidates to rank them provisionally.

It is important to note that the construction of the aggregation procedure is a reflective process; it helps examiners think about their judgments. We have remarked that unguided holistic judgment is prone to inconsistency. In asking the chief examiner to compare pairs of mark profiles, the process risks eliciting inconsistent responses; or rather it risks determining an inappropriate aggregation procedure if it accepts all the responses without question. But part of the purpose of normative measurement is to identify and point out inconsistency to the chief examiner so that he/she may reflect upon and rectify it. Normative measurement is in large part an educative process (French, 1986). Its purpose is to enable the chief examiner to understand his/her judgments better and to improve them in the direction of consistency. Thus, as well as identifying the aggregation procedure, the methods would seek to help the examiner understand how to apply the general principles that guide his/her judgment in the specific circumstances of a particular examination.

The dynamic, reflective aspect of normative measurement cannot be over-emphasised. No ordering of the candidates exists a priori and the chief examiner's judgments are likely to vary throughout the assessment process as information becomes available to him or her. Further, the resulting order is usually only fully defined for a subset of the candidates — those falling close to the grade borderlines. Thus, the concept of a unique, unambiguous order of the candidates (such as is assumed by any version of test theory) is wholly inappropriate within our view of examination assessment.

Three further points should be made. First, the examiner would not be asked to compare an excessive number of pairs of mark profiles; the process should be feasible in the time available. Second, the examiner would not be asked to compare mark profiles that differ in many components. Typically, the pairs of profiles would differ in two components only. Such comparisons are the easiest to make in a consistent fashion. Finally, the chief examiner would never be asked quantitative questions of the form 'What should the weight of Component 2 be?' Such questions may well be meaningless, although they are often asked by present procedures and, indeed, some of the proposals for GCSE use the 'weight' of components in a most arbitrary fashion in determining gradelines. To say that one component is twice as important as another is a figure of speech which may have no quantitative interpretation (French, 1985). All that the procedures proposed here require is that the examiner says which of two marks profiles he/she judges to represent the better overall performance.

We also note that these procedure leave an 'audit trail' of meaningful answers to meaningful questions. This permits open discussion both during and after the awarding process of the standards being applied. It becomes easier to see whether or not the chief examiner's judgments conform to the consensus judgments expected of him or her.

The Use of Descriptive Statistical Techniques

Throughout our discussion of aggregation, we have assumed that chief examiners can compare two mark profiles in terms of the performances that they represent. In other words, we have assumed that, given a mark profile, they will have a fair idea of the qualities exhibited by the candidate's scripts. Thus, before the aggregation procedures can begin, examiners must spend time ensuring that they understand how the various papers performed as assessment instruments. Moreover, they must be satisfied that any marker effects have been minimised and that, as far as possible, the markers have followed the intentions of the marking schemes; in short, that the process of co-ordination has been successful.

Much of the chief examiner's understanding should derive from procedures that occurred long before the examination was set. Papers and marking schemes should have been carefully designed with the assessment aims clearly in mind. Questions, particularly multiple-choice questions, may have been pretested to check that there are no ambiguities and that they are targetted to the general abilities that may be expected of candidates.

None the less, although careful design of papers and marking schemes is essential, it is not sufficient to guarantee that the chief examiner understands the meaning of mark profiles in terms of the performances that they represent. Assessment instruments seldom perform completely as intended. It follows that examiners need procedures to help them comprehend the sort of performances that the papers actually elicited. Undoubtedly, the most important procedure is that of reading scripts. However, time is not available to read more than a sample. Statistical techniques can supplement the information gained from reading scripts with information on general trends that may be found in the entire data set.

Similarly, the various procedures involved in co-ordination should be based primarily on the reading and re-marking of scripts. Again, time constraints preclude doing this on more than a sample of a marker's allocation; and again statistical techniques can be used to supplement the information gained by reading scripts.

Thus, we believe that examiners have need of statistical techniques to help them explore the data in various ways. Statistical techniques are examples of descriptive measurement. In choosing appropriate statistical techniques the following points should be borne in mind.

First, we doubt if high-powered statistical methods based upon complicated models are appropriate tools for these analyses. The problem facing the chief examiner is to identify general trends within the data and, hence, recognise aspects that are atypical. Any model-based analysis which seeks to do this must impose some conception of the form that any general trend is expected to take. We believe that this conception should be as weak as possible. Any fitting procedure inevitably makes assumptions about the relevant conditioning information. It assumes that the distributions of marks have been generated by homogeneous processes. Yet the problem facing the chief examiner is to explore the data set, identify its major features and, particularly, identify any relevant heterogeneity.

Second, it should be remembered that the chief examiners are appointed for their expertise in their subject areas and their general skill in examining. Seldom do they have particular expertise in statistical methodology. Thus, they are unlikely to understand the full import (if any) of, say, a correlation of $0 \cdot 778$ as opposed to $0 \cdot 848$. High-powered statistical analyses may inform research officers of examination boards, who usually have the necessary statistical expertise, but such analyses may not be the appropriate instruments to inform the chief examiners themselves. They need clear, easily understood analyses which do not require them to be statistically aware to more than a modest degree.

For these reasons, we favour the use of exploratory or initial data analytic techniques wherever possible in the examining process. These techniques are designed to help the user explore the data, to see them 'from different angles' (see, e.g., Barnett (1982); Chambers *et al.* (1983); Chatfield (1985); Everitt and Dunn (1983); and Tukey (1977)). As few modelling assumptions as possible are made. Analyses display distributions in ways that facilitate visual comparison. Finally, the techniques rely heavily on the clear, informative, graphical display of data. One need not be a statistical expert to use them. They seem ideal for the purposes of examiners.

We would emphasise that we do see a role for high-powered model-based statistical analyses in the examining process. Inevitably, there will be occasions when exploratory techniques indicate the presence of an anomaly without identifying it precisely. Two distinct investigations may then be carried out in parallel. Firstly, the examiners can try to identify the problem by reading scripts. Secondly, the examination board's research staff may use whatever statistical techniques are appropriate to investigate the data further. However at the end of the investigation it is the chief examiners, not the research staff, who must understand the anomaly.

Concluding Remarks

Throughout our discussion we have sought to emphasise that the tasks facing chief examiners fall into two distinct categories, and that the validity of the procedures used to support the examiners in each particular task depends upon which category the task belongs to.

First, the chief examiners have to establish how their examinations operated. This involves many tasks: they need to investigate whether their assessment instruments have any unforseen biases; whether their teams or markers performed as they should; etc. Various numerical procedures are used to help the examiners here. All have the purpose of enabling the examiners to explore parts of the data before them. Their purpose is to identify general trends in the data and to answer general questions about subgroups of candidates and components. Seldom, if ever, is their purpose to answer questions about individual candidates; and certainly their purpose is never to guide the chief examiners' judgment of an individual candidate. The procedures that the chief examiners need to use here are descriptive statistical ones.

Second, the chief examiners must make judgments about the performance of each candidate in order to award him or her a grade. Taking the decisions that will affect candidates individually and in relation to one another, is a mental process very different from that involved in exploring data; it requires the support of a different type of numerical procedure — that of normative measurement.

The characteristics and structure of descriptive and normative measurement procedures are very different, as might be expected from their different purposes. It is quite inappropriate to use one type of procedure when the other is needed. Too often, to our minds, this distinction has not been appreciated.

Acknowledgements

We are grateful to many people for support and discussion. In particular, we are in receipt of an SEC research grant to develop a computer workstation package which will support chief examiners in their awarding. We have had many informative discussions with members of the steering group set up by the SEC to oversee the project. We are grateful to them all for their advice, given both individually and as a group. Also, we presented and discussed these ideas at a seminar funded by the Nuffield Foundation. MV was supported by a University of Manchester research studentship from 1983 to 1984.

REFERENCES

BARNETT, V. (1982) *Looking at Multivariate Data.* Wiley: Chichester.

BERKELEY, D. and HUMPHREYS, P. (1982) 'Structuring Decision Problems and the "Bras" theoristic'. *Acta Psych.*, 50, 210-252.

CHAMBERS, J. M., CLEVELAND, W. S., KLEINER, R. B. and TUKEY, P. A. (1981) *Graphical Methods for Data Analysis.* Wadsworth.

CHATFIELD, C. (1985) 'The Initial Examination of Data (with discussion).' *J. Roy. Statist. Soc.* A148, 214-253.

CHRISTIE, T. and FORREST, G. M. (1981) *Defining Public Examination Standards.* Schools Council Research Studies, Macmillan: London.

DES (1984) *Records of Achievement: a statement of policy.* HMSO: London.

EVERITT, B. S. and DUNN, G. (1983) *Advanced Methods of Data Exploration and Modelling.* Heinemann: London.

FISCHER, G. W. (1979) 'Utility Models for Multiple Objective Decisions: do they adequately represent human preferences?' *Decision Sci.*, 10, 410-479.

FRENCH, S. (1981) 'Measurement Theory and Examinations'. *Brit. J. Math. Statist. Psych.*, 34, 38-49.

FRENCH, S. (1984) 'The Weighting of Examination Components.' *The Statistician*, 34, 265-280.

FRENCH, S. (1986a) 'Statistical and Decision Theoretic Aspects of Examination Assessment.' Statistical Laboratory, Department of Mathematics, University of Manchester.

FRENCH, S. (1986b) 'The Analysis of Multiple Choice Tests in Educational Assessment.' Paper presented at the International Symposium on Probability and Bayesian Statistics.

FRENCH, S. (1986c) *Decision Theory: an introduction to the mathematics of rationality.* Ellis Horwood: Chicester.

FRENCH, S., SLATER, J. B., VASSILOGLOU, M. and WILLMOTT, A. S. (1987) 'Descriptive and Normative Techniques in Examination Assessment.' Occasional Publication, University of Oxford Delegacy of Local Examinations. OIASL: Oxford.

FRENCH, S. and VASSILOGLOU, M. (1986) 'Strength of Performance and Examination Assessment.' *Brit. J. Math. Statist. Psych.*, 39 (in press).

HOGARTH, R. M. (1980) *Judgment and Choice.* Wiley: New York.

KAHNEMANN, D., SLOVIC, P. and TUERSKY, A. (1982) *Judgment under Uncertainty: heuristics and biases.* Cambridge University Press.

MATHEWS, J. C. (1985) *Examinations: a Commentary.* Allen and Unwin: London.

NOLL, V. H., SCANNELL, D. P. and CRAIG, R. C. (1979) *Introduction to Educational Measurement*, 4th Edition. Houghton Mifflin: Boston.

OCEA (1985) *OCEA Provisional Handbook*: University of Oxford Delegacy of Local Examinations.

PHILLIPS, L. D. (1984) 'A Theory of Requisite Decision Models.' *Acta Psych.*, 56, 29-48.

PITZ, G. F. and SACHS, N. J. (1984) 'Judgment and Decisions: theory and applications.' *Ann. Rev. Psych.*, 35, 139-163.

SLOVIC, P. and LICHTENSTEIN, S. (1971) 'Comparison of Bayesian and Regression Approaches to the Study of Information Processing in Judgment.' *Org. Behav. Human Performance*, 6, 649-744.

TUKEY, J. W. (1977) *Exploratory Data Analysis.* Addison Wesley: Reading, MA.

VASSILOGLOU, M. (1982) MA thesis. University of Manchester.

VASSILOGLOU, M. (1984) 'Some Multi-attribute Models in Examination Assessment.' *Brit. J. Math. Statist. Psych.*, 37, 216-233.

VASSILOGLOU, M. (1986) PhD thesis. University of Manchester.

GRADE-RELATED CRITERIA: THE SCOTTISH EXPERIENCE

MARION DEVINE
Scottish Council for Research in Education

During the past few years in Scotland, reform of the assessment procedures for the Scottish Certificate of Education has been a major concern in education. The Scottish Examination Board has promoted and encouraged the development of grade-related criteria as the basis for the new Standard Grade certificate designed for pupils of all abilities at the end of the compulsory period of schooling. The potential benefits of grade-related criteria are considerable but the difficulties in devising clear statements of criteria at different levels are not to be underestimated. One of the claims made by those who advocate grade-related criteria is that it will be of assistance to teachers in the development of purer criterion-referenced assessment within the classroom. Experience in an action research project* which seeks to support teachers in this particular task has made us aware that the relationship between grade-related criteria and criterion-referenced assessment is not as straightforward as is sometimes assumed. However, given that the Scottish educational system looks to be dependent on an externally assessed leaving certificate for some time to come, the continued development of grade-related criteria with all its imperfections is a genuine attempt to promote wider educational aims across the whole ability range than at present.

The Case for Assessment Reform

Until recently, assessment in schools referred to a system which was designed to discriminate amongst pupils for the purpose of selecting the front-runners for higher education. The assessment took the form of a grade or mark related to some fairly general conception of ability in the subject being assessed. The raw mark was usually less important than the rank order of pupils derived from the marks. In Scotland, formal voice was given to dissatisfaction with this procedure with the publication of 'Assessment for All', the report of the committee set up to review assessment in the third and fourth years of Scottish education i.e. the two years

---

* This project is part of the work of the Schools' Assessment Research and Support Unit of the Scottish Council for Research in Education and is funded by the Convention of Scottish Local Authorities, the Scottish Education Department and the Council itself.

leading up to the Scottish 'O' grade (Dunning, 1977). The Dunning Committee was attracted to 'the notion of criterion-referencing because it seemed to offer a means of anchoring standards of assessment and of presenting reasonable and more encouraging targets for the least able pupils'.

Various factors have played a role in the move away from the traditional norm-referenced assessment towards a form of criterion-referenced assessment. This movement gained momentum in the United States in the 1960s and has since then been widely advocated. A norm-referenced system implied a belief in a static distribution of ability in the community largely innate and unalterable. All academic achievement was believed to be highly correlated with this general ability factor and the main purpose of assessment was to order pupils according to their level of ability. In part it was the development of programmed learning and mastery learning which challenged this assumption and placed the responsibility for the outcomes of instruction on the teacher. Teaching was assumed to be capable of making a difference to the achievements of the pupil and the purpose of assessment was to determine the extent to which the individual pupil had been successful against previously determined targets.

Other less pedagogic reasons had an influence. In Scotland the move to comprehensive education and the raising of the school leaving age meant many more pupils were being entered for 'O' grade than had originally been intended. There was no examination equivalent to the English Certificate of Secondary Education, although some authorities did permit their schools to import CSE Mode III to provide a more relevant course for some of their lower ability pupils. The banding of the 'O' grade at grades A, B, C, D and E had never been fully satisfactory and a radical rethink of the S3/S4 curriculum included the remit to examine 'the purpose, form and structure of the examinations held and the certificates awarded at present . . . with a view to determining, in the light of the changing circumstances of Scottish education, whether or not revision was necessary'.

The subsequent decision to set up an examination system which would cater for almost the whole ability range made nonsense of the traditional notion of using an order of merit as the basis for awards. The form of assessment which was finally decided upon by the Examination Board was that of grade-related criteria; a somewhat distant relation to criterion-referenced assessment.

One Alternative Solution

Brown (1980) defines criterion-referenced assessment as that which 'provides information about the specific knowledge and abilities of pupils through their performances on various kinds of tasks that are interpretable in terms of what the pupils know or can do, without reference to the performance of others'. A great deal of the literature regarding criterion-referenced assessment has concentrated on the need for the refining of criteria in order to provide such specific information and on the difficulties encountered in this process.

Criterion-referenced assessment when used for the purpose of providing feedback to both pupil and teacher is a valuable source of relevant information which can be used to pinpoint specific areas of difficulty encountered by pupils. It gives clear goals to aim for in well-defined areas of learning. However, assessment also has, at times, to serve the purpose of providing a summative statement on the achievements of pupils at certain junctures in their school career. In Scottish secondary schools, this first occurs at the end of the fourth year with the award of a national certificate, formerly the 'O' grade but in the process of being phased out to make way for the Standard Grade certificate. The knowledge to be gleaned from criterion-referencing is a rich source of information to the pupil and teacher who can take account of each assessment as an integral part of teaching and learning. It is, however, difficult to summarise. If the achievements of the pupils were simply listed as a number of statements about what has been achieved, the resulting report would be a fairly bulky document containing far more information than most interested parties would need. It also makes it almost impossible to sort pupils into any order, still one of the functions that industry and many institutions look to the school to fulfil. This is where the notion of a set of grade-related criteria seems to offer an alternative solution. In 'Framework for Decision' (SED, 1982), the Scottish Examination Board accepted that the practicality of criterion-referenced assessment for certification had yet to be established but that it was possible that the grade-related criteria would make it easier for schools to adopt a criterion-referenced approach in the classroom.

The Scottish Pattern

The idea of devising a set of performance criteria which would describe different levels of attainment on a subject-wide basis is unrealistic because of the variety of skills involved. The Joint Working Parties set up in each area were therefore asked to break each subject down into a small number of elements which were considered to encompass the key cognitive aspects. Statements of performance were then drawn up to describe six different levels for each of these 'assessable elements'. For example, those involved with social subjects, viz. geography, modern studies and history, originally decided on four main elements: Understanding, Handling Information, Evaluating and Investigating, the last named being an application of the others in a practical exercise.

Each level is described first of all by a summary statement, a broad descriptor of performance which is then further sub-divided into the extended grade-related criteria (EGRC). For Evaluating in geography, the summary statement for grade 6 (the lowest level) reads as follows:

> Given straightforward information, the candidate has demonstrated the ability to make and support a simple evaluation, to express and support a simple point of view and, with guidance, to identify gross bias and exaggeration.

The EGRC for the same element and grade level are as follows:

> Given straightforward information the candidate can:
> (a) make a simple evaluation of two given possibilities and support the conclusion reached with a straightforward reason;
> (b) express a simple point of view and support it with a straightforward reason;
> (c) identify gross bias and exaggeration in response to guided questions.

These extended grade-related criteria are intended to provide the teacher with the basis for decisions about course construction, teaching and classroom assessment. They also enable teachers to judge the performance of candidates in internal work against national standards. The Scottish Examination Board will use the extended grade-related criteria to set and mark the external examination papers.

The summary statements represent much broader descriptions of expected performance and yet are intended to provide parents, employers and educational institutions with guidance about the nature of the award which is more specific than the information available under the present system.

Potential Benefits

The potential benefits of a system which uses descriptions of performance as the basis for its certification procedures make it an attractive proposition. By making the critera explicit and setting levels of performance which cover the whole ability range, certain features emerge as worthwhile.

Caters for Pupils of All Abilities

The descriptions of performance are hierarchically ordered to provide for pupils of all abilities. The less able pupils who have until now left school with nothing to show for their years of schooling, gain a certificate which indicates what they have achieved. This includes their achievements in areas which have traditionally not been assessed, such as practical skills and oral communication.

Credit Is Given For Success
As each pupil attains a certain grade it enables a positive statement to be made about his/her achievement. Too often in the past the teachers' attitude to assessment was to concentrate on what the pupils had failed to achieve.

Clear Goals To Aim For
The fact that the criteria are in an explicit written form means that the pupils are able to understand the reasons for particular assessments and are able to look ahead to see what must be done to improve their performance. If pupils know what to aim for, they can concentrate their learning on appropriate aspects.

Pupils are Assessed in Relation to a Fixed Target
Pupils are no longer assessed by comparison with their peers and the notion of a pre-determined proportion attaining a certain level is no longer appropriate. Pupil and teacher together can work to achieve the set target.

The Targets Provide a Basis for Course Planning
The extended grade-related criteria provide a checklist to ensure that the necessary skills and concepts have been included in the course. The teaching programme has to be designed to ensure that the pupils have the opportunity to demonstrate whether or not they have achieved the target.

Curricular Development is Promoted
Although there are reservations about the notion of an assessment-led curriculum it is an efficient way of ensuring that teachers as a whole do not ignore certain areas which are deemed to be important. In Scotland the concentration on assessing specific key cognitive aspects of the subject ensures that all teachers conceive their courses to include activities enabling pupils to demonstrate their abilities in these areas. The emphasis on skills and concepts initiated some radical thinking in a number of subjects which had previously been content oriented.

National Standards Apply Within the Classroom
Where certification was based on an order of merit in a final examination, it was not always easy for teachers in one school to

determine how the performance of their pupils in the classroom compared with the performance of pupils nationally. With set targets to aim for and no predetermined proportions of pupils at individual grades, the teachers can judge the standards of their pupils in terms of national standards.

Inexperienced Teachers are Supported

Inexperienced teachers in particular are assisted by the setting of clear targets to assist in their course planning. With little or no past experience on which to judge the standards of their pupils they can be assured of the standards to set and the goals to aim for by referring to the various grade-related criteria.

More Detailed Information Available to End-Users

With each subject being subdivided into its essential elements and each element being described by a summary statement for the individual grades, employers and others can use these summary statements to give them more detailed information about the accomplishments of individual candidates on those areas of achievement which are of interest.

No doubt there are other potential benefits which could accrue from the introduction of grade-related criteria but even the above list contains much that is worthwhile and in line with current thinking about education. However, while working with the grade-related criteria in our action research we did come across some problems which seemed to indicate that fulfilling this potential would not be an easy task.

Problems with the Making of Grade-related Criteria

In Scotland, the devising of appropriate grade-related criteria for each subject was the responsibility of the members of the relevant Joint Working Party. The membership consisted of practising teachers, members of the advisorate and representatives of the Inspectorate, the Scottish Curriculum Development Service and the Scottish Examination Board. The remit of the groups included the requirements to provide for each of the assessable elements, a statement of the performance expected for each level. As mentioned previously there were six performance levels written in two forms, the summary grade-related criteria and the extended grade-related criteria.

The extended grade-related criteria are those which are of most concern to the teacher and to the Examination Board and the difficulties of compiling such statements are not to be under-estimated. They need to be precise enough to give clear guidance to the teacher and the setter of the external examination but yet be relatively content free to avoid a degree of prescription which would be unacceptable. Although knowledge and understanding are not ignored, the bulk of the criteria are written in terms of skills and processes. The transferability of a skill from one context to another is a source of considerable debate at present and, for example, Nuttall & Goldstein (1984) are of the opinion that 'the autonomous existence of a "skill" is itself rather a slippery notion' while Murphy & Pennycuick (1985) argue that there is some tension between conflicting requirements to be both precise and concise. Nevertheless, in Scotland as in other countries, the attempt is being made to develop workable sets of grade-related criteria.

The following are some of the pitfalls which have become apparent as different groups of working parties attempted to respond to their remit. The examples are mostly taken from Scottish material and it should be stressed that our work in this area coincided with the first attempts at drafting the criteria. A great deal of rewriting has since taken place and is still continuing as the members of the working parties take account of the experiences of piloting the system in schools. However, these examples illustrate the very real difficulties that are likely to be encountered. In all examples, Grade 6 is the lowest grade and Grade 1 the highest.

(1) *No Difference Between Two Consecutive Grades*
Assessable Element: Understanding.

Grade 2
The candidate can illustrate fully with several examples the key ideas.
Grade 1
As for Grade 2.

It would be a very miserly teacher who would classify a pupil as Grade 2 if the requirements for Grade 1 were identical. This problem may arise from a more general difficulty that will be returned to later, i.e. the decision to have six grade levels for each and every criterion.

The same example also illustrates another pitfall; the need for the reader of the performance criteria to be aware of, in this case, the key ideas. The summary grade-related criteria intended for employers and others make use of the same phrase, which refers to material defined for the individual topic areas and is not normally available outside the classroom.

D

(2) *Lack of Clear Hierarchy Between Two Consecutive Grades*
Assessable Element: Handling Information.

Grade 5
Given instructions the candidate can communicate given or
obtained straightforward information in a *limited range* of
alternative ways.
Grade 4
The candidate can communicate given or obtained straightforward
information in a *specified* alternative way.

   The ability to communicate in a 'specified' way could
legitimately be interpreted as more simple than communicating in a
'limited range' of ways. If 'given instructions' mentioned in Grade
5 means 'given guidance' this could be made clearer, as it seems
unlikely that no instructions would be given for Grade 4.

(3) *One Grade Stated in Terms of Another*
Assessable Element: Reading.

Grade 4
Nature of Texts: as for Grade 3.
   Summary. The candidate will have occasional uneven success in
retrieving, paraphrasing, explaining and justifying. This will raise
the performance above Grade 5 but it will still fall short of the
accuracy and adequacy of coverage required for Grade 3.
Grade 5
Nature of Texts: as for Grade 3.
   Summary. Overall, the candidate will display the same kinds of
abilities listed for Grade 6 but he will do so on more demanding
texts. He will understand individual points but will not make
connections. He has little success in paraphrasing.

   The above example is stating something which could presumably
be assumed to be true in all circumstances, viz. that Grade 4 is more
demanding than Grade 5 but less so than Grade 3. It refers readers
back to Grade 5 which in turn refers them back to Grade 6. Indeed
in this particular set only Grades 1, 3 and 6 were defined in any
detail, each of the intervening grades being interpolations. Again
this would seem to relate to the more general difficulty of each
Joint Working Party being obliged to set six levels when perhaps,
as subject specialists, they did not see this as the most suitable
solution.

(4) *Performance Levels Dependent on Skills Other Than That Named*
Assessable Element: Problem Solving.

Grade 2
The candidate has demonstrated ability to give a clear written report of an experimental procedure used to solve a problem.

In this particular case, Grade 2 is an enhanced award for a subject, General Science, which is one of the few to be limited to the lower grades only, i.e. Grades 3 to 6. It does appear that the enhanced award will be given more for the candidate's ability to write a clear report than for any specific problem-solving ability.

(5) *Grades Differentiated by Qualifying Adjectives*
Assessable Element: Problem Solving.
The candidate has demonstrated ability to:

Grade 6	Grade 5
draw an appropriate conclusion from *simple* scientific information	draw appropriate conclusions from *simple* scientific information

Grade 4	Grade 3
N/A	draw an appropriate conclusion from *complex* scientific information

Without some kind of definition or exemplar material it may be difficult to come to any consensus on what constitutes simple information and what is complex. Some subjects have sought a way round this problem by providing definitions and/or exemplar material to clarify what is meant by simple, straightforward, complex etc.

(6) *Differentiation by Qualifying Adjectives or Adverbs used in Conjunction*
a Assessable Element: Evaluating.

Grade 6	Grade 5
The candidate has demonstrated ability, given *simple* evidence, to make a *valid, basic* judgment about the actions and/or attitudes of people in the past.	The candidate has demonstrated ability, given *simple* evidence, to make a *valid* judgment about the actions and/or attitudes of people in the past with *limited supporting argument.*

Grade 4
The candidate has demonstrated ability, given *straightforward* evidence, to make a *valid* judgment about the actions and/or attitudes of people in the past, with *limited supporting argument*.

Grade 3
The candidate has demonstrated ability, given *straightforward* evidence, to make a *balanced* judgment about the actions and/or attitudes of people in the past.

Grade 2
The candidate has demonstrated ability, given *complex* evidence, to make a *balanced* judgment about the actions and/or attitudes of people in the past.

Grade 1
The candidate has demonstrated ability, given *complex* evidence, to make a *balanced and extended* judgment about the actions and/or attitudes of people in the past.

b Criteria: Practical Music-making
Student (*almost never, rarely, sometimes, often*) displays a (*reasonable, good, high, exceptionally sensitive*) standard of musical performance and can sight-read, improvise and conduct with (*difficulty, little competence, not always competently, reasonable degree of competence, competence, flair and skill*).

These particular sets of statements are based on juggling with different permutations and combinations of words. The first example depends on rating performance on two different dimensions, both of which are hierarchically arranged.

Diagrammatic Representation

Example (6) a

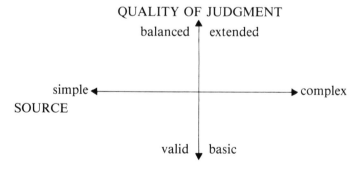

The wording of the performance criteria assumes that there is a near perfect correlation between the two dimensions, i.e. it is not possible to make a valid basic judgement based on complex evidence.

Example b, which is written in a different form to point up the differentiating factors, is a conjunction of three different dimensions, again all assumed to be operating in a lock step fashion: frequency of display, standard of musical performance and degree of competency. This example is further complicated by the degree of competence being attached to three quite different areas of practical music-making, sight-reading, improvising and conducting, which again are presumed to elicit homogeneous achievement patterns. The only way in which the teacher could assess these in practice would be to observe them separately and then aggregate the results in some way. Any interesting differences would be lost by this process.

General Difficulties

For the Scottish Standard Grade certificate, the decision was taken to impose a degree of uniformity on the various subject areas. In the initial stages, all Joint Working Parties were required to arrange each criterion on six levels of performance. This assumed that it was appropriate to assess every skill or subskill at every level and meant in the case of modern studies, for instance, that thirteen separate criteria had each been written as six ordered statements. It has already been shown in the examples above that some subjects found this less satisfactory than others, with a variety of methods being employed to circumvent the difficulty. In English only three grades had been defined, the others being interpolations. In other subjects with perhaps a larger progressive knowledge base, such as mathematics, it had been done by relating the skills to different content appropriate to different levels. Yet others had depended on qualifying adverbs and/or adjectives of varying degree. Certain grade levels for certain criteria were described as not applicable to a few subjects. This may be preferable to artificially forcing all criteria into the same mould of six levels, and more acceptable than writing the same description of performance for two different grade levels. Particularly at the lower levels, differentiation is often dependent on the amount of support given to pupils in carrying out the task. There seems to be no good educational reason why there should be the same number of grade levels for every criterion, and this is borne out by the system being devised in Queensland, Australia. The Board of Secondary School Studies is currently in the process of developing and implementing a new assessment system based on standards of performance in various criteria. In this format there are no pre-determined requirements as to the number of levels for each individual criterion, the actual number being determined through the experience of the subject specialists.

Another general difficulty which will be returned to in the next section is the assumption in many subjects that the hierarchy of skills is a constant, independent of the context in which it is practised. Many of the teachers with whom we worked were of the opinion that, for example, the skill of 'making a valid evaluation from specific information' (Grade 6) could be set at very different levels of ability depending on the nature of the specific information.

Using Grade-related Criteria in the Classroom

One of the claims made in the Government's Consultative Paper 'Framework for Decision' was that the use of grade-related criteria would make it possible for schools to adopt a purer form of criterion-referencing within the classroom. In our present action research we set out to assist teachers in the development of criterion-referenced assessment instruments which would take account of the grade-related criteria as laid down in the guidelines for Standard Grade.

Teachers involved with our project were invited to choose a syllabus area and decide upon a small number of outcomes from that area which they felt were important to assess. They were asked to take into consideration the appropriate assessable elements and the descriptions of performance as outlined in the extended grade-related criteria. For example, one geography department chose the theme Settlement Studies and decided that this area provided opportunities to assess Understanding, Handling Information and Evaluating. Our task was to support the teachers in clarifying the extended grade-related criteria to develop precise definitions which would serve as a basis for criterion-referenced assessment. It quickly became apparent that particularly in the skill of Evaluating, the opinion was that the context in which the skill was practised and assessed would have a major effect on the level of difficulty as experienced by pupils. The context-free statement as a description of performance was open to interpretation over a wide range of ability.

To try to ascertain what the skill of Evaluating might mean in geography, we asked the teachers to take part in a small experiment. This involved a group of teachers individually producing a number of examples of performance related to each of the extended grade-related criteria at each level of difficulty. For example at Grade 5 the extended grade-related criteria read 'express a simple point of view and support it with a limited number of reasons' and an appropriate performance example could be 'after studying the amenities in the local area, suggest with reasons what additional amenities should be provided'. Participants were asked not to discuss the statements with their colleagues at this stage.

These statements were printed out in random order and returned to the teachers who, again individually, matched them to one of the six grade levels.

We then carried out an analysis of the results and found that no single performance example was allocated to the same grade level by all teachers. However, by relaxing the criteria for consensus to an acceptance of a two point distinction (either 1/2, 2/3, 3/4 etc.) by at least six of the nine teachers, we were able to distinguish a set of twenty statements about which there was this limited consensus.

We also isolated 10 statements about which there was least agreement. These 'controversial' statements were each allocated to at least five of the grade levels by the various teachers.

Our next step was to study both of these sets of statements with a view to identifying some general characteristics which might help to ensure greater consensus.

Possible Characteristics

Initial analysis indicated that each performance example related to two factors:
(a) a reference to the context or content;
(b) the nature of the process or skill.

Further study suggested that the consensus statements were characterised by having both the context and the process clearly spelt out in domains which were relatively small in scale. It comes as no surprise that small-scale well-defined descriptions of performance offer the most reliable indicators for differentiating between levels of achievement. It does imply that grade-related criteria can only offer a starting point for the production of criterion-referenced assessment instruments.

A second factor of interest from this experiment was the impossibility of obtaining consensus at six grade levels, our relaxed criteria for consensus being based on acceptance of a two-point distinction. The difficulty of reliably grading behaviour on a six point scale may indicate that for teaching purposes a three point scale may be more manageable and more reliable. Indeed the Examination Board is at present involved in looking for ways and means of simplifying the assessment procedures for Standard Grade, and one of the suggestions likely to be implemented is that the descriptions of performance will be written at three grade levels only.

In many subjects, as the piloting of courses began and feedback was collected from the participating schools, later versions of the extended grade-related criteria showed an awareness of the need to make the process clearer and more focused. For example in the first draft guidelines for geography, one of the extended grade-related criteria for the skill of 'evaluating' read as follows:

'The pupil can demonstrate the ability to make an appropriate deduction from data.'

The same statement written after the benefit of trialling in schools read:

'Given straightforward information the candidate can make a simple evaluation of two given possibilities and support the conclusion reached with a straightforward reason.'

Both of these were intended to demonstrate performance at grade level 6. The first one was general enough to be set at widely varied levels of difficulty, depending both on the complexity of the data and on how the pupil would demonstrate such ability. Other subjects have gone further. For example, in modern studies the section on assessment includes a list of differentiating factors which have been used in compiling the extended grade-related criteria, and defines such terms as straightforward, complex, personal, concrete, abstract and theoretical.

A crucial question relates to the use of the grade-related criteria. Where it is used, as in our action research, to form the basis for formative assessment, i.e. assessment designed to provide feedback to teachers and pupils to assist with teaching and learning, questions of comparability and reliability rarely arise. Where it is to be used summatively as a basis for certification, problems arise in trying to achieve a balance between a statement which is concise enough to provide a summary of achievement to interested parties but yet precise enough to make a reliable assessment possible. The task of the Examination Board to set external examinations based on these criteria is considerable. Issues of validity and reliability must be addressed if the certificate is to gain the credibility of employers and other users.

Grade-related Criteria: Promise or Compromise?

At the 1985 conference of the British Educational Research Association, several speakers asserted that educational policy decisions in relation to assessment and curriculum matters were racing ahead of research and development. When the decision was taken to go ahead with the development of Standard Grade courses in Scotland, a programme of research and development was set up to address some of the issues, including those related to the new assessment procedures. This programme ran parallel to the development and implementation of the first phase of the new system. It was hoped that the piloting of courses and trial examinations would provide substantial feedback on which to evaluate some of the early decisions. Unfortunately, two years of industrial action by Scottish teachers during 1985-87 meant that this feedback was much more limited than had been envisaged. In a paper presented to the International Association of Educational Assessment (1985), Long of the Scottish Examination Board admitted that in many cases the Joint Working Parties responsible for devising Standard Grade courses and assessment strategies had made their decisions before they could take account of research and development findings. However, he went on to say that the Board's agreement to implement the new assessment procedures had been dependent on a full review and evaluation of the system once in operation. This review has already begun.

Already there is evidence that subsequent drafts of the grade-related criteria have attempted to overcome many of the weaknesses of the earlier versions. The statements of performance have been refined and clarified and several subject areas have included, for each extended grade-related criteria at each level, a small number of performance examples. These examples are drawn from the content themes or topics of the relevant subject and are intended to make concrete the skills and processes essential to the subject.

As grade-related criteria become more focused and precise and hence more likely to form the basis for sound reliable assessments, so they bring more rigorous control over what is taught. This conflict is one which will not easily be solved. Paradoxically, a system which was lauded as one which would extend the scope of the classroom teachers to develop their own courses within an overall framework of criteria has resulted in substantial documentation giving guidance on every aspect of teaching and assessment in a detail hitherto unknown in Scottish education. If there was general agreement about what constituted a worthwhile curriculum, precision in the grade-related criteria coud be advantageous. It seems unlikely that such consensus would be possible on a national scale and would inevitably bring about an unacceptable narrowing of the curriculum. In the localised scale of the classroom, specific objectives can be defined for a particular situation and precision of process can be combined with precision of content in a way that is not available to the Examination Board at a national level. Teaching need not, of course, be confined to those areas to be assessed externally, but the backwash effect of public examinations has always been considerable. The commitment demanded from teachers to implement the new and unfamiliar system is such as to leave the average teacher very little time to develop wider aims than those described by the grade-related criteria.

Continuing Developments

As mentioned above, the review of the assessment procedures of
Standard Grade is already underway. The feedback from teachers
and other educators made it clear that the arrangements for
assessment as first developed placed unacceptable demands on the
classroom teacher, and a committee was set up to look into ways
and means of simplifying the system. To some extent the
difficulties which would have attended the introduction of any new
system were exacerbated by the teachers' action. This curtailed the
in-service programme as originally devised and reduced the flow of
information which might have contributed to a rolling programme
of evaluation and improvement. However, at least two of the
recommendations imply a step back from criterion-referencing. It
is suggested that the number of domains to be assessed in each
subject should be reduced and that the grade levels should be
written at three points instead of six. Both of these moves have the
effect of reducing the precision with which one can provide
information about the specific knowledge and abilities of pupils.
This is acknowledged by the proposals for simplification (SED,
1986) which state that:

> 'the contribution which criterion-referenced assessment can
> make to improving the quality of learning and teaching makes
> it desirable to pursue development, but that much has yet to
> be learned before it would be possible to make criterion-
> referenced techniques the sole basis on which certification in
> Standard Grade can take place.'

Has there been anything gained by the move to grade-related
criteria? There is little doubt that a form of externally assessed
Scottish leaving certificate will continue to dominate secondary
education for some time to come. Whereas it can be demonstrated
that criterion-referenced assessment can contribute to an improved
quality of learning within the classroom, it has yet to be shown that
its techniques can be translated into a workable system where
certification is dependent on public examinations. Despite its
imperfections the new system, which is a genuine attempt to
develop a practicable alternative assessment strategy catering for all
pupils, does provide information on their achievements in more
areas and in more detail than that provided by the old 'O' grade.
On the understanding that the programme of improvements will be
continued as the Examination Board evaluates and reviews the
system in operation, perhaps it is appropriate to stop treating
grade-related criteria as a poor substitute for criterion-referencing
and accept it as a fairly complex and imperfect system in a complex
and imperfect world.

REFERENCES

BROWN, S. K. (1980) *What Do They Know?* Edinburgh: HMSO.

LONG, H. A. (1985) 'Experience of the Scottish Examination Board in developing a grade-related criteria system of awards'. Paper presented at 11th Annual Conference of the IAEA, Oxford.

MURPHY, R. J. L. and PENNYCUICK, D. B. (1985) 'Evaluating Current Initiatives in Educational Assessment: Graded Assessments and GCSE'. Paper presented at Nuffield Assessment Seminar Series.

NUTTALL, D. L. and GOLDSTEIN, H. (1984) *Profiles and Graded. Tests: The Technical Issues in Profiles in Action.* London: FEU.

SCOTTISH EXAMINATION BOARD (1984) Standard Grade Arrangements.

SCOTTISH EDUCATION DEPARTMENT (1977b) Assessment for All, Edinburgh: HMSO.

SCOTTISH EDUCATION DEPARTMENT (1982) Framework for Decision. Edinburgh: Scottish Education Department.

SCOTTISH EDUCATION DEPARTMENT (1986) Assessment in Standard Grade Courses: Proposals for Simplification. Edinburgh: Scottish Education Department.

ISSUES IN THE IMPLEMENTATION OF GRADED TESTING

DAVID PENNYCUICK
Education Area, University of Sussex

Introduction

The graded test movement in Britain has been most prominent in Modern Languages, as a result of local initiatives by groups of secondary school teachers dissatisfied with traditional methods of teaching and examining. GOML (Graded Objectives in Modern Languages) schemes are described by Harding, Page & Rowell (1980) and by Harrison (1982). However, there are operational schemes in several other subject areas — Mathematics, Science, Music, Physical Education and Business Studies — and some of these schemes are long-standing. All have in common the three key features of level-progression, success-orientation and curriculum-linking, which are incorporated in the following definition.

> In a graded test scheme, there is a sequence of tests at progressive levels of difficulty, complexity, sophistication and/or syllabus content, which are designed to be taken by students only when they have a high probability of success. Each test is closely linked to the curriculum for the relevant level by means of clear specification of the knowledge and processes to be assessed and of the standards to be attained.
>
> (Pennycuick, 1986.)

There are also several developments in progress under the broader heading of graded assessment (Harrison, 1985) which possess similar features. All three key features are to some extent problematic, and graded testing gives rise to a wide range of curricular, pedagogical, psychological and administrative issues. Some of the more significant of these issues are discussed in this article.* Technical issues such as mastery, validity, reliability and comparability are not included here, but are discussed by Nuttall & Goldstein (1984), Pennycuick & Murphy (1986) and Pennycuick (1986). Murphy & Pennycuick (1986) discuss the relationship between graded assessment and GCSE.

---

* The author has recently completed research on graded tests within the Assessment & Examinations Unit of Southampton University Department of Education. The research was based on a series of case studies of school departments operating graded test schemes in Mathematics, Science and Modern Languages, using the principles of illuminative evaluation and the methodology of condensed fieldwork. The main focus of this research was on the impact of these schemes on teaching, learning and assessment (see Pennycuick, 1986).

Graded Tests as a Vehicle for Curriculum Reform

Many graded test schemes may be placed in the category of assessment-led curriculum development projects. In each case a major curricular and/or pedagogical reform is associated with the assessment framework provided by the principles and structure of the graded tests. Whereas there is a common thread in that learning becomes more pupil-centred, the nature of the reform is dependent on the particular scheme. Thus in Modern Languages syllabuses may be based on functions and notions related to authentic contexts rather than on grammar and syntax. There is much more oral and much less written work; the emphasis is on communication rather than translation. In the Kent Mathematics Project (KMP) the reform is primarily pedagogical; class teaching gives way to individualised learning based on a material bank of workcards, booklets and cassette tapes. In the School Science Certificate (SSC) the curriculum reform is perhaps less pronounced, but nevertheless entails a significant shift towards practical activity by the pupils themselves, as opposed to written work or listening to exposition by the teachers, and there is an increased emphasis on basic skills.

The key features of graded tests are conceptually separate from the curricular and pedagogical reforms associated with the schemes. An immediate question which arises is the extent to which implementation of the reforms depend upon the graded test framework. Could these, or similar, reforms have been introduced without such a framework? Would they have occurred in any case, given the pressures resulting from the almost universal movement to comprehensive secondary education and the raising of the school leaving age to 16? Certainly some assessment system is needed, if only for reasons of status and for reporting pupil achievement.

The view adopted here is that these graded test schemes provide a convenient and appropriate vehicle for reform to take place. Several functions of the schemes support and consolidate the implementation of curricular change.

(a) They provide a learning structure which helps to define and stabilise the classroom situation for pupils and teachers. For example, given the single statement 'We are doing KMP today' at the beginning of a lesson, pupils know what to do and what to expect during that lesson. Schemes can also act as a uniting influence on a department in terms of curriculum, pedagogy and staff relationships.

(b) They provide benchmarks of progress and a means of monitoring individual progress. This is particularly necessary for programmes in which it is not easy to monitor progress because they de-emphasize written work, or where learning is fully individualised.

(c) They provide comparison with what is done in other classes, schools or areas, and hence give status to the scheme in the eyes of parents, teachers and pupils.

It may also be argued that graded test schemes can hasten the dissemination of change.

Another interesting question is whether a graded test scheme could be developed, introduced and sustained *without* significant associated curriculum reform. Any new form of assessment is likely to have some curricular backwash effects, but it would presumably be possible to develop, for example, a progressive series of graded tests for a traditional grammar-based course in Modern Languages. However, this has not occurred, and it might be felt that incentives to develop schemes, and enthusiasm for the operation of schemes, stem at least as much from the prospect of influencing and reforming curriculum and pedagogy as from the graded test principles themselves. Curricular reform is more prominent than the assessment structure in perceptions of the schemes held by many teachers and pupils.

Graded test schemes can act not only as a vehicle for curricular and pedagogical change, but also as a catalyst to stimulate and facilitate such change, and as a lever to exert pressure for change. The graded tests provide a framework, in the form of a progressive series of levels, which is clear in terms of defining firstly the ground to be covered and/or the skills to be acquired, and secondly the standards to be achieved. Although schemes may be aimed at specific target groups the framework does *not* define the age of the pupils to be tested, nor the time to be spent on a given level. There is often scope for flexibility in the ways in which schemes are used within a school, for example in deciding which pupils take which levels, in the order of treatment within a level and the structure of individual lessons, in the tasks assigned to individual pupils, and even in the way the testing is organised (although not all of these would necessarily apply to each scheme). Nevertheless, the content and processes to be assessed, and the methods of assessment, are usually defined with such detail and precision as to confirm that graded test schemes have considerable potential for curriculum control. However it may be noted that schemes rarely cover the whole curriculum in their respective subjects. Restrictions on the scope of the schemes limit the curricular backwash effects of the tests.

Curricular Issues

The progression of levels in graded test schemes may be compared with Gagné's (1968) concept of learning hierarchies. However, the allocation of content and skills to levels by the working parties which develop the schemes is often decided as much on a pragmatic and even arbitrary basis as by a logical analysis of which tasks are prerequisites for which other tasks. Horne (1983) distinguishes between 'causal hierarchies', in which success at a task is *dependent* on success at previous tasks, and 'likelihood hierarchies' in which success at a task is made more *likely* by success at previous tasks. He argues that likelihood hierarchies are not invariant, and that some pupils may respond better to a different order of treatment. Now graded test schemes based on individualised learning (such as KMP) do permit flexibility, and schemes based on class teaching do not prescribe, or even recommend, any order of treatment within a level, leaving this to be decided by school departments or individual teachers. Difficulties in sequencing material may be created by the need to integrate graded test syllabuses with textbook courses. Some schemes, particularly in Modern Languages, draw a distinction between testing syllabuses and teaching syllabuses.

Harding, Page & Rowell (1980, p. 3) state that the first principle of GOML schemes was that the traditional five-year course should be 'broken up into a set of shorter-term objectives, each one leading to the next and each one building directly on its predecessor'. But in some schemes it is common for pupils to bypass one or more levels, which leads to the question of whether a holder of a certificate at level n may be assumed to possess all lower level skills. This assumption may be dangerous.

A related issue is the extent to which pupils retain the acquired skills. Margaret Brown (1983) argues that

> 'for a meaningful graded structure it is necessary for the testing to be restricted to abilities which, once acquired, are relatively permanent. Thus recall of facts and rote-learned algorithms may not be very appropriate contents of a graded assessment if children are able to learn them for a test but liable to forget them rapidly later' (pp. 5-6).

It might be that the probability of retention can be increased by appropriate choice of test content and teaching methods, with the tests forming an integral part of the course. However, the need for effective learning to include continual revision indicates that analysis of learning elements into a linear or branching hierarchy cannot be the only factor in establishing a successful teaching sequence.

Rote learning may be an endemic danger in an assessment system which clearly specifies the tasks to be performed by candidates (the 'curriculum-linking' feature). The more precise the specification, the more candidates will know what the test questions will be, and are able to practise accordingly. Factors encouraging teachers to 'teach to the test' in graded test schemes include not only precise specification of objectives, but also emphasis on success for the great majority of pupils (the 'success-orientation' feature). In some circumstances this might not matter if the specified skills (for example learning to wire a plug) are in fact acquired. Indeed 'teaching to the test' is perhaps not very far from 'relating instruction and assessment closely to the objectives'. But it could still be argued that restriction of the curriculum to the test items themselves is undesirable. One reservation about GOML schemes in general is the possible use of testing syllabuses as teaching syllabuses. This might have consequent negative curricular back-wash effects (e.g. excessive use of English), in addition to overemphasis on testing. Some teachers doubt whether the schemes enable pupils to reach a point at which they begin to use language creatively, but overemphasis on testing can be avoided by by-passing levels. In schemes where learning is individualised, again there is the danger of 'learning to the test', permitting apparent progress without genuine learning, and actual cheating on tests may also have this effect. Cheating may become a greater risk if different pupils take the same test at different times. But it would be a pity to overemphasise the possible negative effects of graded testing. There is evidence (Pennycuick, 1986) that schemes may be handled in such a way as to minimise such effects, and there are also significant positive backwash effects, for example the achievement of greater stress on oral or practical work.

Diagnostic Functions of Graded Tests

The most basic diagnostic use that could be made of graded test results is guidance to pupils on whether or not to continue the subject. But in practice this choice is limited, since many subjects are compulsory, and options may only be available at the end of the 3rd year. Even then the decision is influenced by other factors: intended career, attitude to the subject, results in other subjects and timetabling constraints. Given that study of the subject *is* to be continued after taking a particular graded test level, then pupils who pass may be expected to proceed to the next level, or perhaps bypass one or more levels. If they fail, the situation is more complex. Pupils may possibly be expected to repeat the entire course for the failed level, although this appears to be uncommon. Alternatively, pupils may receive specific remedial instruction before retaking the same level, or even go on regardless to the next level. This last possibility may appear to negate sensible diagnostic use of the test results, but may be the only practicable option in a class-based scheme where teachers may feel that a class is only manageable if all its members are working at the same level.

In principle, pupils are not entered for graded tests until they are likely to succeed, but in practice pupils do sit tests and fail to reach the specified standard. This occurs sometimes through administrative convenience in entering whole classes for tests at the same time, but also because (unlike many mastery learning strategies) schemes do not place stress on formal methods of formative diagnostic assessment by which teachers may know when pupils are ready. Teachers might argue that such assessment may be done informally, but the point is that pupils do fail graded tests, and that diagnostic use may therefore be made of the graded test results themselves, even though this diagnostic function may be limited when the principle of readiness is in fact applied.

There are several points to be made. Firstly Black & Dockrell (1980, p. 12) state that 'diagnostic assessment requires clarity concerning the outcomes of learning intended by the teacher'. The curriculum-linking feature of graded tests ensures that assessment is indeed focused on intended learning outcomes. Clear specification of the knowledge and processes to be assessed assists the diagnostic function, and a wide range of test styles enables a broad spectrum of outcomes to be covered. Secondly, effective diagnostic assessment is essentially descriptive, not numerical. Teachers gain much more information on what pupils have and have not achieved from disaggregated graded test results, that is performance on separate items, than from overall scores. Thirdly, active participation by the pupils themselves may contribute to the process. For example, pupils practising in pairs on oral assignment checklists are not only diagnosing, but to some extent are also remediating, their own deficiencies.

Of course the diagnostic function is only effective if it provides both a process for detecting gaps and weaknesses in students' knowledge and skills *and* some mechanism by which such faults may be corrected:

> 'the over-riding factor in all situations must be that the test should be positioned at a point in the teaching strategy when there will be time to do something about the problems diagnosed' (Black & Dockrell, 1980, p. 31).

A drawback of many graded test schemes from this perspective is the tendency to set tests at the end of the academic year, thus leaving insufficient time available for remedial action. A further serious limitation may be in the time available for teachers to give individual attention. Schemes based on individualised learning are perhaps the most suited to the diagnostic function. Indeed Margaret Brown (1983), in the context of Mathematics, states that

> 'it would seem that the greater the integration between the curriculum and the assessment, to the point where the assessment tasks become identical with the curriculum itself,

E

the more use can be made of the diagnostic benefits of graded testing in the classroom. However this has profound implications in terms of the organisation of the secondary school mathematics curriculum, and must logically lead to individualised or flexible small-group teaching' (p. 7).

She also argues that the more frequent the testing the greater the possibility of using the feedback diagnostically.

So far the diagnostic role of graded tests has been considered only as a provider of information for pupil guidance and the remediation of individual difficulties. These tests can also be used in a diagnostic way to provide feedback on curricular and pedagogical effectiveness, and on the quality of the tests themselves. Thus if it were found that students were consistently having difficulty with a particular graded test item, it would be possible to use that information in several ways at scheme level, such as

(1) to modify or replace the item;

(2) to modify the syllabus content or skill tested by the item, or transfer it to a different level of the scheme.

At school level, teachers can use feedback information to modify the methods used for teaching a particular skill, or to devote more time to it. The use of a grid to record the performance of individual pupils on test items not only assists in monitoring progress, but also provides useful diagnostic information for the course as a whole.

The Concept of Ability, and Suitability Across the Ability Range

The concept of ability will be treated here as if it is a measurable unidimensional pupil attribute. Its use in terms such as 'low-ability', 'mixed-ability' and 'ability range' (within a class or across an age cohort) is often related to the ways in which pupils are allocated to teaching groups. In practice, individual pupils' abilities are usually determined by their (norm-referenced) attainments, commonly measured by performance on tests and/or other forms of assessment. What is included in the assessment depends partly on which features of the curriculum teachers regard as important and assessable, but also on the content of text-book courses or external syllabuses. Where there is setting, account is taken of the possibility that abilities may vary from subject to subject, but for allocation purposes it is convenient to regard ability within a subject as unidimensional, although teachers do of course realise that pupils do not always perform equally well at all aspects of the subject, and may have abilities which are not covered by the assessment system used. Allowance can be made for variation in individual pupils' relative ability over time by building in mechanisms for reallocation.

Questions which arise are whether these norm-referenced concepts of ability and range of ability are appropriate in the context of graded test schemes, and whether some allocation systems are preferable to others for the operation of these schemes. Graded assessment is not designed to discriminate between pupils by measurement of individual differences, but the aim is for the great majority of those working on a given level to achieve mastery. In principle, provided the mastery level is reached, the actual test scores attained, and rank orders of candidates, are not important. But even if test scores are ignored it is still possible to use graded testing to define an ability range, by consideration of the levels reached and individual rates of progress from one level to the next. Within or across class groups, one possibility for differentiation between pupils at the same level is according to when they become ready to take the tests. 'More able' pupils may be defined as those who proceed faster and/or further through the levels, and it would therefore appear that the concept of ability range is still viable in the context of graded tests, even if it is no longer defined in terms of test scores.

If in practice the concept of (differentiated) ability is retained, that is not to say that the meaning of ability within a subject remains unchanged by the introduction of graded testing. Indeed the nature of ability is modified by the schemes in the sense that they assess different types of attainment than do more traditional approaches. For example, ability in writing may be replaced by an emphasis on oral ability or on practical ability. In some GOML schemes the multi-dimensional nature of ability is stressed by the requirement for separate standards to be achieved in reading, listening and speaking. In an individualised learning scheme, the ability to learn by listening to a teacher gives way to the ability to work independently and to learn from workcards. It may well be that individual children occupy different places on the 'ability range' as a result of these different emphases. Perhaps more significantly, many teachers regard the principles of graded testing to be consistent with a wish to play down individual differences in attainment between pupils. But there is no evidence that any significant changes in allocation systems have resulted from the introduction of graded tests.

A major policy issue for graded testing or graded assessment is whether to design schemes for a wide or limited ability range. The target group for the School Science Certificate is 4th and 5th formers who would not be entered for public examinations, and the Cockcroft Report (DES, 1982) recommends the development of limited ability 'graduated' tests in Mathematics. Such schemes do provide an assessment system for less able pupils which goes beyond the individual school, but there is the serious problem of the status of the schemes in the minds not only of the pupils themselves, but also of teachers, parents and employers. However there may also be difficulties for less able pupils taking part in full-ability schemes, who may become disillusioned by lack of visible progress over a long time-span, by repetition of content, and by comparison with the achievements of more able pupils (Margaret Brown, 1983). Even if schemes enable weak pupils to experience initial success, maintaining this is not easy.

It is clearly difficult to design common curriculum and assessment materials which both provide a challenge to more able pupils and offer a realistic chance of success to less able pupils. One advantage of limited-range schemes is that they can achieve an appropriate level of difficulty for their target groups.

However even limited-range schemes may be at a disadvantage for low-ability pupils in that they cannot cater for the possibility of a pupil doing more work at the same level of difficulty (thereby continuing to achieve success), rather than moving up the hierarchy of levels. Once tasks are defined in terms of levels, it may be difficult to convince pupils that progress is being made *unless* they move up the levels.

The desire to make a graded test scheme suitable across a wide ability range may limit its scope, leading to doubts about the scheme for the most able pupils. There may be concern about the transition to A-level courses, and there may be a need to supplement the scheme for able pupils. The pressures of the public examination system and the need for graded tests to lead to some form of national certification has led to the development of Mode 2 or 3 examinations linked to some schemes, requiring certain compromises to be made on graded test principles, but enabling the schemes to be followed by able 4th and 5th year pupils. The problems at the top end of the ability range appear less severe than those at the bottom end, but both appear to increase higher up the age range.

Pupil Motivation

Many graded test schemes state enhanced pupil motivation as a main aim, and it is clear that motivation is a salient issue. In this article motivation will be taken to refer to goal-directed behaviour and 'positive motivation' to mean that pupils' goals include achievement of the graded objectives and that a substantial part of their action during appropriate periods is devoted to the pursuit of that goal.

A major reason for the introduction of graded test schemes is their intended emphasis on success. They are planned to avoid the drawback of traditional examinations whereby many pupils experience a sense of failure both by being compared unfavourably with others and by being presented with tasks which are of an inappropriate level of difficulty. Task difficulty may be defined in normative terms (how well others do) or in subjective terms of pupils' own expectancy of success. Nicholls (1984) argues that in the latter case challenging tasks are preferred — those in which pupils have moderate subjective probabilities of success. Graded tests are designed to provide a challenge while having a high pass rate, and success in the form of 'doing better than others' is replaced by success in 'acquiring skills' and 'passing tests'. As we have seen, this non-competitive form of assessment is not necessarily egalitarian, since some will progress faster and further than others.

It does seem necessary from motivational considerations that passing a graded test is seen to be synonymous with acquiring the tested skills, in other words that the success should be *valid*. Otherwise pupil perception of success may be short-lived. There is a tension in setting cut-off scores which give both a high pass mark and a high pass rate. Whether or not the scheme is certificated it is important for motivational reasons not only that pupils should regard themselves as successful, but also that they should be regarded as successful by others (e.g. teachers, peers, family). Success may be perceived during the tests (when pupils find they can do the tasks), or when pupils are told they have passed, or when certificates are presented, or when pupils receive praise (perhaps when they take certificates home). Motivation may be due partly to encouragement from past (actual) success, and partly to the stimulus of the prospect of future (hypothetical) success. Graded test schemes aim to provide frequent positive reinforcement of pupil motivation by means of short-term goals consisting of readily available targets. The idea that success and motivation can be mutually reinforcing is fundamental to graded assessment philosophy. However the intended emphasis on success is not necessarily realised in practice, and it may be more difficult for graded test schemes to continue the enablement of pupil success than to provide the initial experience.

In the long term there is the question of what will happen if graded tests are extended to more levels and more subjects. Will low-achieving pupils still be well-motivated after they have received a number of graded test certificates, and have seen all their friends receiving them, perhaps many more than they have themselves obtained? Intrinsic motivational factors may be more significant than extrinsic factors such as certificates. However in all three schemes studied by Pennycuick (1986) pupils expressed support for the testing structures, and for the style, content and difficulty level of the tests, and this support extended to some pupils who said they do not normally like tests. The graded tests do act as an incentive for pupils, although older pupils feel that what really matter are public examinations. These act as a major motivating factor by giving national certification, which provides qualifications for further education and enhances employment prospects.

A further possible factor is extra commitment and enthusiasm on the part of teachers, particularly those who have been involved in the working parties developing the schemes, with an associated sense of purpose and of control over the development. If teacher enthusiasm is important in motivating pupils, large-scale schemes developed by examination boards might not necessarily be as successful as those developed locally by groups of teachers. A parallel point is made by Nuttall & Goldstein (1984) who suggest that the *graded* part of graded testing may be relatively insignificant, and that a modular scheme might serve as well. There is case study evidence (Pennycuick, 1986) that pupils are motivated by teachers who make the work interesting, but little to suggest that teacher enthusiasm as a pupil motivator is more important in the graded test context than it is in any other form of teaching.

It was suggested earlier that enthusiasm may be based more on associated curricular reforms than on graded test principles. If the particular syllabus objectives and teaching methods adopted by a scheme are predominant as a motivating factor, new graded test schemes might not necessarily be as successful as existing schemes, unless they are also founded on perceived curricular needs. A good example of such needs is given by the communicative approach to language learning. Pupils like the stress on authentic oral communication which they perceive to be practical, useful and relevant. They enjoy the work partly because they can succeed, but also because they regard the objective of realistic interaction with native speakers to be a valid one. This extends to enjoyment of the actual testing process, and can be reinforced by a genuine sense of achievement on using the language, say on a day trip to France, although this is only a possibility in some areas. Clearly the style of assessment is important from a motivational point of view, as well as the curriculum content and the style of teaching. Another positive factor may be that assessment objectives are clearly defined so that pupils know more precisely what they are expected to do. But there are also negative effects. Pupils can become bored by overemphasis on testing, particularly if the same topics arise in consecutive levels. Where testing is conducted on an individual basis, waiting for other pupils to be tested can create discipline problems in addition to the difficulty that no actual teaching can take place during that time.

There may also be demotivating factors in schemes where

learning is individualised — loss of continuity, lack of perceived relevance, difficulty in understanding the workcards, or possible abuse of the system. In all schemes motivation may be a function of length of involvement with the scheme. In new schemes there may be Hawthorne or other initial effects, although established schemes are still novel to each succeeding age cohort of pupils.

A final possible factor to be considered is that of competition (or its absence). Many pupils do not see themselves as competing with their peers in the sense of striving to excel them, and would not wish to do so, but equally there is a strong desire not to be left behind (Pennycuick, 1986). Pupils are motivated to keep up with their fellows, but competition is rather against targets and standards set by the scheme. Indeed graded tests seem appropriate for a classroom atmosphere in which competition among pupils is discouraged.

No clear picture emerges of what the key motivating factors are, or of the extent to which any improved motivation is a permanent effect. Different pupils are motivated by different factors and combinations of factors, and individuals may react differently in different contexts. The possible results of improved motivation, when it occurs, are that pupils will become more amenable as a result of improved attitudes created by enjoyment and/or satis-faction from achievement and/or perceived relevance of their graded test course. This may lead to several effects, notably better behaviour and greater effort, hopefully reflected in improved performance. Not all teachers are convinced of the disciplinary benefits. For example, an oral approach to language teaching can make lessons more difficult to control. Indeed it may be that discipline must in the first place be such as to permit operation of the scheme!

Nuttall & Goldstein (1984) point out the difficulty of analysing the key ingredients of the success of graded tests in motivating pupils. It appears that schemes can have positive motivational effects, which result from various complex interacting factors, with different pupils reacting in different ways. However, not only do these effects tend to decay with the time individual pupils have been involved with the scheme, but there may also be negative effects. Perhaps the conclusions for teachers are simply not to be overly sanguine about motivational benefits of graded test schemes, and to adopt a heuristic approach to their operation of the schemes with individual groups of pupils in order to maximise potential benefits, while remembering that there are reasons other than purely motivational ones for the development and use of graded tests, for example to provide a vehicle for curriculum reform, or to provide a clear description of pupil attainment.

Staff Perspectives

Graded test schemes permit flexibility in the ways in which they may be used by participating schools, and there are significant variations in practice. Department heads and subject teachers take account of several factors in determining the place of the graded test scheme within the course structure. These factors vary among schools and among schemes, but may include timetabling and setting considerations, resource constraints, and the pressures of external examinations. If the graded test scheme does not provide the entire course it is necessary to mesh work towards the scheme with other work in the subject, with topic selection and sequencing decisions being strongly influenced by the progression of levels. The 'ability' of the pupils and the logistics of testing are other factors affecting decisions about how each teaching group is involved with the scheme.

The temporal organisation of schools, where timetable changes and automatic promotion occur at yearly intervals, does not provide a natural framework for graded testing, in which levels are not designed for a fixed time allocation, but where the intention is that pupils are entered for tests when they are ready. Even in individualised learning schemes there is a tendency to encourage pupils to achieve 'completion' in some sense by the end of the academic year. The principle of readiness is inhibited by the imposition of deadlines, whether the scheme is individualised or based on class teaching. In the latter case, teachers are likely to find it difficult to cope with groups working at different levels, or different stages of the same level. Vertical timetabling may provide at least a partial solution to problems created by the year-group structure of schools (the 'lock-step' system). However, mixed-age classes may only be operable on the basis of modular curricular organisation, which again is likely to require fixed time slots, although if this were done on a termly basis it might become easier for pupils to transfer to a higher level group when ready, or to stay at the same level if not.

The logistics of test administration is a major concern. External administration (e.g. candidate entry, issue of certificates) is a concern for those running the scheme rather than teachers in the schools. It is the internal administration of the tests which creates difficulties for the latter. One is the increase in teacher workload resulting from individualised assessment. Application of the principle of readiness is another. A third problem is the time spent by teachers on testing as opposed to teaching, perhaps leading to boredom and/or reduced pupil progress. Fourthly there are disciplinary difficulties (e.g. preventing cheating, occupying the rest of the class during oral testing, controlling remedial groups taking practical Science tests).

Several possible solutions to these difficulties may be considered. One is to conduct individual testing during lunchtimes, but this would increase workload still further, and does not appear to be realistic in the long term. Secondly, if resources were to become available, a reduction in group size or the provision of cover for teachers involved in testing. The availability of a second teacher would reduce or eliminate all the above difficulties, and some teachers feel that such cover would be the only fully satisfactory solution. Failing that, a third possibility is to reduce the volume of testing by simplifying procedures, reverting to a greater proportion of group assessment, or bypassing levels. It clearly helps if graded tests are seen as a *replacement* for existing school examinations and assessment procedures.

It is not only the logistics of testing which can create an overall increase in teacher workload. Teachers may find periods to be harder work and more exhausting than more traditional teaching. Extra work may be required to integrate scheme and textbook materials into a coherent course. Record keeping to monitor individual progress leads to an increased load. Workload effects on staff are cumulative, depending on the number of classes involved in the scheme. Teachers may be reluctant to extend a scheme to more groups, in order to restrict increased strain to tolerable levels.

The introduction of graded tests appears to require some increased resources in terms of accommodation and materials, and may also pose resource management problems. Teacher comment suggests that the availability of adequate resources is a significant factor in the viability of schemes. These include the provision of textbooks and/or workcards, equipment and consumable materials, and satisfactory acoustics for oral work. Schemes are likely to be funded largely from existing budget allocations, both within the schools and within the LEAs concerned. It is clear that there are substantial hidden costs of LEA-based schemes which have to be absorbed. These may include major time commitments by advisory staff, secondment of teachers, costs of working party and in-service training meetings, secretarial costs and the costs of materials of various kinds (e.g. circulars, test materials, certificates). In general the benefits to the LEAs are non-quantifiable (e.g. pupil motivation, curriculum development, staff in-service training, prestige).

The need for in-service training is stressed by Newbould & Massey (1984) and by Harrison (1985), also by Rutherford (1979) writing in the wider context of criterion-referenced programmes.

'We have found that the problems with locally designed criterion-referenced curricula neither seem to be rooted in the basic concepts and approaches of such curricula, nor in the specific content of the materials which have been developed, rather the problem seems to lie in the fact that school-built programmes, and commercial programmes as well, do not develop a *support system* to accompany the content structure system' (p. 48).

LEA advisers play a key role in such support systems for the schemes studied by Pennycuick (1986). In-service support falls into three main categories, firstly written materials in the form of teachers' guides or circulars, secondly meetings, workshops or courses, and thirdly advisory visits to schools. It appears that the main need for further training felt by teachers is in the style of teaching and testing, not in the principles or administration of the scheme.

It may be supposed that the rewards accruing to individual teachers vary at least in part according to their depth of involvement, and their perceptions of the scheme. Harrison (1985) argues that 'the involvement of teachers in curriculum development improves morale and commitment'. This may extend to all participating teachers, but may be particularly valid for working party members, who are likely to have a strong sense of ownership of the scheme as a result of helping to devise the syllabuses and tests, and therefore a personal stake in its successful operation and dissemination. Teachers who have not been members of the working parties may nevertheless have sufficient commitment to the curriculum and assessment principles behind the scheme for this to compensate for any perceived loss of freedom to plan and develop their own courses, or they may welcome the graded test structure as an aid to curriculum planning.

Even if the scheme is found difficult to operate, staff may persevere since they see advantages for their pupils and perhaps for their own self-esteem. Increased workload is a potential but not necessarily an actual staff demotivator, since teachers may feel that the scheme is worth the effort in terms of results. Staff morale and enthusiasm may be encouraged by a sense of satisfaction in pupil achievement, even if teachers do not particularly enjoy the periods, and may experience a feeling of loss of control during them. A very positive factor is that graded test schemes appear to encourage unanimity of approach and hence departmental unity. Teachers who have adopted a scheme voluntarily are likely to emphasise its beneficial features in their own minds even if they also stress its problems to a researcher. There is the possibility that they may use the scheme as a means of obtaining more resources or recognition. Heads of department in particular may perceive a graded test scheme as a source of departmental prestige by drawing attention to their modernity and commitment, and even as an outlet for ambition. All teachers may experience a sense of pride from their developed expertise in the efficient administration and successful operation of the scheme. However, the overall impression from case study research (Pennycuick, 1986) is that the over-riding reason for teacher support of graded test schemes is that they feel that these schemes benefit the pupils more than whatever they have replaced. It should be noted that many of the points made throughout this section may be true of any curriculum innovation, rather than being specific to graded tests.

REFERENCES

BLACK, H. D. and DOCKRELL, W. B. (1980) *Diagnostic Assessment in Secondary Schools.* Edinburgh: Scottish Council for Research in Education.

BROWN, MARGARET (1983) 'Graded tests in Mathematics: the implications of various models for the Mathematics curriculum'. Paper presented at BERA conference, London, September 1983.

D.E.S. (1982) *Mathematics Counts* Report of the Committee of Inquiry into the Teaching of Mathematics in Schools (The Cockcroft Report) London: HMSO.

GAGNÉ, R. M. (1968) 'Learning hierarchies' *Educational Psychologist* 6, pp. 1-9.

HARDING, A., PAGE, B. and ROWELL, S. (1980) *Graded Objectives in Modern Languages.* London: Centre for Information on Language Teaching and Research (CILT).

HARRISON, A. (1982) *Review of Graded Tests* Schools Council Examinations Bulletin 41. London: Methuen Educational.

HARRISON, A. (1985) 'Graded assessment' in *E206 Block 4 Supplementary Reading.* Milton Keynes: Open University.

HORNE, S. E. (1983) 'Learning hierarchies: a critique' *Educational Psychology* 3 (1), pp. 63-77.

MURPHY, R. J. L. and PENNYCUICK, D. B. (1986) 'Graded assessment and the GCSE' in T. Horton (ed.) *GCSE: Examining the New System.* London: Harper Row.

NEWBOULD, C. A. and MASSEY, A. J. (1984) 'Initial survey of views on aspects of graded assessment'. Report for the Project on the Assessment of Graded Objectives, Midland Examining Group.

NICHOLLS, J. G. (1984) 'Conceptions of ability and achievement motivation' in R. AMES and C. AMES (eds.). *Research on Motivation in Education. Volume 1: Student Motivation.* Orlando, Florida: Academic Press.

NUTTALL, D. L. and GOLDSTEIN, H. (1984) 'Profiles and graded tests: the technical issues' in *Profiles in Action.* London: FEU.

THE NATIONAL CERTIFICATE: AN EXAMPLE OF MODULAR BASED CRITERION-REFERENCED ASSESSMENT IN PRACTICE

JOHN YATES AND JOHN HALL
Scottish Council for Research in Education

January 1983 saw the publication by the Scottish Education Department of *16-18s in Scotland: An Action Plan,* a document which put forward an agenda for the reform of non-advanced further education. In August 1984, following a period of intense activity, the National Certificate was launched. During the development phase teams of development officers and short life working groups were concerned to produce many hundreds of modules (or teaching units), most of which are of 40 hours' duration. From August 1984 the traditional courses in non-advanced further education — City and Guilds, Royal Society of Arts, various SCOTEC (Scottish Technical Education Council) and SCOTBEC (Scottish Business Education Council) certificate courses — were all replaced by the National Certificate, administered by a new body which came into being in March 1985, the Scottish Vocational Education Council. The aim was to produce more relevant education and training for students, with greater flexibility and choice. Although the main client group was 16 to 18 year olds in Further Education, adults also would be catered for and some of the students would be school pupils.

The National Certificate represents the first major implementation in Britain of a modular structure of learning and teaching in which the assessment is continuous, internal and criterion-referenced. It also represents a highly flexible approach to learning, with modules able to be taken alongside or as an extension to SCE Standard grade 'O' grade, Higher Grade or Certificate of Sixth Year Studies in the fifth and sixth years of secondary education. Alternatively it may be taken on a full-time or part-time basis in a College of Further Education, or on a consortium basis with part of the award being provided by a school and part by a college. It may be offered as part of a TVEI Scheme or a Youth Training Scheme. The Certificate itself records the knowledge and practical skills acquired by a student through a programme of modules taken from the National Catalogue, built around personal and vocational needs.

Perhaps the most striking feature of the National Certificate is in the method of assessing student performance. The traditional end

67

of course examination, a centrally administered common assessment instrument based on a sample of the course content, was marked on a norm-referenced basis with students being ranked according to an inferred degree of competence. This has been replaced in the innovation by assessment which is college-based, continuous and criterion-referenced. Assessment is seen to be a cumulative process with a major emphasis being placed on formative as well as summative assessment. It takes place during the 40 hours of the module and only rarely takes the form of an 'end of module' examination. Opportunities are given for remediation and re-assessment to take place. Assessment, therefore, is seen as part of the total curriculum and teaching approach. Thus, although the module descriptors may appear on first reading to be highly prescriptive with clear guidelines on assessment procedures to be followed, and a statement of the performance criteria which the students will have to meet in order to be judged to have fulfilled the learning outcomes, in many modules there is also a stress on the importance of being responsive to the needs of students and to maintain a flexibility of approach. Student-centred and activity-based learning is encouraged wherever possible.

To illustrate what has been stated so far about module descriptors, it may be helpful to look at one module from the National Catalogue. 62103, Reception 1, is taken from the Business and Administration area of the National Catalogue. Three learning outcomes are specified. It is required that:

'The student should:
1. know and perform the role of a receptionist and demonstrate the importance of personal qualities and appearance;
2. communicate effectively with people in a working environment;
3. maintain basic records, and organise a reception area.'

Each of the learning outcomes has corresponding content and context which is given in some detail and the descriptor provides for an internal assessment by the tutor of each particular learning outcome. Thus learning outcome 1 'will be assessed by observation of role-playing which must be adequately carried out', and a checklist for recording student performance is available in the Assessment Guidelines in the descriptor. The performance criteria state that 'a satisfactory performance must be attained covering the following points:

1.1 addressing people correctly;
1.2 courteous and pleasant manner;
1.3 use of tact in an appropriate situation;
1.4 clean and tidy appearance.

On achieving the required level of performance for each item column "A" in the checklist should be ticked and the date inserted. On completion of the learning outcome itself column "B" should be ticked'.

Reception 1, like many other modules in the Business and Administration area, has detailed exemplar material accompanying the module descriptor. This provides examples of how tasks may be set and assessed. Thus in the role-playing exercise for learning outcome 1, staff are referred to an exercise on Reception in Chapter v of 'This Learning Business' by Bitton, Clark and Gresham, and the advice is given that the first 4 role-playing exercises in the chapter are appropriate for learning outcome 1. This degree of detail in the assessment procedures is quite typical of many module descriptors in the Business and Administration section of the Catalogue. Other sections of the Catalogue are not so well supplied.

The Assessment Model

The assessment model in the National Certificate can be described as the dichotomous form of criterion-referenced assessment. Students are assessed purely on the basis of whether they can or cannot perform the task required whether this be a knowledge-based test, the performance of a practical task, or the demonstration of a particular skill or competence in some behaviour. There is no attempt to measure the degree of success, to grade performance within a continuum, or to use multiple cut-scores. In some tests cutting scores have been fixed at a level below which a candidate will be deemed to be unsatisfactory. However, cutting scores need not be fixed until a test has been constructed. The 16-18 Action Plan "Guidelines on Assessment" (SED, 1984c) states that it may not be possible to specify what the actual cutting score should be 'sometimes not until it has been marked', a qualification which, to some extent, undermines the basis of a criterion-referenced assessment system.

There is a major emphasis placed upon the formative aspects of assessment throughout all of the modules within the Catalogue. There is a clear expectation that staff and students will utilise the assessments for diagnostic purposes which might assist in determining the need for remedial instruction should a student fail to achieve a particular learning outcome. In many modules it is envisaged that formative assessment will be built into the teaching approaches, especially where a high proportion of the 40 hours of a module is spent in activities. For example students may be asked to complete a drawing, write a report, produce an artefact, or demonstrate a competence, and all these outcomes of the learning process lend themselves ideally to formative assessment. The main purpose of formative assessment is to assist the student's learning. However, all the modules incorporate forms of summative assessment, and in some instances a task may serve both formative and summative purposes. Thus 'where the thing to be learned is a series of actions, say a planning exercise, or an investigation where the process is as important as the end product, formative assessment can be carried out in the process during its development and the summative assessment can be made after any necessary correction of procedure has been undertaken'.

However, in all cases, staff should try to 'make time available after the summative assessment for remedial action to be taken for those who do not come up to the performance criteria at the first attempt'. (p. 12). This means that assessment should be conducted at an appropriate time during the module immediately after the work to be tested is completed. Moreover summative testing should take place 'between two-thirds and three-quarters of the way through a 40 hour module' so that remedial work and re-assessment should be possible.

Moderation

Although the performance criteria are laid down, and should provide for compatibility of standards between centres offering and staff teaching the module, in many cases satisfactory performance is a matter for the professional judgment of the tutor aided by external moderation procedures. These procedures operate at a number of levels. Firstly, centres offering modules are validated by SCOTVEC to ensure that resourcing is adequate for the modules which it offers and for any new modules it might propose to offer. Secondly there is a system of SCOTVEC subject assessors appointed on a part-time basis to assist in the promotion and maintenance of quality within the National Certificate. An extract from the SCOTEC/SCOTBEC statement of 10 May 1984 states (SCOTVEC, 1986b).

Quality Assurance

It is the view of the Councils that the success of the Action Plan and of the National Certificate will depend in great measure on the extent to which users acknowledge that national quality and national standards exist. It is the intention that the standard of the award should be generally acceptable in the community, to industry and commerce, and to the student. The aim is for the control of standards to be seen as at least as effective as in the existing system, although the methods of achieving this aim will be different.

Validation, moderation and assessment procedures have been introduced to establish and maintain acceptable levels of quality and standard. The procedures have been designed to confirm the student's mastery of the learning outcomes, to reflect the curriculum and objectives and to allow centres flexibility in meeting the needs of individuals and of industry and commerce. National certification is provided by SCOTVEC but centres and teaching staff have a major responsibility in establishing and maintaining standards. A system has been designed which:

(a) encourages centres to develop the arrangements and teaching approaches needed to establish and maintain standards (supported by information, advice and where required, assistance from the Council and its committees);

(b) ensures early identification and remedy of unsatisfactory cases;

(c) provides national standards and certification.

Both Subject Assessment and External Moderation have therefore been seen as important and ongoing functions since the introduction of the National Certificate. . .

Each module in the National Certificate Catalogue is identified as belonging to one of 135 Cognate Groups and Subject Assessors are responsible for assessing modules in the Cognate Group to which they are appointed by SCOTVEC. Subject Assessors are drawn from schools, colleges, central institutions, universities, industry and commerce and have a wide and varied experience which is backed up by a comprehensive training programme. In addition, regular meetings are held to enable Subject Assessors to keep abreast of Council developments and to discuss national standards.

During session 1985/86, Subject Assessors were required to address groups of key practitioners such as regional coordinators, senior centre staff, advisers, to disseminate information on national standards to as wide an audience as possible. These key practitioners then convey this information to other staff within their region, division or centre, thereby ensuring a constant flow of vital information.

Centres offering National Certificate modules are visited by Subject Assessors on a random sampling basis and during a visit to a centre a Subject Assessor will carry out the following duties relating to modules in his/her Cognate Group:

1. obtain details of all assessment instruments and specifications being used by the centre;

F

2. agree that the assessment instruments and specifications are appropriate in type and qualify or request change;
3. discuss any problems raised by the centre in relation to subject assessment;
4. ensure that internal standardisation arrangements (if necessary) are effective;
5. sample the tests, assignments, etc, actually set;
6. sample the responses of candidates;
7. observe, if possible, the performance of students at orals, practicals, etc;
8. prepare a brief report for the Council;
9. recommend approval (or otherwise) of the results of the centre.

Such are the stated aims of SCOTVEC's quality control system. It remains to be seen if the reality always matches the rhetoric. There are some indications from teaching staff that they have their doubts about the effectiveness of moderation and subject assessment and are not yet convinced of the existence of 'national standards'.

Instruments of Assessment

Each module descriptor specifies the assessment instruments to be used for the summative assessment of each learning outcome, and it is necessary to obtain permission from SCOTVEC if a centre proposes to use any other form of assessment instrument. Most modules are likely to require a battery of short tests rather than a single terminal test, each being related to one or more of the learning outcomes. Learning outcomes typically embrace knowledge, skills and behaviours, each assessed by an appropriate instrument, for example a multiple-choice test, the production of an artefact, or the demonstration of a competence in a role-playing situation or a group discussion.

The use of particular assessment instruments is often qualified in specific ways. Thus observation checklists which are commonly used for testing practical skills may specify the number of successive occasions on which a performance has been successful. This type of assessment could be carried out fairly unobtrusively during the course of modular teaching at appropriate times, the teacher using a grid as a cumulative record of student achievement.

In the June 1984 Guidelines on Curriculum and Assessment which accompany '16-18s in Scotland: An Action Plan' a number of characteristics are listed which the learning outcomes should exhibit (SED, 1984b). These include being precise, unambiguous, measurable, few in number, content-related, capable of exemplification, indicative of progression, indicative of minimum competence level and of operating conditions. We shall see later to what extent these characteristics are present in all modules.

Staff Involvement

Perhaps the most radical feature of modular assessment is that it will be undertaken by the teacher of the module, possibly being prepared and certainly being administered and marked by him or her. The external involvement which occurs through the validation of the centre and its modular provision and the external moderation of the assessments does not remove the primary responsibility for assessment which is devolved onto the class teacher, and this fundamentally changes the nature of the relationship which the teacher has to the class. It also enhances the professional status of the teacher. Whereas previously the teacher could sometimes see himself as an ally of the class with the common purpose of outwitting the external examiner, now the teacher has become the assessor with all that this implies for influencing the interaction between teacher and student in terms of such processes as negotiation, the maintenance of objectivity, and the halo effect of the student's impact on staff. Undoubtedly this can create some tension between staff and students. Moreover, some staff have been unwilling to adopt this new role, both because it adversely affects their relationship with students and also because it involves them in much more preparation, marking, and administrative chores connected with the assessment.

On the positive side, the effect of bringing staff into the assessment process is to enhance their professional responsibility. Teachers are made to be more directly responsible for the consequences of their pedagogy. Assessment can be integrated more closely with teaching and learning approaches, and formative or diagnostic purposes can be more directly related to the summative purposes of assessment. Staff become directly responsible for the preparation, marking and return of test materials and this may make them more critical and aware of the impact of their teaching on students, problems which may arise, and the possible solution to difficulties which students may experience in their learning of parts of a module. To the extent that staff cease to be the victims of an external examination system just as much as students, these changes represent a positive gain. Staff are made to feel directly responsible for their teaching in a way which is not possible under any system of external examination. In many respects, modular assessment creates the potential for much more innovative teaching in which the individual teacher is allowed to develop his own method of operation, subject to the safeguard of an external moderation system which, if sensitively implemented, would encourage initiatives and divergent styles of presentation.

A modular system of teaching and assessment based on 40 hour units can allow for much greater flexibility of educational provision than that given by a traditional one-year course with a terminal external examination. In fact one of the reasons for incorporating a modular system into the National Certificate Provision was to permit 'a range of points of entry to and exits from education and training with greater freedom of choice for young people' and 'better opportunities to change areas of study while retaining credit for early achievement' (Scottish Information Office, n/d, p. 4). In addition a modular provision offers scope for being used as a flexible basis for adult re-training.

On the negative side the change in the purposes and procedures of assessment within a criterion-referenced modular provision is likely to lead in the first instance to staff and student work which is dominated by assessment issues. There is a danger that learning outcomes will be taught and assessed one by one in a strictly mechanistic manner. In fact learning outcomes can be dealt with in a variety of ways, in combination or as part of a teaching programme which might include learning outcomes from several modules. Nevertheless the idea of a stimulus, in the form of teaching a tightly defined learning outcome, followed by a response in the form of an assessment of whether the student has assimilated content by demonstrating attainment of the performance criteria through some appropriate assessment, could give rise to a highly mechanistic approach to teaching and learning in which staff and students could feel themselves to be on an assessment treadmill.

By the same token, it is possible for staff to feel in a straitjacket. Inflexible guidelines, extended exemplar materials and insecurity about the maintenance of standards may cause staff to adhere rigidly to the form and content of assessment in the descriptor material.

In National Certificate modules, skills are being assessed in three broad categories: those of knowledge, skills and behaviour, and the emphasis is placed on knowledge, skills and behaviour in use or application. Hence many of the assessments in National Certificate are likely to be undertaken as part of the process of learning, perhaps while involved in some work-based activity, typically by the observation of performance using a checklist. As such, the application of criterion-referenced assessment in this type of situation creates substantial technical difficulties in the achievement of validity and reliability.

Domain Definition

A module of 40 hours must be regarded as close to a minimum period of time during which four or five learning outcomes can be adequately assessed, though of course this will depend upon the size of the class and the complexity of the tasks being assessed. If we examine the assessment instruments being used in relation to the learning outcomes in the module descriptor, the first issue we need to resolve concerns the clarity of the domain being assessed: is it clearly and appropriately defined? Do teachers in fact know what they are assessing? It may also be that the scale of the attainment is unrealistically wide or demanding in relation to the 40 hours of the module, leading to assessment being skimped or the domain insufficiently sampled — even allowing that somehow all the material is taught. Finally, the performance criteria need to be examined for their clarity, ease of use and whether they will constitute acceptable evidence of attainment.

The issue of 'domain definition' is crucial to evaluating the quality of assessment. Modules will typically attempt to limit the contents of the domain through a careful consideration of the aims of the module itself. In order that the assessment should be valid and reliable it is necessary that the performance criteria should adequately reflect the level of knowledge, skill or behaviour which is included in the domain definition for the module, and should be appropriate to the context of assessment. Thus in certain skills, for example shorthand or typing, it is necessary to specify a particular speed and level of accuracy.

Another factor which needs to be taken into account in the construction of criterion-referenced tests associated with modules concerns the detail of the instruments used. While the form of the instrument is specified, it remains possible for the individual teacher or centre to devise the actual contents. In this respect modular assessment accords the teacher considerable professional autonomy and responsibility for developing assessment consistent with a common framework.

If we look at two contrasting modules we can get some idea of the reasons why variations in the quality of assessment may arise. The two examples are taken from modules in the National Catalogue, 01184, *Personal and Social Development: Contemporary Issues,* and 04300, *Introduction to Electronic Systems.*

Personal and Social Development modules aim to develop ways of thinking, feeling and behaving which foster the growth in self-confidence and independence on the part of the student, and which aid the development of communication and inter-personal skills, the capacity for co-operative action, together with planning and decision-making skills. In this particular module, 01184, *Contemporary Issues,* the purpose is to raise awareness of contemporary issues, to develop skills in gathering, interpreting and presenting information and ideas, and in working as a member of a team. There are three learning outcomes:
The student should:

1. Co-operate and participate with others in a small group investigation of a contemporary issue.
2. Contribute to the preparation and presentation of an account of a contemporary issue, working as a member of a small team.
3. Make an effective contribution to group discussion of contemporary issues.

The content/context suggests that students would form groups which would afford them opportunities for activities like planning and decision-making, monitoring progress, and reflecting on experience. Students 'should practise and develop skills in working as a member of a small team, including listening to and watching others, responding constructively to others, expressing ideas in relation to the work in hand, questioning'.

Assessment procedures in this module indicate that formative assessment should operate as an integral part of learning and teaching in the module, and may include self-assessment and assessment by peers as well as assessment by the teacher. Folios of work should be available for inspection by a subject assessor, and students should be issued with record sheets which tell them about what is to be taught and learned and which provide a continuous record of attainment. These records could also be used by the student to inform a third party, for example a potential employer, what has been learnt. The performance criteria demand that the student listens to and watches others, responds constructively to others, expresses ideas in relation to the work in hand, questions others, gathers information, contributes to the preparation of the presentation on the selected topic and to the presentation itself.

This behaviour domain is very extensive and is specified in such a manner as to permit of very large variations in performance. The language used in the performance criteria is full of assumptions and implied value judgments, for example an 'effective contribution', or 'makes relevant contributions'. No attempt is made to provide objective criteria by which these can be judged. In addition the performance criteria state that the student should 'express ideas' and 'question others', but no account is taken of the level or quality of these ideas or questions. In fact given the lack of precision in the performance criteria, it would be very difficult to fail anyone on this module unless they actually refused to take part in group activity.

If we turn to 04300, *Introduction to Electronic Systems,* the learning outcomes are expressed much more exactly.

The student should:

1. be able to identify transducers capable of carrying out listed conversions;

2. assemble known elements into a given working system;
3. develop and assemble simple electronic systems for given functions;
4. know the purpose, operations and limitations of one commercially available system.

Within the assessment procedures, the performance criteria are highly specific. For example learning outcome 1 is assessed by a written/graphical exercise requiring that the student:

a. correctly identifies transducers capable of performing a stated function;
b. names transducers from given symbols correctly;
c. draws the symbols for given transducers correctly;

— the 'stated' functions and 'given' transducers and symbols being listed elsewhere.

The other three learning outcomes are equally specific in their assessment instruments and performance criteria. We might conclude, therefore, that in this module the behaviour domains are reasonable small and that the skills required and the content limit specifications are clearly defined. Learning outcomes and performance criteria are unambiguous, and even the possible uncertainty surrounding learning outcome 4, the choice of a 'commercially available system', is reduced by the need for the system to be based on elements studied within the module. The Learning and Teaching approaches for that outcome in any case specify that the report should be based on information obtained from manufacturers' sales and technical information.

The detailed analysis of module descriptors indicate that there are marked variations in the clarity of language, hidden assumptions and implied value judgments, specificity of performance criteria and the clarity of definition of the behaviour domains and content limit specifications. However, it also suggests that modular assessment can be relatively precise when the language is clear, unambiguous and contains no assumptions or implied value judgments, when the behaviour domain, and content limit specifications are clearly defined and small, and when the performance criteria are clearly stated and objectively measurable. When these conditions are met, modular assessment has the potential for being highly valid and reliable compared to a traditional end-of-course examination system which relies on sometimes inappropriate methods of testing and restricted sampling of course content. However, the examples given may also suggest that some domains may not always be amenable to this treatment. The fact that the Personal and Social Development module descriptor discussed above cannot be regarded as likely to generate high quality assessment does not mean that the skills on which it attempts to focus are any less important. It may, however, call into question the National Certificate approach to such skills.

Organisation

Pressures of time and organisation can develop for staff and students alike. Modular programmes are frequently designed on a sequential basis which means that there is a need to ensure that students complete each module before moving on to another one in linear progression. Staff are required to prepare, administer, mark and record assessments within a definite time period, and they must ensure that there is adequate time for any remediation and re-assessment. In certain circumstances, if the teacher thinks it justified, 'a student may be allowed to proceed to a subsequent module without having attained a satisfactory performance in all of the learning outcomes in a given module' (SED, 1984b). However, ideally, students would achieve one module before proceeding to its sequel. Problems with time seem to be amongst the most common of all the difficulties experienced in implementing the National Certificate modular provision. Some staff are aware of how much additional marking and administration time they now have and the difficulties of remediation and re-assessment are particularly acute in the case of weaker students and students who are absent from initial assessments. Occasionally it is necessary to reduce the 40 hours of teaching time associated with a module to provide for this contingency, and there is also a need to prepare extension work for other students who have completed the required work. Many staff are aware of taking more than 10 per cent of the module time for assessment purposes as well as spending a great deal of their non-teaching time in connection with preparation and recording. Another widely held concern of staff is that recognised standards should be established and maintained. Some colleges now have internal monitoring and moderation procedures and, in some areas, staff from different colleges meet as a group to exchange ideas and information. However, in the eyes of some staff, SCOTVEC moderators and subject assessors have not had the hoped-for impact in establishing national standards and there is little doubt that this affects their perception of the credibility of the National Certificate. The lack of confidence in whether national standards are being achieved is also reflected in a view among many staff that outside users of modules do not understand the new system of assessment with its abolition of norm referencing. The Guidelines (SED, 1984b) in fact draw attention to the implications of a criterion-referenced approach to assessment. Instruments should be chosen to ensure valid testing: 'Every student who has adequately performed the tasks demanded should normally achieve a high score on the test and should not be passed or failed on half, or less, of what was to have been achieved. . . . It follows from this competence-based approach that the student must attain a satisfactory level of performance in *each* learning outcome.' Later in the same section on assessment, the whole question of standard setting procedures is discussed, the conclusion being that draft standards prepared by professionals would be amended in the course of dialogue with a wider audience which could include representatives from the industry. Limitations as to the validity of the assessment for specific occupational needs are recognised on p. 34 of the Guidelines in which it is stated that 'the final occupational fitness test must be determined mainly by the industrial needs specified by particular employers or groups of employers, sometimes in partnership with trade unions. . . . Some skills cannot be tested fully in off-the-job contexts where there are in site requirements. In these cases a moderation agency could operate through a nominated officer, or a part-time seconded tester/assessor (acting as a kind of external examiner or moderator)'. In taking account of the needs of external bodies like industries and professional institutes, it was recognised that it might be necessary for students to take some form of external assessment. If the demand for this kind of assessment arose, it might be met within an integrative module, 'the outcomes of which could subsume those of the set of modules' (p. 28, Guidelines on Curriculum and Assessment).

CRA v. NRA

A particular issue which appears to vex some staff, especially in relation to their views about outside users of modules, is whether the abolition of grading might lead to a lowering of standards and to the de-motivation of more able students from whom very little would now be required in order to meet the criteria of success in modules. One danger is that performance criteria may become very trite indeed, the result being that minimal standards of attainment arise which fail to stretch students of above average ability. The result is that students aim to achieve the minimum threshold and have no incentive to go beyond, resulting in boredom and under-achievement. Of course many students may be similarly de-motivated over a longer period of time by conventional forms of end-of-course assessment, but undoubtedly assessment based on criterion-referencing does create the possibility that given levels of achievement become targets of achievement, with the result that more able students are never stretched to their full potential. On the other hand, the less able are provided with realistic goals, and, accordingly, it might be argued that their level of motivation is enhanced by the change in the method of assessment.

Traditional norm-referenced exams had certain (perhaps illusory) advantages. Potential employers and those charged with selecting students for entry into courses of advanced or higher education were presented with lists of candidates 'ready sorted' according to their examination results and could, if they so wished, either demand a certain level of pass before further consideration was given or just take 'the best' until all their places were filled. The reliability and validity of norm-referenced exam results when used for selection is, of course, open to question, but there seems little doubt that both employers and those responsible for running advanced and higher education courses are used to having this sort of tool at their disposal when faced with making selection decisions. The National Certificate does not provide it. The absence of norm-referenced results, or any other form of grading of students, means that some other selection strategy must be used. The National Certificate attempts to supply the information which will be required by listing on the student's actual certificate, not only those modules which the student has passed, but also the individual learning outcomes he or she has attained. This information, so the argument goes, should be a great deal more valuable to an employer than a simple percentage mark which reveals nothing about what a student can or cannot do. It does, however, require a much greater effort on the part of employers (or other end-users) to interpret all this information which has a greater potential for the end user than the information supplied to the users of traditional examinations.

The Action Plan did not set out to remove all differentiation between students: rather it saw it as being achieved in ways other than by grading of results. The original idea was that students who had successfully completed one module at a particular level of difficulty should then be able to go on to another, more difficult, module and, by thus 'stretching themselves' as far as they were able, demonstrate their level of competence. Differentiation would thus be achieved, not through a grading of results, but by achievement of more demanding learning outcomes.

Conclusion

It is impossible to reach a final verdict on the merits and demerits of criterion-referenced assessment based on a modular system of provision without invoking philosophical questions involving the value of particular educational aims and strategies for achieving them. Modular provision and assessment rests upon a behaviourist theory of learning which owes much to the work of B. F. Skinner and to the ideas associated with programmed learning. Modules are built around discrete units of study in which learning outcomes are assessed by carefully devised instruments which attempt to measure whether the student has attained them through the application of explicit performance criteria. Assessment follows closely upon the teaching of particular learning outcomes within the module. The boundaries to knowledge, skills and behaviour are circumscribed, and assessment is limited by a clear domain definition, relevant performance criteria, and appropriate instruments which satisfy the criteria of validity and reliability. Reinforcement of learning is provided by formative assessment and summative assessment provides the reward. Such a model of instruction is sometimes viewed with alarm by educationalists concerned to inculcate broader values and more diffuse aims such as the development of critical judgment, or an appreciation of liberal values. It is also feared by some that it leads to a fragmentation of knowledge and a narrowing of horizons.

The type of thinking which modular criterion-referenced assessment both encourages and is particularly suited to measure is likely to be of the convergent kind, and to that extent it is difficult to see how the National Certificate can be fully reconciled to a student-centred approach to learning, in spite of the rhetoric of the Action Plan and related literature. There are many references to student-centred approaches which on closer examination turn out to be group-based activities or individualised learning with the situation being carefully structured by the member of staff. This could hardly be described as student-centred in any fundamental sense. In true student-centred learning the student will determine for himself both his educational objectives and the means by which he will attain them, and the role of the member of staff is to act as a consultant and adviser to the student, and as a resource to whom the student may turn for remedial help in case of difficulty. Teaching and Learning approaches are given in the form of suggestions for pedagogic style and methods, but there is a clear expectation that staff and students will adhere to such requirements as the stated instruments of assessment, numbers of learning outcomes and related performance criteria. These are not regarded as available for negotiation in any way, and to that extent National Certificate modules are hardly consistent with a fully student-centred approach to teaching and learning.

The final verdict on modular assessment must include an acknowledgement that it represents an important advance in the field of educational testing. As well as providing an opportunity for defining clear goals in the form of the learning outcomes, the system has the potential for a more rational articulation with employer and end-user demands as well as being flexible in its application to different types of student. However, it must also be acknowledged that some of these same features have negative, as well as positive, implications.

REFERENCES

SCOTVEC (n/d). *Guidelines on Assessment for Subject Assessors.*
SCOTVEC (1986a). *The National Certificate Session 1986-1987,* third edition.
SCOTVEC (1986b). Statement of 10 May 1984 reprinted in *SCOTVEC Journal,* 5, p. 7.
SCOTTISH INFORMATION OFFICE (n/d). *Factsheet 31: The 16+ Development Programme.*
SCOTTISH EDUCATION DEPARTMENT (1983). *16-18s in Scotland: An Action Plan.*
SCOTTISH EDUCATION DEPARTMENT (1984a). *16-18s in Scotland: An Action Plan:* Draft Guidelines on Curriculum and Assessment.
SCOTTISH EDUCATION DEPARTMENT (1984b). *16-18s in Scotland: An Action Plan.* Guidelines on Curriculum and Assessment.
SCOTTISH EDUCATION DEPARTMENT (1984c). *16-18s in Scotland: An Action Plan:* Guidelines on Assessment.

ACCREDITATION OF WORK BASED LEARNING — A NEW APPROACH FOR EDUCATION, TRAINING AND EMPLOYMENT

DAVID MATTHEWS
The Further Education Staff College

Summary

Against a background of the traditions of assessment and accreditation in vocational education and training and in employment, new national policies and initiatives are shown to require a broader base for accrediting occupational competence. The concept of work based learning with its focus on the work role is introduced, together with frameworks which assist in analysis processes. It is proposed that the character of occupational competence makes the application of traditional psychometric approaches to assessment inappropriate. The accreditation of work based learning is intrinsically criterion-referenced; it is linked to the work role and application, not knowledge and theory in their own right; it is multi-dimensional and its interpretation depends on anticipating transfer rather than making broad generalisations about ability. The ordering of this new field of accreditation therefore necessitates new psycho-mathematical models to address the subjective inferential and decision making processes on which it depends.

Introduction — Current Assessment Practices

Accreditation — the public statement of achievement — in employment and in vocational educational and training is dominated by a system of formal qualifications. Their status forms part of a value system based on achievement in secondary and university education.

There is constant debate about the extent to which qualifications represent the achievement of learners. The implications for the world of employment (or desired employment) are particularly contentious. As, for example, Burgess and Adams (1980) and Dale and Pires (1984) discuss, there are those who regard the measures used as unsatisfactory and not relevant to certain processes such as vocational selection. For some the remedy is a radical revision of assessment instruments. For others such considerations as vocational selection are incompatible with education.

There are within vocational education and training many who

83

feel that in their sector all is well — theory-based and knowledge-based examinations and qualifications are well established; all that is needed is an extension of their good practice to the rest of the vocational world. This self-satisfaction disguises the failure to accredit a large proportion of what individual workers have achieved — represented by their demonstrated competence in one or more job. It is partial accreditation, then, which often determines access to additional education and training and affects promotion and transition to other jobs.

Where the workplace has featured at all in formal accreditation, it has involved special assignments as if it were a laboratory or workshop timetabled in on a Friday afternoon. At a greater extreme, in sandwich degree courses a whole year of placement in a company can be represented in the information leading to a degree assessment by no more than a tick against 'completed work placement'.

The intrusion of achievement 'profiles' (as distinct from profile reporting of examination results) into non-advanced further education, stemming very much from the work of SCRE (1977) in secondary education, has enabled many course organisers to work closely with employers to ensure that the content — and to some extent the assessments — in their courses are relevant to the type of work in which students are or will be engaged in the workplace. Even this liaison, however, does not challenge the perception that vocational educational is the primary provider of learning, especially accreditable learning, and it is to provide what it knows best — knowledge and theory.

There are exceptions — notably in the latterday apprenticeship system in the engineering, road transport and the construction industries. There, largely under the influence of the industry training boards, testing of trainees' progress or confirmation of their end-of-programme achievement has come to include much better representation of work-like activity, albeit through specially created tests.

Most assessment in employment and in the workplace itself is not in the main used for accreditation purposes at all (Blum and Naylor, 1968). Its main use is the provision of feedback to the worker and to the organisation, through management or its agents.

Feedback to the individual worker, through frequent, routine reporting or annual appraisals, is intended to encourage improved performance. The information involved in such feedback may also influence internal selection and promotion processes or the identification of specific training needs. Individual performance information is also seen (Drucker, 1974) as an essential component of systems of management in which it is presumed that the individual employee will act rationally if given the opportunity to do so.

Feedback to the organisation is used for evaluation purposes — to judge the effectiveness or general acceptability of some training provision or the reorganisation of a working unit. It is also used in the control of production or other activity, and may be used to identify problems in the work system or to adjust such controlling parameters as the provision of overtime or the recruitment of additional staff.

Like further education and off-the-job training processes, workplace assessment makes use of skills tests or set-piece work samples. Rating scales are used in formative assessment and for evaluation purposes. As in the case of skills tests, the ratings may call for supervisor judgments of quite specific facets of a task — measurements of the dimensions on an engineering component, a check on the completeness of an administrative procedure, monitoring of the inclusion of specific behaviours in livestock feeding or a sales transaction. Other ratings may involve, as in many education profiles, a greater generalisation, perhaps about safety in the workplace, customer contact skills or even ability in the job as a whole.

Gross assessments include measurement of the employee's output. Income may be related to this, as is the case with piece-work and bonus or commission systems used for production workers, sales staff and the managing directors of multi-national companies.

All the assessment approaches involve someone in a supervisory or tutoring capacity reporting specified responses or making a judgmental estimate. Many organisations take some care to ensure that procedures are systematic if not supervisor-proof, but others act without awareness of or concern for the consequences of haphazard measurement. The processes are intuitive to a high degree.

Education and the Workplace — A Comparison

There are both similarities and differences in education and employment assessment practices. They share the issues of who should make judgments and how they should be required to make them — how broad, within what framework, what criteria, on what evidence and with what training for assessors? There are, however, two important differences.

The first, as has already been suggested, concerns the functions for which assessment is used. In education, including further education, and in training which draws heavily on educational traditions, assessment is used formatively *and* summatively.

Assessment is certainly not the same thing as certification, but it is the basis for accreditation of achievement. It seeks in this respect to communicate achievement of the individual to the world outside the institution in which the learning is said to have taken place.

Assessment in the workplace, however, has tended to be about the needs of the employing organisation alone, lacking the dimension of external communication. The purposes of assessment are more immediate.

The second difference concerns the control of events upon which assessment is based. In another context, Landa (1976) suggests a distinction between 'rigorous' and 'non-rigorous' control of learning which is useful here. The distinction is not between well-controlled and badly-controlled, but between the types of control suited to algorithmic processes and those contributing to heuristic ones. There is an analogous contrast between assessment based on, or generated by, the pre-planned events which make up many a syllabus and assessment based on events in the workplace which are not so predetermined, at least not for learning or assessment purposes. The distinction is between input-led and outcome-led processes.

A New Context for Accreditation

The start of the most recent wave of central government intervention in vocational education and training is associated with the publication of the New Training Initiative (MSC, 1981). This proposed changes to post-16 vocational education and training affecting the transition of young people to work, long duration skill training and education and training opportunities for adults. It placed particular emphasis on new types of accreditation and new means of enabling progression and access.

The Youth Training Scheme followed, superseding the Youth Opportunities Programme, but designed on the basis of experience with the Unified Vocational Preparation programme (Levy, 1985). Its major impact on the transition to work is not free of criticism, either in terms of implementation or policy orientation. Finn (1985) has captured many of the policy arguments.

Nevertheless, whatever the interpretation of policy makers' and implementers' motives, the emphasis in YTS on work experience as a source of learning opportunities has provided a major challenge to assumptions about worthwhile provision being achievable only through off-the-job or similarly learning-dedicated provision. Furthermore, the issues involved have implications far beyond YTS.

In Scotland, a new National Certificate was developed for post-16 students in the Further Education sector. Perhaps the most distinctive feature of the reorganisation was the modularisation of provision, but there was also a significant acceptance of the principle that learning in the workplace could eventually be recognised for accreditation purposes (Oates, 1986a).

More recently, the report of the Review of Vocational Qualifications (MSC/DES, 1986) and the subsequent government White Paper (DE/DES, 1986) have led to the creation of the National Council for Vocational Qualifications. The Council, in turn, has gone about forming a framework for vocational qualifications. Despite an unhealthy obsession with creating a constricting system of levels (Oates, 1986b), the Council is seeking to ensure that vocational qualifications are able to capture occupational competence, to make qualifications more informative, and to include assessment carried out by employers 'in industry' (sic).

There are practical arguments too for extending accreditation to include learning in the workplace. Education-based or education-like assessments and qualifications are not designed for prediction of, nor representation of, competence in a job. They may capture many qualities and achievements, but it is hardly radical now to suggest that they cannot capture them all. There is an *accreditation gap* — a difference between what is formally accredited to the individual and the substantive achievement relevant to such purposes as progression, selection or guidance. Much of this is bound up in what we characterise as 'experience'.

Work Based Learning

In one of his several studies of principles of management, Drucker (1974, op. cit.) writes about the requirement for *continuous learning*:

'There is a need for workers, whether unskilled, skilled or knowledge worker, to be trained for new skills. Continuous learning does not replace training. It has different aims and satisfies different needs. Above all it satisfies the need of the employee to contribute what he himself (sic) has learned to the improvement of his own performance, to the improvement of his fellow workers' performance, and to a better, more effective, but also more rational way of working. . . . Continuous learning needs to be organised as a formal session the way it is done in Japan. But it always needs to be organised.'

In his discussion of 'Alternance Training', Jallade (1982) discusses the value of 'the linking of practical training obtained by the exercise of vocational activity at the place of work with

G

theoretical training obtained in a training service, organisation or establishment'. He accepts that there are technical and industrial relations difficulties inherent in accreditation, but favours the award of 'diplomas' over the more covert processes of recognition which management might prefer.

Levy (1987), in reporting development work initiated under the New Training Initiative, has proposed the following operating definition of 'work based learning':

> '*Linking learning to the work role,* and having three inter-related components, each of which provides an essential contribution to that learning process. These three components are: *structuring learning in the workplace; providing appropriate on-job learning opportunities; identifying and providing relevant off-job learning opportunities.*'

The definition does not seek to elevate either the workplace or off-the-job training to a prime position. Rather, decisions about learning, design of learning and accreditation are to be appropriate to the work role — a concept attaching to the individual, and wider than the duties entailed in a single job.

Frameworks for Occupational Competence

The commitment in the New Training Initiative to credit transfer and progression and to the recognition of previously unrecognised achievement is not constrained by traditional occupation boundaries. There is, therefore, a need for new, common frameworks to express occupational competence in such a way as to highlight the relevance of achievement in one area for future work or learning in another.

Activity in the workplace can too easily be viewed as merely sets of tasks. While in some cases this is a pretty fair approximation of the truth, given the lack of autonomy granted to employees, it ignores a range of skills critical to competent performance of a job. Mansfield and Mathews (1985) have proposed an embryonic framework for the description of occupational competence. In discussing the nature of competence in a job, they proposed three classes of skills. Firstly, and conventionally, those to do with *tasks*. Secondly, those to do with *task management* — the skills of dealing with several, often competing tasks; the skills of handling contingencies and the unforeseen. Thirdly those skills exercised in dealing with the *role/job environment* made up of other people and health and safety factors.

A complementary and more highly developed framework is that of the Core Skills. Core Skills are defined (MSC, 1984; Matthews, 1987) as 'those skills which are common in a wide range of tasks and which are essential for competence in those tasks'. The definition of the skills is similar to that of the earlier Generic Skills (Smith, undated), but unlike these and, for example, the CPVE 'Core' (JBPVE, 1985), the Core Skills are dimensions or facets of occupational competence rather than free-standing, independently demonstrable actions.

The 103 skills of the framework are organised in four areas — the application in work activity of *number* (quantity, dimension, symbol, numbers; using processes of mathematisation, calculation, estimation, interpretation), *communication* (purposeful use of spoken and written word and action in obtaining and transmitting information), *problem solving* (planning, decision making and monitoring) and *practical* skills (involved in preparing for, carrying out and finishing off physical activity).

Without comprising a syllabus or curriculum, the Core Skills define part of the agenda for the accreditation of work based learning. Processes of 'core analysis' (for example, Prescott, 1986; Mansfield, 1985) show how Core Skills can be identified in workplace and other activity and can assist three macro-functions — learning, design and accreditation.

The Component Processes of Accreditation

Accreditation is not simply a matter of certification, nor of assessment plus certification. Without recognition within some user population a certificate could not be counted as having any value. The *interpretation* of a certificate and any other products of assessment should therefore be seen as part of the accreditation process, and should inform both assessment and certification.

The function of interpretation is not to provide a neutral commentary on presented information. It certainly cannot be objective. Interpretation, like assessment and certification, is both goal-setting and value-setting. It forms part of selection (however much selection practice leaves to be desired). It is part of guidance and counselling. It contributes to the perceived status of a programme or an organisation, and affects the ways in which a learner may see certification as a reward. The process of evaluating learning provision through achievements of the learners is yet another form of interpretation, and like the other forms requires decision making based on probabilistic information.

Accreditation is the generating, handling, evaluating and interpreting of information, the 'stuff' of the accreditation process. Information is generated through measurement or observation of performance and aggregated or generalised to form an assessment. In work based learning, as elsewhere, it is vital to distinguish between the measurement of a performance and the assessment of competence.

Certification follows assessment, but also may structure it. In anticipation of interpretation, it involves further generalisation, aggregation or selection of assessment information, and the presentation of what results from these processes.

Constraints in Measuring Competence

Three characteristics of competence at work combine to make the accreditation of work based learning technically distinct from the vast proportion of assessment and certification processes at large in the U.K. until now. Firstly, occupational competence must be criterion-referenced, not for directly ideological reasons, but in recognition of the character of work. Secondly, the interpretation of achieved competence demands considerations of *transfer* rather than generalisation of achievement. Finally, assessment and interpretation of the different facets of competence have to be based on subjective inference from holistic activities rather than statistical inference from focused items.

Criterion-referenced Character of Occupational Competence

In employment the acceptability or non-acceptability of a worker's activity and its results is substantially criterion-referenced. It is true that the evolution of the criteria may be rather chequered, involving the gradual institutionalising of norms, designers' requirements, administrative and customer needs, and so on, but this does not change the realities which accreditation must address.

Glaser and Nitko (1970) describe criterion-referenced tests as being representative of a specific domain of tasks. Martuza (1977) considers criterion-referenced tests to be a subset of domain-referenced, being those tests which are designed to inform decisions about mastery rather than domain status. We can broaden these concepts in two ways. We can address all measurement of performance, not just those things we call tests. We can create job or occupational competence domains containing not so much tasks as functions and skills (which include behaviours) to specifiable standards. We should, for example, include all three components of job competence described above. Skills should be expressed in a vocabulary which is not unnecessarily exclusive to individual jobs. The Core Skills introduced above are designed to provide this vocabulary.

Occupational competence is multi-dimensional. The acquisition of skills in jobs and training does not adhere to hierarchies. Achievement in one aspect of a job may be quite independent of performance in another. To attempt to disguise the heterogeneity — for example, by creating composite measures — is to attempt to force competence to conform to the psychometric conventions which dominate educational and psychological measurement.

The Role of Transfer

The multi-dimensionality also limits the degree to which achievement can be presented as general. There can be little justification, for example, for reading into competence in a job some broad measure of ability to perform in any other job. Even so, as Anastasi (1968) says of tests, all labels tend to suggest more generality than the instruments possess and, further, instruments tend to be chosen to satisfy wider criteria than they are intended to cover. The interpretation of achievement in, say, guidance and internal or cross-company selection has therefore to deal explicitly with processes of *skill transfer* rather than the generalisation of abilities.

Skill transfer is, roughly, the carry-over effect of learning in one situation to a later occasion in the same or different situation. If this results in quicker or more effective subsequent learning, the transfer can be said to be positive. There is much debate (for example, Annett and Sparrow, 1985) as to just how transfer occurs. Various supposed mechanisms require some generalisation of skills, but this is of a quite different order from what would be described as generalisation in tests of ability or in composite or profile educational qualifications.

Anticipating transfer — identifying the potential for transfer — is not a trivial act. Fleishman and Quaintance (1984) emphasise the problem, in generalising research findings, of relating one task to another in a classification system. If we add to this the dependence of achievement on the nature of the opportunities for learning, the type of support given and critical motivation factors, the complexity of interpretation becomes clear. Transfer is always a matter of degree, and the reality of transfer is the subject of individual as well as contextual differences (Matthews, 1986). The interpreter's best strategy, perhaps, would be to see in what way previous learning could be *harnessed,* and the natural process of transfer enhanced.

The Importance of Inference

In describing skill in such a way as to highlight the common facets of competence, the Core Skills help the identification of potential transfer — and do this for learners/workers themselves as well as for those who make decisions about them.

As facets of occupational competence rather than skills represented by free-standing tasks, however, Core Skills are detected by inference from activity of some higher order of aggregation. The process of inference is subjective (judgmental) rather than statistical. It is a process needed in the assessment of any skill for which 'application' cannot be separated from 'possession'. Events are holistic and do not isolate individual skills for the assessor's convenience. This is as true of a skills test in motor vehicle repair as it is of a routine stock taking task.

Work Based Learning and the Psychometric Tradition

Given the criterion-referenced nature of occupational competence, the non-general manner of its interpretation and the type of inference used to detect skills, there is a need to review the types of statistical model which are appropriate for ordering the quality of assessment.

Psychometric testing is concerned with the scaling of individual differences, and as Lyman (1978), for example, contends, the vast proportion of testing has been developed along psychometric lines. This applies equally well to examinations. The normal distribution is the basis of such testing, and, as Lewis (1986) argues, progress in test theory has been made by treating its problems as those of statistical inference. Testing which does not conform to the conventional models is hardly deemed worthy of the name. The major investment in the statistical ordering of testing has been committed away from the area of criterion-referenced assessment. Unfortunately, occupational competence cannot be made to fit the norm-based models.

Within test development the major concerns have been, in addition to the discriminating power of tests, the reliability and validity of instruments. There is in the estimation of validity of tests a perennial problem of identifying criteria in the real world which are adequate for validating tests. Much validation, therefore, depends on factor analysis studies among sets of tests, or at least on inter-test consistency. Domain-referenced assessment, and criterion-referenced assessment in particular, seem more suited to content-orientated validity rather than construct.

In the evaluation of skills tests, supervisors' assessments and other measures considered to relate to competence, reliability rather than content validity has dominated. And, as Wolf (1985) has shown, the control of assessment carried out by supervisors or instructors in training locations is difficult. Even when standard procedures are defined, in addition to random error and systematic error in-built to an instrument there are significant, systematic errors associated with the individual assessor.

The workplace, an essential location in work based learning (though not the only one), cannot suddenly become more amenable to testing procedures. There will always be, in workplace tests, lower accuracy and precision in comparison with assessment instruments used in controlled settings. It is no use, therefore, seeing such tests as rather feeble equivalents to ability tests or knowledge examinations.

This is not, it must be emphasised, an inadequacy of the workplace or of work based learning, but the inappropriateness of the psychometric tradition for this new context. The decision that someone is competent needs to be determined on the basis of information flowing from performances during work experience and on-the-job and off-the-job learning, and by means of judgments against multiple criteria. The models needed are those which can contend with this requirement and the types of constraint already described.

We need to examine, therefore, not the process of differentiation or improving individual test items in isolation, but that of optimising decision making under uncertainty. The new technical foundation for accreditation which this implies will need to incorporate criteria drawn from outside the assessing/accrediting agency for the examination of utility, not just reliability and validity (Dunnette and Borman, 1979). Without such foundation, accreditation of work based learning, failing to conform to the psychometric tradition, will lack coherence and remain an intuitive art, not subject to evaluative processes.

We need to build up a number of psycho-mathematical models of the whole of the accreditation process, drawing on, in addition to utility theory and multiple criteria analysis, the study of human judgments, decision theory and Bayesian statistics. Bayesian approaches are particularly suited to dealing with the weighing of evidence and sequential revision of judgment which may come to characterise assessment in work based learning and its interpretation.

Strategies for Development

The technical development of accreditation processes — assessment, certification and their interpretation — must be complemented by implementation. Researchers and developers need to engage in a process of 'developmental dissemination' in which the compromises between principles, practical constraints and acceptance by the user are worked out and revised continuously. To attempt anything else would be a denial of present realities — that staff in further education, and trainers and employers are attempting to do what they can, albeit with varying degrees of success. People do not react well, on the whole, to handed-down bright ideas, but respond more favourably to processes in which they or their peers have some investment.

Such a strategy is similar to that reported by Harrison (1983) in examining the development of profile reporting of examination results. He too draws together a number of views which suggest that the technical proficiency of an instrument in isolation provides a less good evaluation than consideration of the decision consequences of its use.

There are, moreover, a number of developments and lines of thinking which have already taken forward the accreditation of work based learning in both technical and implementation terms.

One approach to specifying competence for accreditation purposes has been developed by the Yorkshire and Humberside Association for Further and Higher Education (YHAFHE, 1986) in their system of functional modules, known as Learning and Assessment Modules (LAMs). These express competence in terms of functions, free of artefacts or other details which emphasise the uniqueness of tasks rather than their similarities. The YHAFHE work also takes in some aspects of task management skills and discusses possible ways of accrediting skills of dealing with the role/job environment. The work depends heavily on Core Skills analysis, but this is applied without analysing a task to within an inch of its life and stripping it of meaning.

In terms of educational conventions, the development shows that the workplace is accessible to processes of moderation, although the price for this may be a tendency for trainers and others to interpret the modules as input models rather than the outcomes modules they are intended to be.

Further, it shows how roles within accreditation can be allocated in a way similar to the breakdown of the accreditation process described earlier in this paper. The personnel who are in a position to observe or measure the performance in the YHAFHE scheme of things are not, generally, trained assessors. As Brown (1983) suggests they should be, they are observers who gather information. They identify and record behaviours and reactions. They do not decide what they mean.

Another way of specifying performance for assessment purposes is the use of 'standard tasks' as benchmarks to locate the activities in any workplace within a framework defined by the scope of each activity and the performance criteria applying to it (Evans, Brown and Oates, 1987). Development of standard tasks has experienced some drift from their original conception (Mathews, 1987 op. cit.), but they continue to have considerable potential for calibrating workplace activity.

Perhaps the greatest culture shock for conventional assessors faced with work based learning is the sacrifice of comparability in measuring performance according to the circumstances of work experience and the contingent events of integrated on-the-job and off-the-job learning. In looking at the *consequences* of assessment, however, comparability is needed not in the measurement of performance which generates information but in the generalisation and aggregation of that information. It is also a goal for interpretation. Dealing with problems of comparability so that accreditation judgments are somewhat better than merely disaster-proof will be a major task of the development process.

In the service of this, there may be particular value in Wickert's (1967) distinction (albeit in the context of selection assessment) between 'broad band' and 'narrow band' information. Broad band information, as its name suggests, is inferred from widely based events, rich in a little information about a number of attributes. Narrow band information, in contrast, derives from much more targetted events or instruments, used to deal with specific uncertainties about an individual learner.

This gives a clue to one way of augmenting workplace and other circumstantial measurement with more artificial but focused tests (even knowledge tests!) within a single decision making framework. What is critical is that the framework retains the directedness to the work role characteristic of work based learning.

REFERENCES

ANASTASI, A. (1968) *Psychological testing* (third edition). New York: Macmillan.

ANNETT, J. and SPARROW, J. (1985) *Transfer of learning and training*. Sheffield: Manpower Services Commission.

BLUM, M. L. and NAYLOR, J. C. (1968) *Industrial Psychology*. New York: Harper and Row.

BROWN, F. G. (1983) *Principles of educational and psychological testing*. New York: Holt, Rinehart and Winston.

BURGESS, T. and ADAMS, E. (1980) The present inadequacy. In BURGESS, T. and ADAMS, E. (eds.) *Outcomes of education*. London: Macmillan.

DALE, R. and PIRES, E. (1984) Linking people and jobs: the indeterminate place of educational credentials. In Broadfoot, P. (ed.) *Selection, certification and control*. Falmer: The Falmer Press.

DE/DES (1986) *Working together — education and training*. London: HMSO.

DRUCKER, P. F. (1974) *Management: tasks, responsibilities, practices*. London: Heinemann.

DUNNETTE, M. D. and BORMAN, W. C. (1979) Personnel selection and classification systems. *Ann. Rev. Psychol., 30,* 477-525.

EVANS, K., BROWN, A. and OATES, T. (1987) *Developing work-based learning: an evaluative review of the YTS Core Skills Project*. Sheffield: Manpower Services Commission.

FINN, D. (1985) The Manpower Services Commission and the Youth Training Scheme: a permanent bridge to work? In DALE, R. (ed.) *Education training and employment: towards a new vocationalism?* Oxford: Pergamon.

FLEISHMAN, E. A, and QUAINTANCE, M. K. (1984) *Taxonomies of human performance: the description of human tasks*. Orlando, Florida: Academic Press.

GLASER, R. and NITKO, A. J. (1970) *Measurement in learning and instruction*. Pittsburgh: Learning Research and Development Centre, University of Pittsburgh.

HARRISON, A. (1983) *Profile reporting of examination results*. London: Schools Council/Methuen.

JALLADE, J.-P. (1982) *Alternance training for young people: guidelines for action*. Berlin: CEDEFOP.

JBPVE (1985) *Certificate of Pre-Vocational Education — Parts A and B*. London: Joint Board for Pre-Vocational Education.

LANDA, L. N. (1976) *Instructional regulation and control*. Eaglewood Cliffs, NJ: Educational Technology Publications.

LEVY, M. (1985) Curriculum development in YTS. *Local Government Policy Making*, July.

LEVY, M. (1987) *The Core Skills Project and work based learning*. Sheffield: Manpower Services Commission.

LEWIS, C. (1986) Test theory and 'Psychometrika': the past twenty five years. *Psychometrika, 51* (1), 11-22.

LYMAN, H. B. (1978) *Test scores and what they mean* (third edition). Eaglewood Cliffs, NJ: Prentice-Hall.

MANSFIELD, B. (1985) Getting to the core of the job. *Personnel Management*, August.

MANSFIELD, B. and MATHEWS, D. (1985) *Job competence — a description for use in education and training*. Blagdon: The Further Education Staff College.

MARTUZA, V. R. (1977) *Applying norm-referenced and criterion-referenced measurement in education*. Boston, Mass: Allyn and Bacon.

MATHEWS, D. (1986) *The accreditation of 'ability to transfer skills and knowledge to new situations'*. Blagdon: The Further Education Staff College Information Bank.

MATHEWS, D. (1987) *The development of the YTS Core Skills — derivation and characterisation*. Blagdon: The Further Education Staff College Information Bank.

MSC (1981) *A new training initiative — an agenda for action*. Sheffield: Manpower Services Commission.

MSC (1984) *Core Skills in YTS: Part 1*. Sheffield: Manpower Services Commission.

MSC/DES (1986) *Review of vocational qualifications in England and Wales*. London: HMSO.

OATES, T. (1986a) *Work based learning and modular accreditation: an analysis and a methodology for a development project*. Blagdon: The Further Education Staff College Information Bank.

OATES, T. (1986b) *The RVQ levels — a critical review and recommendations for development strategy*. Blagdon: The Further Education Staff College Information Bank.

PRESCOTT, B. (1986) *Competence Analysis Flow Chart*. Blagdon: The Further Education Staff College.

SCRE (1977) *Pupils in profile.* London: Hodder and Stoughton/Scottish Council for Research in Education.

SMITH, A. D. (undated, but distributed 1978) *Generic Skills: keys to job performances.* Ottowa: Employment and Immigration Commission.

WICKERT, F. R. (1967) Some implications of decision theory for occupational selection. In Payne D. A. and McMorris, R. F. (eds.) *Educational and psychological measurement.* Waltham, Mass: Blaisdell

WOLF, A. (1985) *Work Based learning: trainee assessment by supervisors.* London: University of London Institute of Education.

YHAFHE (1986) *Work-based assessment and its accreditation.* Leeds: The Yorkshire and Humberside Association for Further and Higher Education.

THE ASSESSMENT OF COMPETENCIES

Consultant

This chapter will be devoted to the assessment of soft skill competencies. These include the ability to communicate effectively, the ability to identify problems, and the ability to work with others.

It is important at the outset to distinguish the competencies we will be concerned with here from the much narrower and more specific competencies which have dominated the Competence Based Education movement. Despite the fact that relatively little attention has been paid to them, these wider competencies are of considerable importance. Thus, they are listed in many official reports as central goals for education.[1] The views of those who wrote these reports are supported by research. One cluster of research studies [2] has shown that most people agree that the main goals of education include fostering such qualities as initiative, the ability to work with others, and the ability to understand and influence society. Another group of studies have shown that these are indeed the qualities which are most important to success at work and in leisure and to economic and social development.[3] Yet

---

[1] Relevant reports include the Plowden Report (1966), the Scottish *Primary Memorandum* (SED 1965), *Education in Schools* (DES 1977), the Munn Report (1977), the CBI, the YTS Objectives Document (MSC 1985) and the TVEI Aims (MSC 1984). Those who promoted comprehensive education often sought to redirect secondary education toward aims in this area (see Raven 1977) and such aims also figured prominently among the aims of Nuffield Science and the Schools Council Integrated Science Project.

[2] Morton-Williams *et al.* (1968); Morton-Williams, Raven and Ritchie (1971); Raven *et al.* (1975); Raven (1977); Bill *et al.* (1974); De Landsheere (1977); Johnston and Bachman (1976); CES (1977); and MacBeath (1981).

[3] Research carried out over the past 25 years shows that the economic and social development of societies, and effective job performance within them, is dependent on the development of such qualities as initiative, modernity, the ability to work with others, the ability to lead and to follow, the willingness to listen and communicate, and willingness to try to understand the workings of organisations and society and take on oneself responsibility for doing something about them. The relevant research on the overall development of societies has been reviewed by McClelland (1961) and Inkeles and Smith (1974). Studies of the factors which make for effective job performance within societies have been reviewed by Raven (1984). However, reference may be made to the work of Klemp, Munger and Spencer (1977) with naval officers, McClelland and Dailey (1973) with foreign service workers, McClelland and Burnham (1976) with managers, and Flanagan and Burns (1955) and the ITRU (1979) with operatives and supervisors. Mention must also be made of the work of Roberts (1969) with entrepreneurs, Taylor and Barron (1963) with scientists, MacKinnon (1962) with architects, and Price, Taylor and others (1971) with doctors.

these goals are generally neglected in the educational system.[4] One of the reasons for their neglect is that there are no generally accepted means of assessing them — whether for formative or summative purposes.[5]

Some observations made in one of the few schools which do foster these qualities effectively will illustrate some aspects of the assessment problem.[6] In this class, most of the pupils' education took place in interdisciplinary, enquiry-oriented, project work grounded in the environment around the school. In the course of this work, one pupil had become an expert on the distribution of different species of butterfly in the locality; another on the history of a particular agricultural implement; another on the relationship between improvements in that implement and changes in the social structure of the community; and another on the current social structure of the area — who knew whom and what they talked about.

Traditional tests and examinations would not do justice to the outstanding achievements of each of these children. To do so it would be necessary to have different scales for each child.

---

[4] Evidence that the wider goals of general education are neglected is summarised in Raven (1977), but specific reference may also be made to the fact that Raven *et al.* (1975) found that teachers said that they devoted little effort to achieving such goals and that pupils said they were poorly attained. The CES (1977) and MacBeath *et al.* (1981) found the same thing in Scotland. The IEA found both that the educational processes which were implemented were unlikely to lead to their attainment and that they were in fact poorly achieved (Torney, Oppenheim and Farnen, 1976; Raven and Litton, 1976; Litton, 1982). Likewise HMI (1980) found that these wider goals were neglected and poorly attained by primary schools in Scotland, and this was confirmed by Varley and Raven (1983), Raven and Varley (1984) and Raven, Johnstone and Varley (1985). On the other side of the Atlantic, Johnston and Bachman (1976), Bachman *et al.* (1978), Johnston (1973), Flanagan (1978) and Goodlad (1983) have all found that they are neglected (see Raven 1986 for an account of the implications of Goodlad's work).

[5] See Raven (1977); Raven (1984); Raven, Johnstone and Varley (1985) and Raven (1984). Other reasons for their neglect include the following: (i) relatively little progress has been made toward clarifying the nature of the qualities which are to be fostered or the processes to be used to promote their development; (ii) the qualities to be fostered are value-laden — and many teachers shy away from value-laden activity; (iii) many teachers and managers lack confidence in their ability to manage independent, thoughtful people who take initiative and responsibility for their own actions; (iv) there are no satisfactory means of giving teachers, students, employees, supervisors or managers credit for their achievements in these areas; (v) public servants — including teachers — are not generally expected to attend to, and find better ways of meeting, the needs of, their clients; nor are there means of giving them credit for involving themselves in the frustrating, difficult and demanding business of innovation, and, finally (vi); although our research points to the conclusion that these qualities can best be fostered in the course of individualised educational programmes (or work experience) in which students practise and develop them in the course of undertaking tasks they care about, there are no tools to help teachers, managers, or supervisors to manage such individualised developmental activities.

[6] See Raven, Johnstone and Varley (1985) for details.

However, there are also more serious problems: for example, the first pupil mentioned above had developed the *competencies* of the scientist. He had learned to *invent* ways of making his observations; he had learned to notice things which no one had noticed before; he had learned not only how to find information in journals but also how to use what he did find to stimulate that kind of lateral thinking which is required to make use of the information that is obtained; he had learned to write to, telephone, and visit university lecturers; and he had learned to invent ways of summarising his data and communicating it to others — and not just in writing. The other pupils mentioned above had developed the competencies required by the historian or sociologist, rather than a 'knowledge' of 'history' or 'sociology'.

Traditional tests are unable to testify to the development of such competencies.

But there are still more serious problems. The pupils had worked as a group. One pupil had become an ideas man. Another a spokesman who represented the demands of the class to the authorities. Another a negotiator. Another a communicator who presented the work of the class to visiting dignitaries. Another specialised in cooling things down when tempers flared. Another in getting the group to listen to ideas. Another in curbing those who were tempted to disrupt the work of the group.[7]

How are we to give these children credit for these idiosyncratic competencies? How are we to give the teacher credit for having fostered them? How are we to help other teachers to manage the individualised, competency-oriented, educational programmes which are required to foster such qualities? The answer to all of these questions depends on developing appropriate assessment procedures.

The Nature of Competence: A Preliminary Discussion[8]

In an attempt to discover a basis for such assessment procedures we may first examine one of the competencies which has been mentioned — initiative — a little more closely.

The first feature of initiative to which attention may be drawn is that it is self-motivated. It does not make sense to describe as 'initiative' any behaviour which the individual concerned has had to be told to display. Next, it should be noted that, if an individual is to take a successful initiative, he has to devote a great deal of time, thought and effort to the activity. He has to take innovative

---

[7] Those who are interested in finding out how this was done should turn to Raven, Johnstone and Varley (1985).

[8] Details of the theoretical framework which is developed below will be found in Raven (1984).

action, monitor the effects of that action, and learn from those effects more about the problem he is trying to tackle and the appropriate strategy to use. He has to wake up at night to seize on flickering glimmerings of understanding on the fringe of consciousness and bring them to the centre of attention so that they become fully conscious and usable. He has to anticipate obstacles in the future and invent ways of circumventing them. He has to get help from other people. He has to build up his own, unique, set of *specialist* knowledge to tackle the problem.

No one is going to do any of these things unless he cares very strongly indeed about the goal in relation to which he is attempting to take initiative. The valued goal is therefore of crucial importance. In practice it turns out that the valued goal can be in a particular content, such as developing a knowledge of the properties of alloys. Alternatively, it may be a particular *type of behaviour* which the individual values. Examples of the latter include inventing better ways of doing things or getting people to work together effectively.

What we have just said implies that one must assess values, pre-occupations, or intentions prior to any attempt to assess ability — for important abilities will only be displayed in relation to valued goals. It therefore does not make sense to attempt to assess abilities except in relation to valued goals.

What has been said also implies that it does not make sense to attempt to assess separately the cognitive, affective, and conative[9] components of activity. For an initiative to be effective these components must be in balance.

These observations conflict markedly with many traditional canons of psychometry. We have asserted that one cannot assess abilities independently of values. It is, therefore, essential to adopt a two-stage (*not* a two-factor) approach when assessing these qualities. We must first assess an individual's values, and then, and *only* then, assess his abilitiy to bring to bear a wide variety of effective cognitive, affective and conative behaviours to achieve his valued goals.

Our observations also suggest that such qualities are factorially complex. It is the individual's willingness to do a number of independent and different things which will result in successful goal achievement. The person concerned has to analyse, get help from

---

[9] The conative components — those which have to do with will, persistence, and determination — have been sadly neglected in psychology, although it is of interest that Dockrell and Broadfoot (1977) and Hope (1985) found that a factor comprising ratings of these qualities was one of the main ways in which teachers discriminated between their pupils. Much earlier MacArthur labelled such a cluster of variables as 'Factor X' (MacArthur 1951). 'But persistence *in relation to what*?' I am inclined to ask.

others, and develop his own understanding of (and influence) the workings of social and political systems. His ability to do any of these things in pursuit of his goals is unlikely to be closely related to his willingness to do others. Yet the *more* of these independent things he does in pursuit of his goals, the more likely he is to be successful. On the other hand, if he does any one of these things particularly well, it will, to some extent, compensate for his failure to do others. The implication of these observations is that factor-analysts have been wrong to argue that important human qualities can only be meaningfully assessed by adopting scales made up of items which are highly correlated with each other. Our reflections suggest that, far from needing to make use of factorially pure scales, we need to make use of *indices* made up of items which are as little correlated with each other as possible.[10]

The conclusion to which this discussion points is, then, that it is necessary to make use of *indices*, covering a maximally heterogeneous cluster of relevant behaviours — rather than maximally homogeneous scales — to assess important human qualities.

In actual practice, it turns out that detailed cognitive-affective maps of people's interests, perceptions and expectations in each such area are a great deal more revealing than any overall measures. In other words, category-based descriptive statements about people are more useful than profiles of scale scores.

Institutional Structures

It would be wrong to give the impression that people are aware of their distinctive concerns and values. They are not. They simply do not know how different are their concerns and priorities from those of others until these have been brought out into the open. Until then, they tend to assume that other people share their own priorities, perceptions and goals.

This is, however, only the tip of the iceberg, because the way in which other people with whom one has contact think over-whelmingly determines the way one thinks oneself. These shared thoughtways are the main determinants of behaviour.

Important perceptions, thoughtways and understandings include beliefs about how things *should* be done, who should relate to whom, and about what. They include other role expectations as

---

[10] While it may be thought that the viewpoint developed here might be reconciled with traditional factor analytic theory by focusing on qualities like 'the ability to make one's own observations', a little reflection shows that this is not the case. Our argument is precisely that such qualities cannot be assessed independently of valued goals. They have no *generalised* meaning. They therefore cannot be assessed by factorially pure scales.

well. What does one think it is appropriate to do oneself? What does one think others expect one to do? How does one think others *should* react? How does one actually expect them to react?

The institutional framework in which a person lives and works influences his behaviour directly, obliquely, and indirectly: *directly* through the constraints which it places on what he can do; *obliquely* through the concepts, understandings and competencies which he is able to practise and develop; and *indirectly* by influencing his motivation — his beliefs about how it is appropriate for him to behave and how others will react to various behaviours on his own part. The assessment of the institutional context of behaviour (both perceived and actual) is not, therefore, independent of the assessment of competence. As a result we have devoted considerable attention to assessing people's social perceptions and expectations. This has unexpectedly led us directly into assessing perceptions of how organisations and societies work — into assessing 'political' perceptions — into assessing perceptions of organisational and political hierarchies and understandings of concepts like participation, majority decision-taking, and managerial responsibility and accountability. We have found that people's understandings of such terms are central determinants of their competence.

Recapitulation and Re-statement

In the course of these remarks I have introduced some ideas which it has taken us many years to develop and which contrast sharply with many traditional assumptions in psychology and education. For this reason it may be useful to re-present the same ideas in a different way, making use of a 3-dimensional diagram proposed by Ron Johnson and shown in Fig. 1.

Johnson argues that behaviour is a resultant of three sets of variables: skills and abilities, motivation, and the situation in which people find themselves.

For our purposes we can substitute 'components of competence' for 'skills and abilities' and 'values' for 'motivation'.

So far so good. But we have also argued that:

(1) components of competence will only be developed and displayed whilst the individual is undertaking tasks he cares about. They cannot be abstracted in the way the diagram suggests and assessed independently of motivation. Motivation is *an integral part* of competence;

(2) effective performance — the resultant — is much more dependent on the number of independent and substitutable competencies which are brought to bear in a wide variety of situations in order to reach the goal, than it is on the level of

H

John Raven

FIGURE 1: JOHNSON'S MODEL

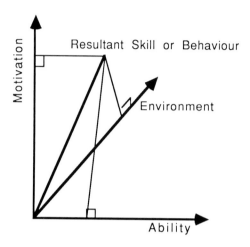

competence or ability displayed in relation to any one of them in a particular situation. It is the total number of competencies which the individual displays in many situations over a long period of time in order to reach his valued goals that we need to assess, not his level of ability in relation to any one of them (although, in an ideal world, it would be nice to know that too!). And an *overall* index of a person's 'ability' or 'motivation' is virtually meaningless;

(3) the situation in which an individual is placed influences the values which are aroused and the competencies which are practised and developed directly . . . quite apart from its influence on the behaviour which emerges at the end — when a person with a particular pattern or motivation and abilities is placed in a particular situation;

(4) the diagram does not sufficiently emphasise the potential of the environment to transform people. It gives the impression that a change in some feature of the environment will lead to an increase (or decrease) in the quality or frequency of a particular behaviour, with the motivation and ability of the actor remaining the same. But, in the course of our research, we have encountered situations in which consideration by a group of pupils of what a particular pupil was good at and liked doing, and the creation of opportunities for him to pursue those activities to the benefit of the group, resulted in the *transformation* of that pupil — rather than simply a higher level of a particular behaviour. The process has more in common with the transformation of a chemical substance when brought into contact with another chemical (environment)

than with the resolution of a field of forces in physics — which is what Johnson's diagram leads one to envisage.

Despite these limitations, the diagram is useful because it emphasises (i) that it is important to assess all three sets of variables, (ii) that behaviour is a product of all three sets of variables, (iii) that the components of competence can only be assessed in relation to a task the individual cares about, (iv) that behaviour is influenced by the individual's perceptions of the situation in which he is placed, his understandings of the way the organisation works, and the reactions he expects from others, and (v) that people will only display the levels of competence of which they are capable if they define the situation in which they are placed as one which will enable them to undertake activities they care about.

Having shown that 'resultant' behaviour may not be at all what one wishes to assess, it is useful now to use the same three-dimensional model to illustrate that other people's ratings of that resultant are still less satisfactory — for what a rater sees depends on his own values and priorities, what he takes to be the demands of the task and situation, and his subjective ability to manage the ratee — with his specific values, priorities and talents, and which may well differ from those of the rater. Many teachers lack confidence in their ability to manage groups of independent, thoughtful, questioning pupils, and this both makes them unwilling to create situations in which such qualities could be developed and displayed and has a marked effect on the interpretation they place on such behaviours when they are displayed.

In the remainder of this article we will see how it is possible to assess all the components illustrated in Johnson's diagram and to combine them together in order to produce a measure of the 'resultant'. But we will also see that the detailed assessment of a pupil's cognitive-affective map of the whole situation is of much greater value than the single figure computed to index the resultant. Yet it is only the resultant which any external observer — such as a teacher — sees through his dark, value-and-ability-polarised glasses.

A Model of Competence, Motivation and Behaviour and its Assessment

We return now to the task of elaborating our model of competence and the way in which its components are to be assessed. We have seen that it is inappropriate to try to assess the self-motivated competencies which make for effective behaviour except in relation to activities which the person concerned values. We have also seen that there is a large number of components of competence, that many of them are relatively independent of each other, and that these competencies are cumulative and substitutable.

This way of thinking about competence may be made more concrete by reference to Grid 1.

On it, some of the types of behaviour which an individual may value have been listed across the top. These behaviours have been grouped into the three clusters (Achievement, Affiliation, Power) identified by McClelland in 1958 and confirmed empirically in our own previous work.[11] Down the side are listed a number of components of effective behaviour which, if present, are likely to result in the overall activity being successful. These components of competence include cognitive activities like making plans and thinking about obstacles to goal achievement, affective activities like enjoying the activity or hoping a necessary but distasteful task is completed, and conative activities like determination and persistence. However, also listed are a number of other factors which contribute to successful performance — like having the support of others and believing that one's behaviour is consistent with both one's own and others' views of what it is appropriate for someone in one's position to do.[12]

The importance of separating these value and efficacy components in assessment can be re-emphasised by taking another example. An individual who values success at football may show a great deal of initiative in relation to football, be very sensitive to feedback from his environment, seek the help of others to improve his performance, seek out new techniques and ideas, be sensitive to minor cues which suggest ways in which he might improve, be sensitive to the approval or disapproval of his peers, have the willpower to persist in the face of difficulty and be able and willing to persuade local politicians to provide a pitch. Nevertheless, if the ability of this same person to engage in these complex, cognitive, affective, social, and conative activities is assessed in relation to performance at mathematics — a goal which, for the sake of argument, we may assume he does not value — then one might erroneously conclude that he is unable (and not just unmotivated) to engage in the activities we have mentioned. Teachers, psychologists, and managers have, in the past, too frequently been guilty of drawing such erroneous conclusions.

Attention should be drawn to the fact that, while this model is readily comprehended as a model designed to help us to understand and assess motivation — the styles of behaviour an individual values and his ability to pursue those goals effectively because he

---

[11] Raven, Molloy and Corcoran (1972); Raven (1977).

[12] These components of competence are spelt out in more detail in Raven (1977) and Raven (1984).

A MODEL OF COMPETENCE

GRID 1

Valued styles of behaviour

Components of effective behaviour	Achievement				Affiliation					Power		
	Doing things which have not been done before.	Inventing things.	Doing things more efficiently than they have been done before.	Finding better ways of thinking about things.	Providing support and facilitation for someone concerned with achievement.	Ensuring that a group works together without conflict.	Establishing warm,convivial relationships with others.	Establishing effective group discussion procedures.	Ensuring that group members share their knowledge so that good decisions can be taken.	Articulating group goals and releasing the energies of others in pursuit of them.	Ensuring effective compliance with one's demands.
Cognitive											
Thinking about what is to be achieved and how it is to be achieved.											
Anticipating obstacles to achievement and taking steps to avoid them.											
Monitoring the effects of one's actions to discover what they have to tell one about the nature of the situation with which one is dealing.											
Making one's value conflicts explicit and trying to solve them.											
Having an appropriate understanding of how society works.											
Believing that other people whose opinion one values will expect one to engage in activity.											
Believing one's actions to be in the best interests of mankind.											
Affective											
Turning one's emotions into the task.											
Selecting tasks one enjoys and facing up to the need to complete necessary but unpleasant tasks.											
Anticipating the delights of success and the misery of failure.											
Conative											
Putting in extra effort to reduce the amount of risk involved in the activity.											
Summoning up energy, determination and will-power.											
Persisting in the face of difficulties.											
Habits and Experience											
A range of appropriate routine, but flexibly contigent, behaviours each triggered by cues which one may not be able to articulate and which may be imperceptible to others.											
Experience of the satisfactions which have come from having accomplished similar tasks in the past.											

tends spontaneously to do many of the things which he needs to achieve his goals — it is, in reality, a model of competence.

Relationship Between Descriptive Statements and Profiles

Grid 1 can be used to identify the behaviours people value and the components of competence they tend to display in pursuit of them. For any one person, an assessor can, after having made relevant observations, enter ticks in the appropriate cells under the behaviours the person values. By adding up the ticks in any one column one can obtain an index of how likely it is that the person concerned will undertake that kind of behaviour effectively. By summing the scores obtained in adjacent columns, under one of the overall headings, scores which indicate the probability that a person will reach achievement, affiliation and power goals can be obtained. This yields a profile which is directly comparable with those published by McClelland, and which he (misleadingly) refers to as a motivation profile.

It is important to note, however, that, because (as has been indicated) the grid should be considerably extended, the procedure would become cumbersome if it were applied wholeheartedly. A way round this problem will be suggested shortly.

Heterogeneous Indices or Internally Consistent Factor Scores?

Not only must values be assessed as an integral part of the assessment of competence: the components of competence we have identified cannot be meaningfully analysed or identified in factorial or dimensional terms. Indeed, the attempt to examine the internal consistency of McClelland's motive scores using factor-analytic procedures has made for a great deal of unproductive argument as well as for invalid criticism of his work. The scores obtained by summing down the columns in our grid are, quite obviously, not uni-dimensional. Indeed, the more independent and heterogeneous the competencies over which we sum the better — provided, of course, such competencies relate to goal achievement. Factor analysts argue that such heterogeniety shows that the scores which are obtained are not uni-dimensional. Quite right. But they then go on to argue that they are not meaningful. Quite wrong. No one would argue that multiple regression coefficients are meaningless simply because they are derived from summing over a large number of independent variables.

Overall Indices v. Detailed Descriptive Statements

In practice, a description of the types of behaviour an individual values, and the competencies he shows a spontaneous tendency to display in the course of trying to reach them, gives much more useful information than a total score. Such a description is radically different from a profile of scores across a series of factorially independent dimensions. The assumptions behind a factorial profile are that behaviour is best to be described and understood in terms of people's relative scores on a small number of dimensions. The assumption behind the model developed here is that behaviour is best to be understood by identifying people's values, perceptions and expectations, and the components of competence they tend to display spontaneously in pursuit of their valued goals.

'Atomic' v. 'Variable' Models

The difference between factorial profiles and descriptive *statements* can be illustrated by taking examples from physics and chemistry.

Physicists have shown that the behaviour of a projectory is best described in terms of some such equation as:

$$s = ut + \tfrac{1}{2} \, ft^2$$

(the distance travelled can be calculated from the initial velocity multiplied by the time elapsed plus half the acceleration multiplied by the square of the elapsed time).

The factor analysts' model is analogous. It asserts that the degree of leadership an individual will display is a function of his scores on a number of other variables, such as extroversion and intelligence.

Unlike physicists, chemists have found a quite different type of equation to be most useful in their work. They argue that substances and the environments in which they are placed are best to be described by listing the elements of which they are composed and the relationship between these elements. The descriptors (elements) are drawn from a large set known to all chemists. The elements which are not present do not need to be listed. The behaviour of the substance in a particular environment is then described by making use of equations which permit of transformation (rather than monotonic combination).

$$Cu + 2H_2SO_4 = CuSO_4 + 2H_2O + SO_2$$

(Copper plus sulphuric acid yields copper sulphate, water and sulphur dioxide).

It is here being argued that human beings might best be described and understood by adopting a model which has more in common with that used by chemists than that used by physicists. Such a model would enable us to indicate an individual's values and the components of competence he shows a spontaneous tendency to display, and the features which characterise his environment, without restricting us to the small number of variables which characterise factor-analytic models.

It is not, in fact, difficult to reconcile some such model with the facts to which factor analysts point as a justification for their model. They point out that most human traits are correlated with each other. They go on to argue that it is unnecessary to retain a large number of independent dimensions, or categories. However, many of the correlations are of the order of $0 \cdot 2$ and most are of the order of $0 \cdot 3$ to $0 \cdot 5$. Even the latter leave some 75 per cent of the variance on one trait 'unexplained' by the variance on the other. There is, therefore, a *good* chance that someone who is not good at one thing will be good at another. Even factor-analysts point out that this is because the second ability has probably caught the interests of the person concerned and, therefore, been practised and developed. While the factor-analyst's model does, in fact, provide for such possibilities (by including provision for specific factors) these are generally neglected in practice. If we were forced to state our case in factor-analytic terms, we would therefore find ourselves arguing that the important things to record about an individual are his specifics, not his generalities.

We may now attempt to push our chemical analogy a little further. Following this model we might find ourselves writing a *summary* description of an individual and the environment in which he lives and works. This might take the following form (the symbols which are used are exemplary only, and should in no way be taken to suggest that we have developed even a preliminary version of a more complete table of 'human elements'):

$$Ach_4Pow_3;Auth_4PartCit_2;NuP_4HostP_3;DP(T)_1$$

Such a statement might be interpreted to mean that the individual showed a spontaneous tendency to display four components of competence in pursuit of achievement goals, three in pursuit of power goals. He endorsed four items contributing to the set dealing with authoritarian perceptions of society and only two of the set dealing with participatory citizenship. Four components of his environment were supportive of his goals: his manager modelled achievement behaviour but did not delegate, encourage participation, nor create developmental tasks for his subordinates. There was hostile press from other people in the individual's environment. Concern with efficiency and effective leadership was scorned. The task which the individual was set had little developmental potential: it was a routine task which prevented the person concerned developing perceptions and expectations appropriate to innovation.

If the equation were written in some way which permitted of movement, one would conclude that the individual would be likely to become frustrated and lose his motivation to engage in achievement and leadership behaviours.

In fact, of course, such summary statements could be filled out in a great deal more detail, and very usefully too. One could identify exactly what type of achievement or power behaviour the individual thought it was important to engage in; one could identify exactly what competencies he brought to bear in pursuit of each; one could identify the particular perceptions and expectations which encouraged and prevented him from engaging in such behaviour; one could say more about the role models to whom he was exposed by managers, colleagues and subordinates; and one could say more about the tasks set and their probable effects on his future development and motivation.

Before leaving this discussion it is worth reiterating that such *statements* about people *and the environments in which they are placed* enable us to handle the transformational processes which occur in homes, schools and workplaces. (Incidentally, YTS is above all else about the potential of the workplace to *transform* those who pass through it. The potential of workplaces to do this has been widely noted.[13])

Technical Feasibility

Ample evidence of both the feasibility of implementing measurement procedures based on the model of competence and its assessment outlined above, and of the validity of the data so obtained, has now been obtained.[14]

Interestingly, different procedures have proved useful in individual assessment (for guidance, placement, and development purposes) and for programme evaluation. For individual assessment, the model is most elegantly implemented in the form of Behavioural Event Interviews or Reports.[15] The problem is that the successful use of this approach is dependent on specialised training for both interviewers and scorers. For programme evaluation it is

---

[13] E.g., Flanagan (1978); Bachman *et al.* (1978).

[14] The *general* model has been validated in a series of studies such as those of Klemp, Munger and Spencer (1977); Huff *et al.* (1982); McClelland and Dailey (1973); Pottinger (1979) and Winter, McClelland and Stewart (1981). To date we have used value-expectancy methodology in four studies: in an evaluation of an adult education programme which was intended to 'encourage mothers to embrace their unique and irreplacable role in promoting the development of their pre-school children' (Raven 1980), in an evaluation of project-based, enquiry-oriented education grounded in the environment around primary schools and which aimed to achieve the wider goals of general education (Raven and Varley 1985; Raven, Johnstone and Varley 1986), as a basis on which to develop *The Edinburgh Questionnaires*, in a preliminary survey conducted with those Questionnaires (Raven 1984) and in a cross cultural study of values and competencies associated with the economic and social development of a number of different countries (the U.S., Hawaii, Samoa, Tonga, New Zealand, Japan, Singapore, Hong Kong and Canada) (Graham, Raven and Smith 1987).

[15] Spencer (1983); McClelland (1978).

the value-expectancy model which has proved most satisfactory. The problem with it is that one is dependent on the skills of the professional researcher to (a) determine the precise questions to be asked and (b) interpret the mass of category-based data obtained.

Because of their potential from the point of view of developing measures which do not require extensive training to administer and interpret, assessment procedures based on value-expectancy theory hold out the greatest promise. What is most attractive is that, in the short term, they offer the possibility of a half-way house. There is now no doubt that the methods can be used to document the effects of educational programmes and highlight the defects in those programmes. We are therefore in a position to place the accreditation of *courses* (or teachers) which aim (or claim) to foster soft-skill competencies on a sound basis. That done, one would have much more confidence in the assessments made by the teachers and the students involved in those courses. One would, in effect, have demonstrated that the teachers had created situations in which students could practise and develop soft skill competencies. That is, they must have created situations in which it would have been possible to *observe* students exercising important competencies in the course of undertaking tasks they cared about. Ratings of, or statements about, such behaviour would therefore have a good chance of being meaningful.

But value-expectancy methodology has greater potential than this. One of the chief problems with using value-expectancy-instrumentality methods to assess *individual* competence is their cumbersomeness. This could be overcome by computerising their administration so that the questions which any one person is asked are tailored to his emerging pattern of interests.

The importance of doing this must not be underestimated. The development of summative assessment procedures is not the only urgent task facing educators. There is, for example, ample evidence that one of the most important unmet felt needs of pupils is for guidance to help them to identify, develop, and get recognition for their talents.[16] This need is recognised by both the MSC (TVEI)[17] and Burgess and Adams.[18] Yet there are currently no procedures which can meet the need. It is also clear from our more recent work[19] that teachers need tools to help them to manage multiple, individualised, soft-skill-competency-oriented, educational programmes. It would be possible to use value-expectancy theory to develop procedures which have the potential to yield tools which

---

[16] Morton-Williams *et al.* (1968); Morton-Williams *et al.* (1972); Raven (1977); MacBeath *et al.* (1981); Centre for Educational Sociology (1978); Flanagan (1978).

[17] MSC TVEI and YTS Aims.

[18] Burgess and Adams (1985).

[19] Raven, Johnstone and Varley (1985).

would meet both needs. And from there it would be but a short step to cumulate the data obtained to generate meaningful summative assessments derived from information otherwise stored invisibly within the students' heads.

The Assessment of Competence Using Value-Expectancy Methods

In this section value-expectancy-instrumentality methodology will be discussed in more detail. The procedures are designed to get inside people's heads and assess the (re-interpreted) three dimensions of the Johnson model, and compute their resultant. The methodology enables us to assess people's values, their perceptions of relevant features of their environment, what they expect the effects of their actions to be and how much importance they attach to each of those consequences. The consequences which are examined include those arising from the individual's own competence (or the lack of it) and those arising from other people's expected reactions to his or her behaviour. If appropriate, the individual's confidence in their ability to deal with the reactions they expect from other are also documented. The methodology then enables us to combine these bits of information together in order to calculate the strength of the resultant disposition to undertake different tasks effectively.

It is easiest to introduce the theoretical basis of value-expectancy-instrumentality methodology by reference to the work of Fishbein. In the late 60s, Fishbein[20] stimulated a paradigm shift in the then quiescent area of 'attitude' measurement by emphasising, and finding an elegant way of handling, something which everyone had always known — but which had not been taken into account in the theories or practice of attitude measurement current at the time (and which is still neglected in the measurement of personality and abilities). This is that behaviour — such as buying biscuits or using contraceptives — is primarily determined by multiple beliefs and feelings which come into play in particular situations rather than by single underlying 'attitude' or personality variables.[21]

Fishbein made two fundamental contributions to our ability to think about, and handle, these issues. First, he focused attention on

---

[20] Fishbein (1967); Fishbein and Ajzen (1975). However, see also Vroom (1964), Porter and Lawler (1968), Feather (1982), and Mitchell (1982).

[21] This is the explanation of the still widely encountered statement that 'there is little relationship between attitudes and behaviour'. It is true that there is little relationship between behaviour in a particular situation and scores on a single, factorially pure, attitude or personality scale. But there is a very close relationship between behaviour and 'attitudes' [or behaviour tendencies] indexed by identifying and summating the perceptions, beliefs and feelings which come into play in the particular situation, using the techniques under discussion here.

something which has been repeatedly emphasised in this paper, namely that it is the respondent's attitude toward, or value for, *the behaviour in question* — and not his value for the object of the behaviour — which it is important to assess. One should study the respondent's attitude toward *using* those contraceptives — rather than his attitude toward the contraceptives. Second, he found a means of tying together three well-established, empirically-based, theoretical viewpoints about behaviour determination in psychology and sociology.

The first of these traditions holds that an individual will be inclined to engage in an activity if he is relatively certain that the activity will lead to satisfactions which he values. The second holds that he will be more likely to do something if he feels that the behaviour is consistent with his self image — with the sort of person he wants to be. The third viewpoint is that an individual will be more likely to engage in a behaviour the more certain he is that other people expect him to do so and the more dependent he is on a favourable reaction from those people.

There is considerable evidence[22] to support each of these viewpoints taken individually. The predictive validity of measures based on any one of them is typically of the order of 0·4. The beauty of Fishbein's work was that, for the first time, it enabled us to assess each set of variables more systematically and then to tie the three sets of variables together. The method of combining and weighting the component parts is itself supported by a considerable body of empirical research. The effects of these developments is that predictive validities of 0·8 to 0·9 are not uncommon.

Before moving on, attention may be drawn to ways in which Fishbein's model parallels that developed above in connection with Grid 1. There we argued that the capacity to undertake a valued activity effectively was multiply determined and that it was dependent on bringing to bear a number of relatively independent, but substitutable, competencies each having cognitive, affective, and conative components. It was argued that effective behaviour depends on having an appropriate self-image, on perceiving oneself as having the support of relevant reference groups, and on having an appropriate institutional framework in which to work (i.e., on *shared* beliefs about priorities, relationships and ways of doing things).

In non-technical language, what the Fishbein version of value-expectancy-instrumentality theory does is to ask people what they think the consequences would be if they were to engage in any particular behaviour and then to weight those consequences with the importance attached to each. Three domains of possible

---

[22] This evidence is reviewed in Raven and Dolphin (1978).

consequences are systematically studied. These may loosely be called *personal* consequences, *self-image* consequences, and *reference groups' reactions*.

The *personal* consequences which are studied include such things as 'I would enjoy doing this'; 'It would take up a great deal of time which I would prefer to devote to other things'; 'I would have a lot less money for other things'.

The *self-image* (or, more correctly, personal normative belief) consequences include such things as 'No self-respecting person would do this'; 'It is my duty to do this'; or 'I would be working for the long term good of mankind if I did this'.

The *reference group* consequences include 'My grandmother would object to my doing this'; 'My workmates would encourage me to do this'; and 'God will punish me if I do this'.

Each of these perceived consequences has to be weighted by the importance attached to (or motivation to comply with) them: What my grandmother thinks won't have much influence on my behaviour if I don't *care* what she thinks.

So, to apply the model fully, one has first to find out how *certain* the person we are assessing is that, if he engaged in the behaviour, each consequence would follow and then how much *importance* he attaches to those consequences. One then multiplies the certainty ratings by the probability ratings and adds up the resulting figures.

To use value-expectancy-instrumentality theory to index the likelihood that people will display selected competencies in the course of undertaking tasks they care about we first identify tasks they have a 'felt need' to carry out by asking them to complete a Quality of Life Questionnaire (see Fig. 2a).

On this Questionnaire they are first asked to indicate how *important* various features of the environment are to them and how important they think it is to be able to do various things at work. Thereafter they are asked to say how *satisfied* they are with each of these same features of the environment and with their opportunity to do each of the things they have said they would like to do. Their responses are then examined, and an item which they have rated both important and unsatisfactory is selected.

The *Consequences* Questionnaire is then used to explore their perceptions of the consequences of trying to do something about this discrepancy. What do they think would happen if they tried to persuade other people to do something about it? What would happen if they tried to do something about it themselves?

The consequences which are studied cover the domains identified in Fishbein's model: they include such things as conflict with other values, whether doing it would enable them to be the sort of person they want to be, and their perceptions of how their reference groups would react.

FIGURE 2a: THE ASSESSMENT OF THE COMPONENTS OF COMPETENCE

An Illustration from the Edinburgh Questionnaires.
(Note:This is a schematic representation only; it does not bear a direct relationship to the questionnaires)

(a)The Process

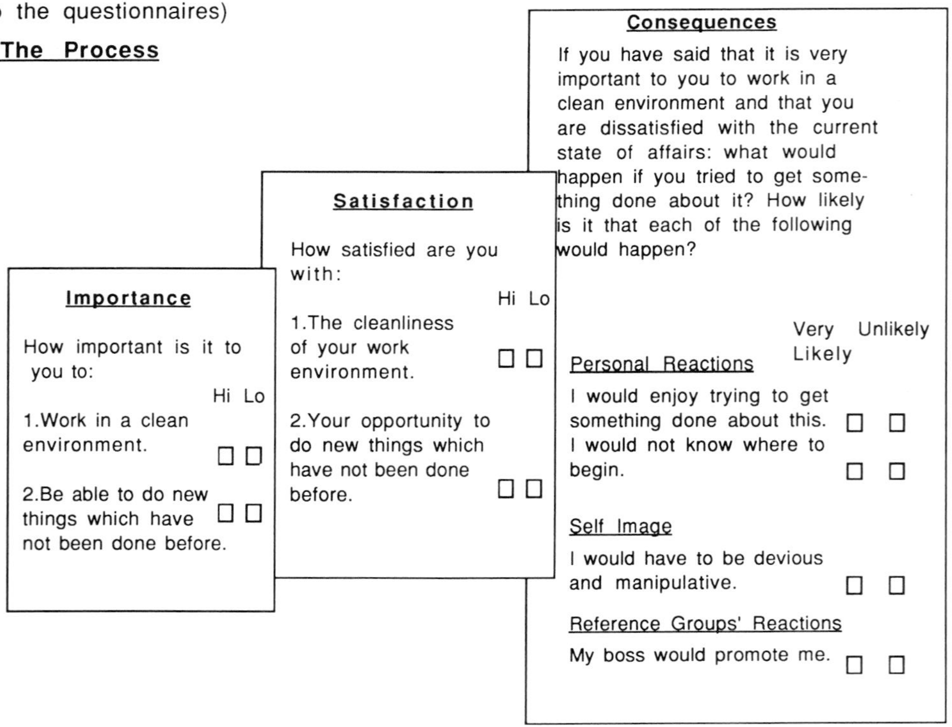

Importance

How important is it to you to:

             Hi Lo

1.Work in a clean environment. ☐ ☐

2.Be able to do new things which have not been done before. ☐ ☐

Satisfaction

How satisfied are you with:

             Hi Lo

1.The cleanliness of your work environment. ☐ ☐

2.Your opportunity to do new things which have not been done before. ☐ ☐

Consequences

If you have said that it is very important to you to work in a clean environment and that you are dissatisfied with the current state of affairs: what would happen if you tried to get something done about it? How likely is it that each of the following would happen?

         Very Unlikely
         Likely

Personal Reactions

I would enjoy trying to get something done about this. ☐ ☐

I would not know where to begin. ☐ ☐

Self Image

I would have to be devious and manipulative. ☐ ☐

Reference Groups' Reactions

My boss would promote me. ☐ ☐

The process may be illustrated by taking an example: supposing we are interested in exploring the perceived consequences of trying to persuade one's fellows to behave in a more responsible manner. Those concerned would first be asked what they think the *personal* consequences would be. In fact they often think that trying to do this would make them uncomfortable and unhappy, leave less time for other activities they value, and demand abilities which they feel they do not possess. In the absence of these abilities any attempt on their part to persuade other people to behave in this way would demand a great deal of effort, lead others to think that they were 'getting above themselves', and the whole thing would be a disaster. They would look, in their own eyes, and in the eyes of others, very foolish indeed.

After they have been asked what they think the general consequences would be, they are asked whether the sort of person they would like to be would do these things — and what sort of person *would* do them. They sometimes feel that the sort of person who would try to persuade his fellows to behave more responsibly would be a rather pious, priggish killjoy, and that, to be successful, they would have to be devious and manipulative. They may not themselves wish to be any of these things.

Finally, they are asked how others would react: would their friends support or reject them, would their superiors condemn them because they would have exposed the latter's behaviour as self-interested, rather than concerned with the good of all employees; would they, like Socrates, be deprived of their lives or livelihoods for having been concerned about the long-term social consequences of their actions?

If one cumulated these results one would have a clear assessment of the strength of the individual's disinclination to engage in the activity! (See Fig. 2b.)

But, by going through the process we have described, one obtains a great deal more useful information than this single index. In the case just described, one would have learned a great deal which would be of value in helping one to devise an individualised, generic-competency-oriented, developmental programme to help the individual, if he so wished, to resolve value conflicts and thus release energy into his chosen task, and to practise and develop competencies he requires to reach his goals. He could, for example, be brought to pay more attention to the probable long-term social consequences of not behaving in a socially responsible way. He might be encouraged to meet other people who *had* behaved in a responsible way and not been punished or forced to behave in ways which were incompatible with being the sort of person he wants to be. As a result of getting to know them he might learn how to persuade other people more effectively without having to be

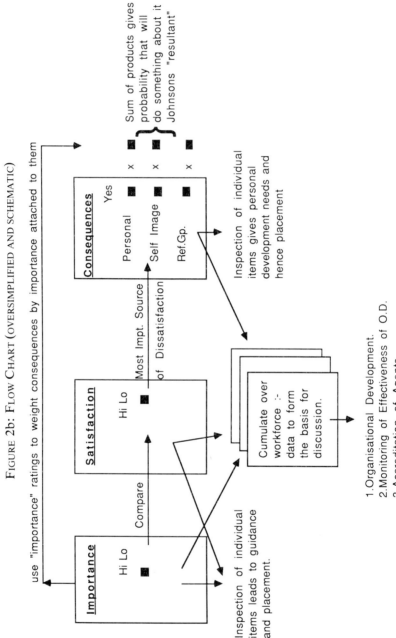

FIGURE 2b: FLOW CHART (OVERSIMPLIFIED AND SCHEMATIC)

obnoxious. He could be helped to practise the skills required to obtain the co-operation of others.

Classroom Climate Measures

Not only would the information be of value in making it possible to design an *individual* programme of development for this particular pupil: the data would, if collected from all pupils in a class, be of value in enabling the teacher (or an external accrediting agency) to assess the quality of the teacher's overall programme of placement and development and his or her ability to release the know-how, goodwill, and enthusiasm of all his pupils — and thereafter improve his or her performance in both these respects.

This is the basis for the final suggestion to be made in this paper. We have already seen that this methodology can be used to document the effects of educational programmes and to highlight deficiencies in them. We have argued that such assessments would enable us to place the validation of courses on a sound basis. Let us now back up one step. It is a relatively straightforward matter to determine the presence or absence of classroom processes which are likely to lead to the identification and development of the talents of each pupil.[23] Having established that a particular teacher did in practice create such a climate, it would (as we have already seen in another context) be but a short step to trust his or her assessments of individual students.[24]

The Question of Validity

In the course of our research we have shown that value-expectancy-instrumentality measures of the sort which have been described differentiate between different groups of people in a way which seems to be related to their life style and seems in some way to account for the differences in their life situation.[25] We have shown that they are sensitive to the effects of educational programmes and able to pinpoint deficiencies in those programmes.[26] We have shown that they are able to provide explanations of unanticipated, and in many ways counter-intuitive, effects of those programmes. We have shown that they generate data which seems to contribute to an explanation of the plight in

---

[23] Raven (1977); Walberg (1979-85); Howard (1982).

[24] This would place the procedure advocated by the Scottish Examination Board (1985) for Social and Vocational Education on a firm basis. For this syllabus the SEB does not require teachers to assess individual pupils' social and vocational competence. It insists only that they certify that the *course* was likely to lead to these outcomes. This is something we are in a position to validate. From there it would be but a short step to trust the teachers' judgment about individuals.

[25] Raven (1984); Graham, Raven and Smith (1987).

[26] Raven (1980); Raven and Varley (1985).

which Britain finds itself and which seems to help to explain the relative position of other countries. We have shown that they generate data which enables people, as individuals or as a group, to take a look at their beliefs, attitudes, priorities and expectations and ask themselves whether they like the look of what they see and, in particular, its probable consequences and, if not, what they could do about it.[27]

All this evidence suggests that the measures have some validity. Yet we still encounter the view that 'the measures are not as good as measures of academic attainment'. It is therefore appropriate to note just how shaky that argument really is. Sixty per cent of the variance in O level grades is due to differences between examiners; only 40 per cent is due to differences between students. The difference between an A and a D grade is typically only eight raw score points.[28] Because of this, the student variance in grades is primarily determined by presentation; not by differences in academic knowledge — although this is the construct which grades are widely thought to index. Fifty per cent of the knowledge assessed in examinations is generally forgotten after one year and 75 per cent after two years. The knowledge on which such assessments are based is, therefore, not only out of date when it is taught — it is also unavailable when it is needed. It follows from these remarks that O level grades have little construct validity as indices of academic knowledge. Just as importantly, they have zero predictive validity to *occupational* performance. (Although they account for about nine per cent of the variance in future academic performance, some may feel that an inability to explain 91 per cent of the variance in the criterion leaves something to be desired.) Yet not only do these assessments determine what teachers and students do in schools: the total costs of generating them amount to a not insignificant proportion of the costs of the 'educational' system.

Conclusion

We have seen that, in part stimulated by the MSC, there is now a powerful movement afoot to develop some form of certificate — and, in the case of YTS and the Scottish National Certificate, a *statement*-based certificate — for all. Equally, there is growing concern that the accreditation of agencies in YTS and performance appraisal in the educational system be placed on a sound basis. There is a widely acknowledged need for improved guidance procedures (though this problem, like the others we have discussed, has proved intractable). The way therefore seems to be open to

---

[27] Raven (1984).
[28] Spencer, E. (1979, 1983).

capitalise on the suggestions made in this paper. This applies both to developing tools which will help teachers to help students to identify and develop their talents and to developing means of certifying the outcomes. The one real barrier is the fact that the short-term, fragmented and modularised orientation of the MSC and SCOTVEC programmes is incompatible with the long-term individualised, interdisciplinary, project-based, soft-skill-competency-oriented programmes which are required to identify, develop and assess soft-skill competencies.

Address for correspondence: JOHN RAVEN, 30 Great King Street, Edinburgh.

REFERENCES

BACHMAN, J. G. *et al.* (1971) *Youth in Transition III: Dropping Out — Problem or Symptom?* Ann Arbor, Michigan: The Institute for Social Research.

BACHMAN, J. G., O'MALLEY, P. M. and JOHNSTON, J. (1978) *Adolescence to Adulthood: Change and Stability in the Lives of Young Men.* Ann Arbor, Michigan: The Institute for Social Research.

BILL, J. M., TREW, C. J. and WILSON, J. A. (1974) *Early Leaving in Northern Ireland.* Belfast: Northern Ireland Council for Educational Research.

BURGESS, T. and ADAMS, E. (1986) *Records of Achievement at 16.* Windsor: NFER-NELSON.

CENTRE FOR EDUCATIONAL SOCIOLOGY, University of Edinburgh. (1977) *Collaborative Research Dictionary.*

DE LANDSHEERE, V. (1977). On Defining Educational Objectives. *Evaluation in Education* 1, no. 2, p. 73-190. Oxford: Pergamon Press.

DEPARTMENT OF EDUCATION AND SCIENCE (1977) *Education in Schools: A Consultative Document.* London: HMSO.

DOCKRELL, W. B., BROADFOOT, P. M., *et al.* (1977) *Pupils in Profile.* Edinburgh: The Scottish Council for Research in Education.

EISNER, E. W. (1985) *The Art of Educational Evaluation.* Lewes: The Falmer Press.

FEATHER, N. T. (1982) Actions in Relation to Expected Consequences: an Overview of a Research Program, p. 53-95 in FEATHER, N. T. (ed.) (1982). *Expectations and Actions: Expectancy-Value Models in Psychology.* Hillside, New Jersey: Erlbaum.

FISHBEIN, M. (1967) Attitudes and the Prediction of Behaviour. In: Fishbein, M. (ed.), *Readings in Attitude Theory and Measurement.* New York: Wiley.

FISHBEIN, M. and AJZEN, I. (1975) *Belief, Attitude, Intention and Behaviour*. Reading, Mass.: Addison Wesley.

FLANAGAN, J. C. (1976) *Planning Life and Career Goals: A Cluster of Materials and Manuals*. Monterey, Calif.: CTB/McGraw-Hill.

FLANAGAN, J. C. and BURNS, R. K. (1955) The Employee Performance Record. *Harvard Business Review, 33*, 95-102.

GOODLAD, J. (1983) *A Place Called School*. New York: McGraw-Hill.

GRAHAM, M. A., RAVEN, J. and SMITH, P. C. (1987) Identification of High Level Competence: Cross-Cultural Analysis between British, American, Asian and Polynesian Labourers. To be published in *Organisation Forum*.

HMI (Scotland) (1980) *Learning and Teaching in Primary 4 and Primary 7*. Edinburgh: HMSO.

HOPE, K. (1985) *As Others See Us: Schooling and Social Mobility in Scotland and the United States*. New York: Cambridge University Press.

HOWARD, E. (1980) *Some Ideas on Improving School Climate*. Colorado: Department of Education.

HOWARD, E. (1982) *Instrument to Assess the Educational Quality of Your School*. Denver: Colorado Department of Education.

HOWARD, E. (1982) Involving Students in School Climate Improvement. *New Designs for Youth Development*. Tucson: Associations for Youth Development Inc.

HOWARD, E. (1982) *Successful Practices for Making the Curriculum More Flexible*. Denver: Colorado Department of Education.

HUFF, S., LAKE, D. and SCHAALMAN, M. L. (1982) *Principal Differences: Excellence in School Leadership and Management*. Boston: McBer & Co.

INKELES, A. and SMITH, D. H. (1974) *Becoming Modern*. Harvard University Press.

ITRU (1979). *The A-Z Study: Differences between Improvers and non-Improvers among Young Unskilled Workers*. Cambridge: The Industrial Training Research Unit.

JOHNSTON, L. (1973) *The American High School: Its Social System and Effects*. Ann Arbor, Michigan: Institute for Social Research.

JOHNSTON, L. D. and BACHMAN, J. G. (1976). Educational Institutions *in* Adams, J. F. (ed.): *Understanding Adolescence*, 3rd Edition, 290-315. Boston: Allyn and Bacon.

KLEMP, G. O., HUFF, S. M. and GENTILE, J. D. G. (1980) *The Guardians of Campus Change: A Study of Leadership in Non-Traditional College Programmes*. Boston: McBer & Co.

KLEMP, S. O., MUNGER, M. T. and SPENCER, L. M. (1977) *An Analysis of Leadership and Management Competencies of Commissioned and Non-Commissioned Naval Officers in the Pacific and Atlantic Fleets*. Boston: McBer.

LITTLE, A. (1983). Employers and Qualifications: Learning from Developing Countries. *International Review of Applied Psychology. 32*.

MacArthur, R. S. (1951) *An Experimental Investigation of Persistence and its Measurement at the Secondary School Level.* PhD Thesis, University of London.

MacBeath, J., Mearns, D., Thomson, B. and How, S. (1981) *Social Education: The Scottish Approach.* Glasgow: Jordanhill College of Education.

McClelland, D. C. (1958) *in* Atkinson, J. W. and McClelland, D. C. *Motives in Fantasy, Action and Society.* New York: Van Nostrand.

McClelland, D. C. (1961) *The Achieving Society.* New York: Van Nostrand.

McClelland, D. C. (1973) Testing for Competence rather than for 'Intelligence'. *Amer. Psychologist, 28,* 1-14.

McClelland, D. C. (1978) *Guide to Behavioural Event Interviewing.* Boston: McBer.

McClelland, D. C. and Burnham, D. H. (1976) Power is the Great Motivation, *Harvard Business Review, 54,* No. 2.

McClelland, D. C., and Dailey, C. (1973) *Evaluating New Methods of Measuring the Qualities Needed in Superior Foreign Service Workers.* Boston: McBer and Co.

MacKinnon, D. W. (1962) The Nature and Nurture of Creative Talent. *American Psychologist, 17,* 484-94.

Mitchell, T. R. (1982) 'Expectancy-Value Models in Organisational Psychology'. p. 293-312 *in* Feather, N. T. (ed.) (1982): *Expectations and Actions: Expectancy-Value Models in Psychology.* Hillside, New Jersey: Erlbaum.

Morton-Williams, R., Finch, S., Poll, C., Raven, J. and Ritchie, J. (1968) *Young School Leavers.* London: HMSO.

Morton-Williams, R., Raven, J. and Ritchie, J. (1971) *Sixth Form Teachers and Pupils.* London: Schools Council/Books for Schools.

MSC (1984). *TVEI Review, 1984.* London: MSC.

MSC (1985). *Developing the Youth Training Scheme as Part of an Integrated Vocational Training Provision.* Statement of Intent.

MSC (1985). *Two-Year YTS: Guide to Scheme Content and Quality.* Sheffield: MSC.

MSC/DES (1985). *Review of Vocational Qualifications in England and Wales: Interim Report.*

'Munn' Report (1977). *The Structure of the Curriculum.* Edinburgh: HMSO.

'Plowden' Report (1966). Central Advisory Council on Education. *Children and their Primary Schools,* Vols. 1 and 2. London: HMSO.

Porter, L. W. and Lawler, E. E. (1968) *Managerial Attitudes and Performance.* Homewood Illinois: The Dorsey Press.

Pottinger, P. S. (1976) Techniques and Criteria for Designing and Selecting Instruments for Assessing Teachers. *In* Leviottov, B. (ed.), *Licensing and Accreditation in Education.* Lincoln, Nebraska: Nebraska Curriculum Development Center.

Pottinger, P. S. (1977). *Competence Testing as an Alternative to Credentials.* Boston: McBer.

PRICE, P. B., TAYLOR, C. W., NELSON, D. E. *et al.* (1971). *Measurement and Predictors of Physician Performance: Two Decades of Intermittently Sustained Research.* Salt Lake City: University of Utah, Dept. of Psychology.

RAVEN, J. (1977) *Education, Values and Society: The Objectives of Education and the Nature and Development of Competence.* London: H. K. Lewis; New York: The Psychological Corporation.

RAVEN, J. (1977) On the Components of Competence and their Development in Education. *Teachers' College Record, 78,* 457-475.

RAVEN, J. (1980) *Parents, Teachers and Children.* Edinburgh: The Scottish Council for Research in Education.

RAVEN, J. (1980) The IEA Civics Study as a Study of General Education. *Studies in Educational Evaluation, 6,* 15-20.

RAVEN, J. (1980) The Most Important Problem in Education is to Come to Terms with Values. *Oxford Review of Education, 7,* 253-72.

RAVEN, J. (ed.) (1983) The Relationship Between Educational Institutions and Society paying special Attention to the Role of Assessment. Whole Issue: *International Review of Applied Psychology, 32,* No. 4. (The issue includes a paper by J. R. with the same title.)

RAVEN, J. (1984) *Competence in Modern Society: Its Identification, Development and Release.* London: H. K. Lewis.

RAVEN, J. (1984) Some Barriers to Educational Innovation from Outside the School System. *Teachers College Record,* vol. 85, 431-43.

RAVEN, J. (1984) The Evaluation and Improvement of Provision for General Education. *In* Skilbeck, M. (ed.) *Evaluating the Curriculum in the Eighties.* London: Hodder and Stoughton.

RAVEN, J. (1986) A Nation Really at Risk: A review of Goodlad's 'A Place Called School'. *Higher Education Review, 18,* 65-79.

RAVEN, J. and DOLPHIN, T. (1978) *The Consequences of Behaving: The Ability of Irish Organisations to Tap Know-How, Initiative, Leadership and Goodwill.* Edinburgh: The Competency Motivation Project.

RAVEN, J. and DOLPHIN, T. (1978) *Toward Value-Expectancy Measures of Human Resources.* Edinburgh: Competency Motivation Project Paper No. 49.

RAVEN, J., HANNON, B., HANDY, R., BENSON, C. and HENRY, E. (1975) *A Survey of Attitudes of Post Primary Teachers and Pupils, Vol. 1: Teachers' Perceptions of Educational Objectives and Examinations.* Dublin: Irish Association for Curriculum Development.

RAVEN, J., HANNON, B., HANDY, R., BENSON, C. and HENRY, E. A. (1975) *A Survey of Attitudes of Post Primary Teachers and Pupils, Vol. 2: Pupils' Perceptions of Educational Objectives and their Reactions to School and School Subjects.* Dublin: Irish Association for Curriculum Development.

RAVEN, J., JOHNSTONE, J. and VARLEY, T. (1985) *Opening the Primary Classroom.* Edinburgh: The Scottish Council for Research in Education.

RAVEN, J. and LITTON, F. (1976). Irish Pupils' Civic Attitudes in an International Context. *Oideas*, Spring, 16-30.

RAVEN, J. and LITTON, F. (1982) Aspects of Civic Education in Ireland. *Collected Original Resources in Education, 6* (2), F4E7.

RAVEN, J., MOLLOY, E. and CORCORAN, R. (1972). Toward a Questionnaire Measure of Achievement Motivation. *Human Relations, 25*, 469-92.

RAVEN, J. and VARLEY, T. (1984) Some Classrooms and their Effects: A Study of the Feasibility of Measuring some of the Broader Outcomes of Education. *Collected Original Resources in Education 8,* No. 1, F4 G6.

ROBERTS, E. B. (1968) A Basic Study of Innovators: How to Keep and Capitalize on their Talents. *Research Management, XI,* 249-66.

ROBERTS, E. B. (1969). Entrepreneurship and Technology *in* Gruber, W. H. and Marquis, D. G. (eds.). *The Human Factor in the Transfer of Technology.* Cambridge, Mass.: MIT Press.

SCOTTISH EXAMINATION BOARD (1985) *Scottish Certificate of Education: Social and Vocational Skills on the Standard Grade. Revised Scheme for Moderation of Internal Syllabuses and Assessment Arrangements.*

SCOTTISH EDUCATION DEPARTMENT (SED) (1965) *Primary Education in Scotland.* Edinburgh: HMSO.

SPENCER, E. (1979) *Folio Assessments or External Examinations?* Edinburgh: Scottish Secondary Schools Examinations Board.

SPENCER, E. (1983) *Writing Matters Across the Curriculum.* Edinburgh: The Scottish Council for Research in Eduction.

SPENCER, L. M. (1983). *Soft Skill Competencies.* Edinburgh: The Scottish Council for Research in Education.

STANSBURY, D. (1976) *Record of Personal Experience, Qualities and Qualifications* (plus tutor's handbook). South Brent: RPE Publications.

STANSBURY, D. (1980) The Record of Personal Experience *in* Burgess, T. and Adams, E. *Outcomes of Education.* Basingstoke: MacMillan Education.

TAYLOR, C. W. and BARRON, F. (eds.) (1963) *Scientific Creativity.* New York: Wiley.

TORNEY, J. V., OPPENHEIM, A. N. and FARNEN, R. (1975) *Civic Education in Ten Countries.* New York: John Wiley, The Halsted Press.

VARLEY, T. and RAVEN, J. (1983) A Survey of the Extent and Nature of Out-of-School Visits by Primary Schools in Lothian and Fife Regions. *Collected Original Resources in Education.* Vol. 7, No. 2. F4 D13.

VROOM, V. H. (1964) *Work and Motivation.* New York: J. Wiley.

WALBERG, H. J. (ed.) (1979) *Educational Environments and their Effects.* Berkeley, CA: McCutchan.

WALBERG, H. J. (1984) Improving the Productivity of America's Schools. *Educational Leadership, 41*, No. 8, 19-30.

WALBERG, H. J. (1985) Classroom Psychological Environment *in* Husen, T., and Postlethwaite, N. (1985) *International Encyclopaedia of Education*. London: Pergamon.

WALBERG, H. J. and HAERTEL, D. (1980) Validity and Use of Educational Environmental Assessments. *Studies in Educational Evaluation, 6*, 225-238.

WINTER, D. G., McCLELLAND, D. C. and STEWART, A. J. (1981) *A New Case for the Liberal Arts*. San Francisco: Jossey Bass.

ISSUES IN THE ASSESSMENT OF AFFECTIVE CHARACTERISTICS

W. B. DOCKRELL
University of Newcastle upon Tyne

The assessment of the affective characteristics of pupils has become of more general concern with the advent of profiling and records of achievement. Assessing, recording and reporting affective characteristics is of course not new in schools. Teachers have been making these assessments of their pupils and reporting them to parents, using them in references or to complete forms from prospective employers, but usually up to now in an informal unstructured way. Ingenkamp's strictures on this traditional approach 'At the moment we have the disquieting situation in which teachers make their judgments like amateurs in the field of those objectives which are often regarded as the most important; and are subject to all those prejudices, stereotypes, distortions, etc. to which all people are exposed when they have only their common sense to rely on' (Ingenkamp, 1977) may seem harsh, but in many cases are all too accurate.

Evaluating the Affective Outcomes of Schooling

Profiling has given prominence to the assessment of individual pupils, but specific curricula and particular school systems have affective aims. As for curricula, TVEI, for example, is concerned with attitudes as well as skills and must be judged by the extent to which it fosters 'enterprise' as well as by increased knowledge of the role of technology in modern society. Popham has warned us that if we ignore the affective outcomes in our evaluations they are likely to be neglected. 'Talk is notoriously cheap, and until it is backed up with tangible techniques for promoting and measuring important kinds of learner affect there is considerable chance that the current vocal support for affective education will fade quietly away' (Popham, 1975). There have, of course, been evaluations which have addressed themselves to the affective outcomes of educational programmes (Brown, 1976; Harlen, 1976) but these outcomes have generally been neglected.

The case for affective aims for a school system was put most eloquently in the Scottish report on the structure of the curriculum in the secondary school. 'In educating young people it seems irresponsible to ignore their emotional and moral natures, or to assume that the educational process should not concern itself with their attitudes and values. . . . We believe, therefore, that schools

127

should seek to contribute to the development of such dispositions as the following: to be concerned for other people and to show compassion for them; to be capable of co-operating and forming relationships with them; to be tolerant and fair; . . . to be resourceful, self reliant and hard-working' and so on (Scottish Education Department, 1977). It is possible to assess affective education at a national level as Torney and her colleagues demonstrated (Torney, Oppenheim and Farnen, 1975). Yet the assessment of the affective outcomes of education was dropped from the programme of the Assessment of Performance Unit, thus omitting one of the four major sets of aims of the school system.

Individual schools too have affective aims. Wake has suggested that schools should extend the proposals in Curriculum 11-16 (Department of Education and Science, 1983) to cover moral education. There should be a list of questions for heads and senior staff about overall objectives; for heads of department in consultation with their colleagues about objectives, methods and content in their subjects and cross curricular linking; and for heads and heads of department about what knowledge, skills, concepts and attitudes are necessary (Wake, 1986). If Popham, as quoted above, is correct about the importance of evaluation, schools need to address the crucial issue of the assessment of attitudes as well as of skills and concepts.

There is general commitment to affective aims at national and school level and for specific programmes and curricula. There are examples of evaluations which take account of affective outcomes but they are relatively few. Some schools, however, have attempted their own systematic evaluations of the affective outcomes of units or programmes.

An example of evaluation within schools of the affective outcomes of a programme is the work of two groups of Geography teachers. They evaluated the effect on pupils' attitudes of their teaching about third world countries. They wanted to know whether or not they had indeed made their pupils more 'concerned for other people' and more likely to show compassion for them (SED, 1977). Each group of teachers prepared a questionnaire designed to assess the attitudes of their respective classes. Because they wanted to assess the effect of their teaching they gave the questionnaires to their classes before and after the unit and so were able to measure change.

The questionnaire prepared by the first group of teachers told the pupils to 'imagine that your class has collected £20 to donate to charity. The money is to be given out in £5 units. Using the list of charities below, show how you would distribute your donations by putting one tick under each £5 opposite the charity of your choice'. The charities included cancer research, sports equipment for the school and Help the Aged as well as a range of third world charities. The questionnaire was administered to a year group of more than 200 pupils. Even before the unit was taught, third world charities were attracting a great deal of sympathy from the pupils. 79 per cent of them said that they would wish to contribute to health clinics for the third world. The provision of clean water had attracted the support of 71 per cent. After the unit had been taught, support for these causes went up to 85 per cent and 84 per cent respectively. Inevitably support for some other causes had to come down.

The questionnaire prepared by the second group of teachers was a little more complex. In this case the pupils were told that 'a world banking organisation had set up a world cities improvement fund. Money is to be given to projects aimed at improving the quality of life in the cities of the world'. Two cities were described. One of them was called Slumsville, U.S.A. and the other Shanty Town, India. The instructions went on 'the projects listed below are designed to help the two cities, decide which projects are the most urgent. Put them in order of importance in the boxes below'. The projects included modernisation of old houses in Slumsville, clean water supplies for Shanty Town and restoring the ancient temples in Shanty Town. The three most popular causes before the unit was taught were all from Shanty Town, health clinics, clean water and helping the people to build their own simple houses. Ninety-four per cent of pupils had put at least one of these among their top three. That went up slightly to 96 per cent.

The teachers had an answer to their question. They had influenced their pupils' attitudes to the third world and not in a vague undifferentiated way. There was a cognitive component too, which showed a greater realisation of the importance of clean water and medical services. They had achieved both sets of objectives, greater understanding and greater sympathy. But the teachers had learned something else. The children were already very sympathetic to the third world, even before Bob Geldof, Bandaid and Sportaid. They now could ask whether their attempts to influence attitudes were necessary. Perhaps their time could be more effectively spent in some other way. The crucial point is that teachers can assess their impact on attitudes by using relatively straightforward techniques and can obtain information that will enable them to rethink their teaching.

Assessing Individuals: The Views of Teachers and Parents

The affective outcomes of particular curricula, of the programme of an individual school or of a school system, may be the important questions for education generally, but teachers find the assessment of individual pupils a more pressing issue. Some teachers are reluctant to make assessments of their pupils' affective characteristics, though most teachers accept both that schools have a role in the affective development of pupils and that teachers have a responsibility for assessing and reporting in this area. In a survey of Scottish teachers (Forsyth and Dockrell, 1979) 84 per cent of teachers agreed the aims of education included the affective development of pupils as proposed by the Munn report quoted above. Eighty-eight per cent of teachers thought that schools should keep a standardised comprehensive record for all pupils that included assessments of affective characteristics, and that it should be used for guidance within the school. Eighty per cent of them thought that it should be also used as a basis for references for school leavers. The vast majority of teachers, then, accepted that the affective development of their pupils and its assessment was a part of their responsibility.

Parents too believe that schools have a role in the affective development of children and that they should receive reports on behaviour; on attitudes such as effort, enterprise, interest and co-operation; and on some aspects of personality — for example shyness and friendliness. They also thought that these assessments should be used for references to prospective employers (Dockrell, 1985; McKay and Dockrell, 1983).

Issues in the Assessment of Individuals

The majority of both teachers and parents are agreed that assessments of pupils' attitudes and other personal characteristics should be made. If it is decided that these assessments are to be made (and since they are now virtually universal the decision is in effect either to stop making them or to put them on a more defensible basis) the chosen system must be fair and accurate if it is to be acceptable. Whatever the purpose of the assessment, formative or summative, no matter who it is made by, pupils as self assessment or teachers, the assessment must be accurate it if is not to mislead.

Assessments should be fair in three ways. A statement should report typical and not unusual behaviour. Assessments by different teachers of the same pupils should be consistent. If one teacher makes or approves a statement as indicating 'perseverance' which another teacher will not accept, then the pupil understandably will be confused. Assessments of different pupils by a single teacher should be comparable, for pupils will inevitably compare them and feel a justifiable sense of injustice if the same behaviour elicits different comments from a teacher — unless, of course, the different basis has been understood and agreed beforehand. As with accuracy, assessments should be fair, whether they are made by teachers or whether they are self-assessments accepted or validated by the school.

Assessing, recording and reporting cannot be entirely separated, for whatever is to be reported must be assessed and recorded, though it may be that a school might assess and record more than is put into a report. Additional information may be gathered as a basis for counselling, for discussions with parents or as a backup for formal reports. Decisions about the nature and purpose of the report will inevitably determine procedures for assessing and recording.

A major issue is whether the report should be structured or unstructured. Should guidance be given to pupils or teachers about what is to be included, or should there simply be an invitation to record whatever activities or personal qualities they wish? An open-ended personal record allows for great diversity among individuals and imposes no constraints upon schools or individual teachers. The final report can reflect more fully the achievements of any individual than can a structured report. Openendedness and structure can, however, be combined. The Scottish Headteachers (Dockrell and Broadfoot, 1977) recommended both the inclusion of a structured report and provision for an open record. If the decision is to go for an entirely open report, thought will have to be given to recording and use. If a record is too bulky it may not be read, and if reports are too diverse they are open to misinterpretation.

A more structured approach gives rise to a different set of issues. The first is the purpose for which the assessments are to be used. Both parents and teachers want them to be used for two distinct purposes, the first formative during the course of education and the second summative at the end of schooling. Bloom, Hastings and Madaus (1971) assert that 'although it may not be good practice to assign a summative grade for affective behaviour, it is often desirable to evaluate a student's affective behaviour formatively. Such an evaluation is diagnostic in that it can indicate to the student his progress towards the attainment of such outcomes. The point is, however, that feedback to the student, not the assignment of a grade, should be the purpose of making a formative evaluation of affective objectives'.

The initial emphasis in profiling was on the final report (Dockrell and Broadfoot; 1979, Swales, 1978) but more recently there has been an increasing recognition of the value of formative assessments (Stratton, 1985). It is important to distinguish between these two purposes, for the form and content of the reports might differ in the two cases. Parents want either a written comment which refers to their own child, or an oral report at a parents'

evening or at a personal interview with guidance staff. Employers'
forms on the other hand often ask simply for a tick in the relevant
box as a norm-referenced assessment comparing the pupil for
whom the report is being prepared to others of the same age in the
school or in the community in general.

Parents want a formative report to be comprehensive, covering a
range of different aspects including negative ones, but they expect
the summative statement whether in the form of a profile, record or
reference to focus on those aspects of a youngster which would be
helpful. Employers are usually interested only in those
characteristics which are relevant to their specific employment.

Deciding What to Assess

The decision about the characteristics to be assessed is more
complex than it might at first seem. It is a task for the school
community. Parents know what aspects of their children it is that
they want the schools to tell them about, but different groups of
parents might have different expectations. Parents of children at
church schools, for example, might have made their choice of
schooling on the grounds that such schools would be concerned to
encourage the development of particular attributes and a
commitment to certain values, in a way that would not be
appropriate in state schools. Different ethnic communities, too,
might have different emphases if not different objectives that
would need to be taken into account in formulating the assessment
and reporting programme.

Groups of parents or teachers might produce their own lists of
aspects of pupils that they would like to see covered, but it is
sometimes necessary to stimulate discussion with an established
list. While the list would be chosen as a stimulus, its content might
be taken to have a significance that was not intended and in any
case might become the agenda for discussion. The initial list should
be chosen, therefore, either because it thought to be appropriate if
not definitive or because it is likely to evoke responses from the
group.

Any list emerging from an initial discussion is likely to be too
extensive to be usable and to include items which appear to overlap.
It will therefore need to be simplified, as the experience of a
number of schools demonstrates. For example, a department in one
school had a system with five assumed traits. Each trait was
assessed by reference to a set of descriptive statements, 25 of them
in all. A research team analysed their assessments using factor
analysis. A number of rotations were made. The first was a
principal components varimax rotation. This most nearly met the
teachers' assumptions that each statement belonged exclusively to a

designated trait. The second analysis sought a factor structure that corresponded to the teachers' hypothesised factors to see whether their groupings could be obtained reasonably satisfactorily from the intercorrelations. Three oblique rotations were made with a heuristic purpose, to see whether a plausible set of traits could be discerned that were intercorrelated.

None of the factor analyses supported the teachers' groupings. The teachers' five assumed traits were not measured by the assessments that they made. The oblique rotations were not very helpful. They grouped the items in what appeared to be rag-bag factors which could only be labelled 'goodness' or 'badness'. In the other factor analyses two factors emerged, 'confidence/leadership' and 'dependability' (or less flatteringly 'conformity' or 'docility'). This latter factor included much of what teachers call general class behaviour and perseverance. What they were assessing under those headings went so closely together that in their actual assessments the teachers were in effect treating that as a single trait (Dockrell and Black, 1980).

A later study carried out in another school (Black and Dockrell, 1980) included the whole of a year group (n = 356) and all the teachers teaching those pupils (n = 70). The year group chosen was in the middle of the secondary programme, so the assessments were to be used formatively. These teachers did not begin with an assumed set of traits. Instead it was decided to cover as wide a range of affective characteristics as possible, so that the assessments would be useful both for guidance and teaching purposes. They also wanted a smaller set of variables for reporting. Again the teachers' assessments were factor analysed by the research team. The analyses were made by department. The hypothesis was that in a school organised by subject department, with a highly differentiated subject specific curriculum and with teachers permitted to teach only the one or two subjects for which they were qualified, there might well be differences between departments in the characteristics developed and assessed. Bacon's well-known aphorism about the effects of different disciplines might apply in the affective domain if not in the cognitive, especially when the departments making the assessments included not only Bacon's mathematics and English but aesthetic subjects like art and music and activities like physical education and outdoor studies.

The teachers were given the full list of 27 characteristics and asked to indicate which of these they felt most appropriate to assess in their own subject and to add any that they felt had been omitted. The teachers examined the responses from their own departments and arrived at a consensus about what would be appropriate for them. They then made the assessments. As in the previous study

these were factor analysed by the research team. The analyses were
made department by department.

There were two factors running across all departments which
were labelled 'conscientiousness/perseverance' and 'confidence'.
In addition there was in some departments an additional small
factor. The history teachers seemed to be assessing 'originality'.
Chemistry and physical education (boys) teachers were assessing
'willingness to share'. In physics the additional factor was
'relationships with peers' and in business studies it was
'attentiveness'. These factors were all small and might not be
stable. The factor patterns of individual teachers, however, seemed
to be largely congruent with those of their departments. While they
might reflect the emphases of different subjects, for example
attentiveness in the case of business studies, or the concerns of
different departments, for example willingness to share in the case
of physical education, it is equally possible that they reflect the
idiosyncracies of individuals or small tightly knit groups.

The findings from these two studies were not surprising. The
earlier analyses of the data obtained in the Pupils in Profile study
had suggested that most of the variance in those assessments of
affective characteristics could be explained by two major factors
which were labelled 'perseverance' and 'enterprise' (Dockrell and
Broadfoot, 1977). Other researchers had found much the same.
Greaney (1974) had found four factors, but the two major ones
'satisfactory   classroom   behaviour'   and   'group   leadership'
accounted for 38 per cent of the variance. Airasian, Kellaghan and
Madaus (1977) reported that in each of four related studies two
factors, a classroom behaviour factor and a social behaviour
factor, accounted for 75 per cent of the variance. Others have
reported   similar   findings   (Hallworth   and   Morrison,   1964,
Ingenkamp, 1979, Morrison, McIntyre and Sutherland, 1965). It
was put best by Hope (1977) who in his analysis of the Scottish
mental survey data found very similar factors which he said
discriminated between 'even tempered plodders' and 'pushful
innovators'.

These findings are perhaps best understood in terms of 'implicit
personality theory' first proposed by Bruner and Tagiuri (1954) and
later developed by Jackson and his associates (Jackson, Chan and
Stricker, 1978). Observers make inferences about the personal
attributes of others and act on these inferences. This implicit theory
does not necessarily tell us about the psychology of human
personality but about the naïve implicit personality theory of an
individual, or in this case of a group. What the factor analyses have
done is to make explicit the implicit theory lying behind teachers'
assessments. If this interpretation is correct, teachers currently act
on a limited number of dimensions of personality even when a large

number of assessments is made. Increasing the apparent range of assessments does not increase the range of aspects of pupils actually reported.

It does not follow that assessment of affective characteristics of pupils should be restricted to these two dimensions even though teachers' assessments currently are limited in this way. It does however mean that a decision has to be made either to accept that teachers' assessments are limited and to work with only these two dimensions, or to try to expand the range. This latter option would presumably require an extensive programme of training.

It is clear that it would be foolish to set up an elaborate system and to assume that a large set of assessments is producing a correspondingly large amount of information. That does not appear to be the case. The working party of the Headteachers' Association of Scotland when it received the Pupils in Profile report decided to recommend that the affective part of the profile should consist only of the two dimensions (Dockrell and Broadfoot, 1977). When the reports of the current experiments with profiles and records are available, English educators will be faced with the same decision: either a limited and justifiable set of dimensions or a more extensive set of categories which give a spurious impression of greater comprehensiveness. Whether the third option, training, is viable remains to be demonstrated.

How to Make the Assessments

The next question is: how can the assessments be made more accurate? One way of doing this is by making the assessments and reports descriptive and not judgmental. The procedure followed in the studies reported above involved the use of crucial indices (Black and Dockrell, 1980). Flanagan (1956) developed a critical incident technique which was used subsequently as a means of creating performance records in industry (Flanagan, Miller and Burns, 1955), as a teacher recording system for personal and social development programmes (Flanagan, 1956) and as a parental system for child observation (Flanagan, Pumroy and Tuska, 1966). In his 'Teachers' Guide to Social and Personal Development' (1956) Flanagan says 'teachers should not be expected to write down everything a child does. . . . Briefly, (the critical incident method) involves noticing what the children do during the course of the school day, and singling out those activities which are indicative of strengths or weaknesses in a crucial area of personal or social behaviour'.

Flanagan's system requires teachers to keep a written record of pupils' behaviour over a period of time. This focus on observing and recording behaviour is the key to an accurate report. The

K

record need not of course be compiled by a teacher or other supervisor — it can be a self report. Flanagan's technique was modified by the Scottish team. This modification was called 'crucial indices' to distinguish it from Flanagan's original, but also to recognise its derivation from his work. The Scottish modification of Flanagan's technique involved observing pupil behaviour in school or on the playing field, selecting those examples of behaviour that were thought to be indicators of the chosen characteristics at a particular level, reaching agreement about which behaviours were crucial and using them as bench marks for future observations.

It is worth noting at this point that all the groups of teachers that the Scottish team worked with wanted to record and report the affective qualities at different levels. They did not think that pupils either did or did not display 'enterprise' or 'persistence' but that all pupils were more or less enterprising or persistent. They wanted to recognise in their reports that all pupils exhibited the desired characteristics to some extent, but also the extent to which they exhibited them. They assumed in other words that the characteristics to be observed and assessed were on a continuum. Indeed the very notion of progress implies a path that the pupils move along.

An example of the use of this technique is found in an early study where a technical studies department of seven teachers had wanted to assess four pupil characteristics including 'effort'. They had been using a subjective one-to-six scale from 'good' to 'bad' but wanted to improve inter-rater and rater-rater consistency. To do this they had to agree what was meant for example by 'Effort 4'.

Each teacher was asked to write down independently examples of behaviour that he or she had observed and thought exemplified each of the characteristics at each part of the scale. Table 1 lists some of the statements that the teachers made for effort. Some of these statements are judgments, for example 'Does not waste time talking'; others are generalised descriptions, like 'A pupil who is prepared to work steadily from the beginning of the period to the end'; but some are reports of actual behaviours, like 'Voluntary preparation for practical work done at home, e.g. drawings etc.'. All the statements were randomised and returned to the teachers with the instruction to allot, again independently, each of them to the characteristic and level that they thought appropriate. The purpose was to achieve a common understanding of the meaning of the terms and levels. Many of the statements were differently categorised by the teachers and were discarded. Others were eliminated because they were not descriptions of actual behaviours. Some were deleted because they were very similar to others. Only seven of the 18 statements in Table 1 survived this review. The gaps

TABLE 1

Actual Behaviours Offered by Teachers as Exemplars of Effort

A pupil who is prepared to work steadily from the beginning of the period to the end.

As soon as one process/job is completed the pupil is eager to get on with the next one.

Does not get put off by awkward or difficult problems, works them out and sees the job through to completion.

Tends to engage in window gazing.

Very seldom asks questions.

Voluntary preparation for practical work done at home, e.g. drawings.

A pupil is given a task to perform and works at it until it is completed.

Always reluctant to start work.

Requires constant prodding.

Starts work willingly, is reluctant to finish.

Does not waste time talking.

Gives up easily when faced with a problem.

Doesn't waste any time.

Slow.

Enthusiastic.

An eager beaver who is not put off by awkward or difficult situations.

A real plodder who does not give up easily.

Continues to work even when faced with a difficult task.

---

were mainly in the middle. It was easier to agree on examples of extreme behaviours than to find those which discriminated among the middle grades. The teachers were therefore asked to repeat the exercise until there was a number of examples for each point on the scales. This iterative procedure was also used in the other Scottish studies to arrive at agreed reference behaviours for each level of the chosen characteristics.

Table 2 gives examples of the descriptors of effort that the teachers used to make their assessments. The statements did not compromise a comment bank but were exemplars. The teachers did not search for these specific behaviours in every pupil: rather they used the statements to provide an agreed definition of the characteristics and levels. They provided a set of anchor scales. The teaching in this department was so organised that the pupils were being taught by more than one of the teachers in different class groups and Teacher 5 was teaching two groups that included some of the same pupils. The teachers assessed all pupils in their groups, so there were two assessments for some pupils. Table 3 shows the mean difference in the assessments made of individual pupils by pairs of teachers, and in the case of Teacher 5 the mean difference in the assessments of those pupils that he assessed twice. In the 14 cases where groups were assessed more than once, in only five instances was the mean difference in excess of one point. Some variability in pupil behaviour with different teachers might be expected, but some of the inconsistency remaining in the

TABLE 2

Agreed Exemplars of Effort

1 As soon as one process/job is completed the pupil is eager to get on with the next one.

Does not get put off by awkward or difficult problems, works them out and sees the job through to completion. Voluntary preparation for practical work done at home, e.g. drawings.

Makes attempt to continue working without further instruction.

---

2 Works steadily.

Works well in class when given a job to do.

---

3 Works erratically, sometimes eager and keen, at other times lazy.

If a certain job really interests him he will work hard, but if the job in hand does not appeal very little effort is applied.

---

4 Interest wanes if success is slow to come.

Easily satisfied with an inferior job.

---

5 Requires constant prodding.

Spends too much time window gazing.

---

6 Even when pushed this pupil will look for excuses to stop work.

Will actually destroy or "lose" an item of work rather than attempt to complete it.

assessments is presumably attributable to disagreements among the teachers. Inter-rater reliability is, however, remarkably high. The difference between the two sets of assessments made by Teacher 5 might also arise from some small variability in the behaviour of the pupils in the two situations, or more likely from inconsistency in the teacher's assessments. In either case intra-rater reliability in the case of this teacher is very high. The teachers themselves reported that the use of crucial indices represented a considerable improvement on their previous practice.

TABLE 3

Mean Difference in Score for Groups Assessed Twice

Teacher	1	2	3	4	5	6	7	x
1	—	0·78	1·12	1·00	—	0·73	—	0·91
2	0·78	—	0·90	0·75	0·33	—	0·00	0·55
3	1·12	0·90	—	—	1·11	1·25	—	1·10
4	1·00	0·75	—	—	—	—	—	0·88
5	—	0·33	1·11	—	0·67	1·28	0·67	0·81
6	0·73	—	1·25	—	1·28	—	1·25	1·13
7	—	0·00	—	—	0·67	1·25	—	0·96

Statements of actual behaviours observed by teachers or reported by pupils anchored in scales defined by crucial indices are both accurate and fair. They provide a sound basis for the formative use of assessment during the course of schooling. If they are used for summative purposes, they recognise that the behaviour reported occurred in the rather special situation of the school and make no claim to easy generalisability to the entirely different circumstances of tertiary education, the training centre or the workplace.

Using the Assessments

A manageable system for the use of the observations poses another set of problems. If they are to be used only for tutorial guidance and for no other purpose, there is no great difficulty. The records in many schools are kept by the pupils. They bring them to their tutor periods for review and target setting and take them away again. No copy is kept centrally. This kind of record can be used as a basis for discussion with parents if such a use has been agreed beforehand. Pupils too can take the cumulative record with them when they leave school, as a final report. It is however likely to be bulky and not easily accessible to anyone but the pupils themselves, nor is it available in the school to be used when writing references or completing tertiary education or employer's forms.

If a more manageable document is required as a basis for school reports, and most teachers and parents endorse the summative use of affective assessments, then consideration has to be given to the content and form of the document and to the collation and summation of the assessments. Such a document might also provide a suitable basis for reports to parents.

If the experience of the Scottish schools reported above is accepted, the content would be descriptions of typical behaviour with respect to a limited number of agreed aspects of pupils. The format of the document would then have to provide for a series of such statements, made or selected by teachers. Whether or not the statements should be accompanied by some indication of the level that they represent or not is a matter for consideration. Some schools like to make explicit the hierarchical nature of their assessments, others prefer to keep them implicit. A choice has to be made in the light of the general philosophy of the school.

The simplest and quickest system is one where teachers select from a limited number of statements. They may be selected from a list and copied on to report forms or profiles, or they may be printed on a form and ticked by teachers. A more sophisticated approach developed by some education authorities and schools is to have a computerised system with item banks of statements from which teachers choose the appropriate ones for each individual pupil. These are undoubtedly efficient, quick and easy to use. All three approaches, however, are necessarily limited. Even if they consist of descriptive statements they are relatively few and may come to serve as absolute expectations of pupils rather than as exemplars of what is to be observed.

A recent development of the use of computers is a programme with a standard form and exemplars and space for the pupils to insert descriptions of their own behaviour. Only the agreed target level need appear on the VDU and not the full set of categories. The statement need not be printed until it is agreed. Earlier statements can be discarded as new targets are reached and only the final achievement printed or, of course, all statements can be retained as a record of progress if that is more appropriate.

An alternative approach is the system described in Pupils in Profile (1977) suitably adapted. It allows the affective assessments to be recorded at the same time as the academic marks. A single entry provides an individual pupil report and a class record. The reports from the various teachers for each pupil are easily collated and need not be transcribed. It is more flexible and can be less stereotyped than other systems, but is more time consuming.

Whatever the approach adopted the technology is important. However desirable a record or profile might be, it wil not survive or not be used effectively it if is not manageable.

Conclusion

The current experiments with profiles and records of achievement in England have faced many schools for the first time with the issues that are involved in the assessment of affective characteristics. Schools are under pressure to institute practices that will have long term consequences for pupils, for schools' commitment to the broader aims of education, for pastoral systems and not just for reporting. It is important that they at least be aware of the solutions that other teachers have found to the problems that face them.

REFERENCES

AIRASIAN, P. W., KELLAGHAN, T. and MADAUS, G. F. (1977) The stability of teachers' perceptions of pupil characteristics. *Irish Journal of Education, 11,* 74-84.

BLACK, H. D. and DOCKRELL, W. B. (1980) Assessment in the affective domain. Do we, can we, should we? *British Educational Research Journal, 6,* 197-203.

BLACK, H. D. and DOCKRELL, W. B. (1984) Criterion Referenced Assessment in the Classroom. *Scottish Council for Research in Education.*

BLOOM, B. S., HASTINGS, J. T. and MADAUS, G. F. (1971) Handbook on Formative and Summative Evaluation. McGraw Hill.

BROWN, S. (1976) Attitude Objectives in Secondary School Science. Stirling University, Educational Monographs 1.

BRUNER, J. S. and TAGIURI, R. (1954) The perception of people. *The Handbook of Social Psychology* (ed. LINZEY, G. and ARONSON, E.). Addison Wesley.

DOCKRELL, W. B. (1980) Teachers' assessments of their pupils' affective characteristics. *Enfance 4/5,* 295-299.

DOCKRELL, W. B. (1985) Reporting assessments of pupils' attitudes and personality. International Association for Educational Assessment, Annual Conference, Oxford.

DOCKRELL, W. B. (1987) The assessment of childrens' affective characteristics. *British Educational Research Journal, 13,* 3-13.

DOCKRELL, W. B. and BLACK, H. D. (1980) Assessment in the affective domain — what can be done about it? Impact of Tests on Education (ed. DOCKRELL, W. B.). Educational Testing Service.

DOCKRELL, W. B. and BLACK, H. D. (1986) Assessment in the affective domain. Schulgerechte Diagnose (ed. PETILLON, H., WAGNER, J. W. and WOLF, B.). Beltz Verlag.

DOCKRELL, W. B. and BROADFOOT, P. (1977) Pupils in Profile. Hodder and Stoughton.

FLANAGAN, J. C. (1949) A new approach to evaluating personnel. *Personnel, 26,* 35-42.

FLANAGAN, J. C. (1956) Teachers' Guide for the Personal and Social Development Programme. Science Research Associates.

FLANAGAN, J. C., MILLER, R. B. and BURNS, R. K. (1955) *The Performance Records Manual.* Science Research Associates.

FLANAGAN, J. C., PUMROY, S. S. and TUSKA, S. A. (1956) Parents' Booklet for Understanding and Developing Children's Behaviour.

FORSYTH, J. P. and DOCKRELL, W. B. (1979) Curriculum and Assessment, The Response to Munn and Dunning. Scottish Council for Research in Education.

GREANEY, V. and KELLAGHAN, T. (1972) Cognitive and personality factors associated with class placement of pupils. *Irish Journal of Education, 6,* 93-104.

HALLWORTH, H. J. and MORRISON, A. (1964) A comparison of peer and teacher ratings in a secondary modern school. *British Journal of Educational Psychology, 34,* 285-281.

HARLEN, W. (1976) Progress in Learning Science. The Schools Council.

HOPE, K. (1985) As Others See Us. Cambridge University Press.

INGENKAMP, K. (1977) Educational Assessment. National Foundation for Educational Research.

JACKSON, D. N., CHAN, D. W. and STRICKER, L. J. (1978) Implicity Personality Theory, Is It Illusory? Educational Testing Service.

McKAY, N. and DOCKRELL, W. B. (1983) What parents want from teachers' assessments and school reports. *British Educational Research Association,* Annual Conference, London.

MORRISON, A., McINTYRE, D. and SUTHERLAND, J. (1965) Teachers' personality assessment of primary school pupils. *British Journal of Educational Psychology, 35,* 306-319.

POPHAM, W. J. (1975) Educational Evaluation. Prentice Hall. SED.

CONSULTATIVE COMMITTEE ON THE CURRICULUM (1977). The Structure of the Curriculum in the Third and Fourth Years of the Scottish Secondary School. HMSO.

STRATTON, N. (1975) Profiling in Schools. City and Guilds of London Institute.

SWALES, T. (1978) Records of Personal Achievement. Schools Council.

TORNEY, J. V., OPPENHEIM, A. N. and FARNON, R. F. (1975) Civic Education in Ten Countries. Wiley.

WAKE, R. (1986) Catholic Education in School. *The Month, 19,* 248-251.

IT'S MA FAITHER THAT HITS ME

Some Pupils' Views on the Importance of Schools Reports and
their Repercussions

H. D. BLACK
Scottish Council for Research in Education

N. McKAY
Clydebank High School

The years between 1980 and 1985 saw substantial changes in assessment practices in Scotland. The most public changes were those
made to the leaving certificates. A new 'Standard Grade'
examination was introduced for 14-16 year olds to replace the
'O-Grade'. Its distinguishing characteristics are the provision of a
certificate which caters for the whole age group and the adoption of
a 'grade-related criterion' model of assessment design — an
approach explored in Marion Devine's paper in this collection. A
'National Certificate' was introduced which replaced the existing
complex and often overlapping provision from existing agencies
such as SCOTBEC, SCOTVEC, City and Guilds, Pitmans etc. The
assessment model for this is described in the paper by Yates and
Hall.

Inevitably, however, it is not surprising that this period of
development in certification had a parallel in assessment in the
classroom and in school reporting practices. This hypothesis was
substantiated when, in preparation for a study of the perceptions of
school-based assessment undertaken by the Scottish Council for
Research in Education in 1980-82, a national survey of reporting
practices in Scottish secondary schools was conducted by SCRE.
While in the majority of cases these reports had not been changed
in the recent past, 25 per cent of schools claimed to be modifying or
considering modifications to their reports, and it was clear that
experimentation was taking place in a number of ways.

It is data from that survey and a detailed follow-up of pupil
views of practice in four case-study schools which this paper will
describe. It outlines the various forms of change which were found
to be taking place and then briefly describes the four case studies
which were the focus of the research. In relation to these case
studies it describes what pupils think should be the focus of reports,
discusses findings on the extent to which various aspects of the
reports appeared to be understood by pupils, and outlines their
perceptions of what reports are for.

Innovation in School Reporting

The innovations noted fell into three categories. These comprise modifications of format, modifications of content and format, and more radical modifications associated with changes in philosophy or principle.

Modifications in format ranged from those where the change was minimal to others which represented entirely new views on how to communicate with parents. The former, for example, included reports where 'grade' and 'effort' statements were based entirely on letter grades. Thus, for example, in one school the term 'grade' meant different things according to the course being followed. For those following non-certificate courses it comprised five, ranging from 'A' — excellent to 'E' — unsatisfactory. Pupils attempting O-Grade or Higher courses were rated on a four-point scale from 'L' — good pass to 'X' — pass unlikely. Similar distinctions were made for pupils on other types of courses. In all, the pupils and parents had to master 20 codes in order to decipher the report.

In another school the report comprised a computer print-out stating the name of the school, the pupil's name, the class and a list of subjects taken along with the mark and the class average. Printed on a sticky label, this was gummed to a report sheet and handed out to the parents. Quite what the impact of this 'lazy' use of computer facilities was in the homes where they arrived remains to be seen, and one of our colleagues suggested that the school might save itself further work by peeling off the label, slapping it on the forehead of the appropriate pupil, and sending the youngster home without bothering with an envelope.

Computer print-out formats, however, were not limited to this rather suspect approach. In other schools, formats very similar to existing traditional reports were used, but all numerical and grade information was printed out by the machine, leaving space only for written comments by the teachers. This perhaps represented a more acceptable utilisation of modern technology.

Perhaps more interesting were examples of reports which combined format changes with changes of content. In particular, one Region had devised a computerised reporting system which not only included the more traditional information such as the mark and class average and the place of the pupil in relation to the rest of his year group, but also included comments which were derived from a bank of statements. Quite how the impersonality of the computer print-out sustains the apparent interest in the individual of a written comment is open to speculation. Nevertheless there was in this approach a recognition of the need for individual comments in each subject alongside grades or marks, which is recognised as desirable by both parents and pupils alike.

Changes in reports incorporating modifications in philosophy or principle were perhaps the most interesting, but were equally the least frequent. Broadly speaking there were two types, the first reflecting a move towards differentiation in the learning tasks and expectations for individual pupils, and the other representing a move towards profiling typically on a subject basis.

An example of the former at first glance appeared very similar to a traditional report. However, further study showed that attainment gradings were given under columns labelled as 'core', 'extension 1' and 'extension 2'. The report, therefore, reflected the move in the school towards a 'mastery learning' philosophy in all departments. There was evidence in our more detailed studies of such reporting that, unless special care is taken in making clear to the users of the reports what is meant by these distinctions, much confusion can result. Nevertheless, what this represented was an example of school policy on pedagogy leading the reporting requirements placed on teachers rather than the reporting requirements dictating the pattern of pedagogy which is so often the case in schools.

The profiling approach manifested itself in a number of ways. In some schools it was obvious that the policy was to allow individual departments to develop forms of report which were appropriate to their needs as they saw them at that time. Thus, for example in one report, while Science gave a letter grading on up to 13 units of work in S1 and S2, and also reported on behaviour, effort, progress, co-operation, interest, care and skill, Modern Studies gave only a single overall grading. Clearly the amount of information provided by the Science department was substantially greater than that in Modern Studies, which must have left the parent with some problems in comparing progress in the two. As it was clear from interviews which we carried out with parents that the more detailed profile information was broadly welcomed, one presumes that in the long term, policy will be to move towards a profile in all subjects.

The format of such reports varied considerably. In some cases the school had devised a single sheet which incorporated reports from each subject. This, however, severely restricted the space available for comment and is probably a doubtful means of economy. More typical, however, were the booklets of reports produced individually by departments. Many of these appeared to give important diagnostic information which would be of value to the parent in supporting the child. The reservation we would have about the style of some of these was that variation in subject must have created considerable problems of interpretation for the parents.

The Case Study Reports

The object of carrying out the national survey was to identify examples of innovation in reporting which appeared worthy of study in greater depth, and four such schools were invited to co-operate with us in our research. School A was chosen because it had been actively involved in an action research project in affective assessment, and had come to include comment on a number of such areas on its report. Furthermore, the teachers had spent some considerable time in arriving at the components to be included, and it was therefore felt that this would be a source of information on the issues relevant to affective assessment and reporting. School C was involved in the introduction of criterion-referenced reporting in both S1 and S2. The focus in this case was initially for reporting purposes, although it was hypothesised that this would have a backwash effect on pedagogy and curriculum. In school D the impetus to the new reporting system was modification to pedagogy and curriculum. The school policy was to introduce diagnostic assessment in all departments, and the reporting system was in the process of modification to embrace the needs of departments working within such a policy. School P was chosen because it was using the 'Pupils in Profile' (SCRE, 1977) reporting system in the final two years of compulsory education with pupils who were following largely 'non-certificate' courses.

Extensive semi-structured interviews of approximately one hour were carried out with 30 pupils in school C, 15 in school P, and 12 in each of schools A and D. With the exception of school P, where only 'non-certificate' pupils were interviewed, a structured random sample was used, drawing an equal number of pupils from each Mathematics set.

What Do Pupils Think Should be Reported on?

In schools C, D and P each of the pupils was asked what he or she considered to be appropriate foci for school reports, and whether there was anything which they considered it inappropriate for teachers to report on. In school A the focus was solely on pupil perceptions of the reporting of affective characteristics.

The data suggested that the elements of reporting could be divided into three distinct sets. The first comprised components where there was little controversy amongst pupils about their inclusion. The second set was characterised by components on which there was some dispute, which was either from a small number of respondents, or relatively trivial in nature. The third set comprised components which were clearly controversial to a substantial number of respondents and which are worthy of consideration in greater depth.

In the first set two components of reports stand out as being acceptable to all, or at least a considerable majority of the pupils. The first of these is predictable, and the other perhaps less so. The former was the inclusion of subject attainment, which was mentioned by a majority of pupils in all schools in an unprompted context, and by all pupils when further prompted. The way in which this achievement was reported was, however, more controversial and is discussed below.

Perhaps less predictably, some form of statement on pupil behaviour and relationship with teachers was mentioned in the unprompted context by a majority of pupils in all schools. In school G, for example, more pupils mentioned this variable without prompting than they did subject attainment. In school P, when a list of possible inclusions was offered to them as a means of prompting, 12 of the 15 respondents chose to mention this variable, and only one pupil expressed mild concern that perhaps discipline should not be included. Even he conceded, however, that had he smashed a couple of windows that term, this might receive appropriate mention on the report.

"Things should be put in only if they are bad, you know, like smashing a window. That's because you could get a hammering at home."

Other variables which were mentioned by a substantial number of pupils, and whose inclusion was questioned by none, were attendance and punctuality.

The two areas which appeared to be somewhat controversial were the inclusion of a cognitive subject profile and a set of basic skills. The extent to which these were a source of controversy, however, varied amongst the schools, and it should be recognised that a methodological limitation of the study was that the pupils had varying degrees of acquaintance with these two aspects of reporting.

In school D, where the diagnostic approach was associated with a cognitive profile approach at the reporting stage, the pupils were specifically asked to compare a detailed report with a more general report. All the pupils said that they preferred individual subject reports which provided achievement profiles. This, they claimed, enabled them to see what exactly they were good at and poor at. One respondent also claimed that it told his parents what work had actually been covered. In school C, where similar ground was covered in asking respondents about the criterion-referenced report, a favourable attitude to achievement profiles was also noted.

In school P, however, one-third of the respondents specifically said that they would prefer not to have a subject breakdown. The reasons for wanting such a breakdown amongst the majority were essentially the same as in schools D and C, i.e. to show up strengths and weaknesses which were covered up by the overall marks. The exclusion of such breakdowns was not so cogently argued, however, and was typically because the pupils could not see the point of it. Although the numbers are small, it may be important to note that the group of pupils who did not see the subject breakdown as being useful comprised those who claimed not to be concerned about receiving reports, and who saw the home follow-up to be no more than a parental expression of satisfaction or dissatisfaction.

The reporting of basic skills was considered in school C, and to a greater extent in school P. In the former, basic skills were reported in the criterion-referenced report of a number of subjects. The considerable majority of pupils considered this to be acceptable. The main justification was to let parents know what progress was being made, so that extra help could be given if necessary.

In school P, however, there was more controversy. One-third of the respondents had reservations and in one case the condemnation was quite forthright:

> 'There shouldn't be stuff about basic skills; some of the descriptions aren't fair like "can't do an essay" — anyone can do that. Sometimes teachers are not fair. If a teacher doesn't like you he might put something down for badness.'

One pupil contended that teachers do not know their pupils well enough to judge them in the detailed way required by the profile, and two others suggested that the skills listed were apparent only in the home or in situations outwith the school. The information was seen as being 'useless' both to parents (who know these things already) and to employers (who find out about the basic skills in which they are interested at interview).

Even amongst those wholeheartedly in favour of the principle of such assessment, the qualification was added that teachers need to see pupils for four to six periods a week in order to know them well enough to make such assessments. A number of respondents also doubted the ability of teachers to make such assessments across the curriculum. Many of the skills they felt were apparent in only a few subjects, and so teachers should assess only those most closely related to their own subject discipline.

In the set of components coming in for most criticism there were again two particular areas. The inclusion of school extra-curricular activities was explicit in the reports of schools P and C, and the data suggested that this did not have the wholehearted support of the respondents. The issue of the assessment of personal characteristics was raised in all four schools, and again it was clear that this was an area of substantial controversy.

In school P, four pupils chose specifically to state that they were in favour of including school activities, and five chose to make their opposition explicit. The reasons for considering inclusion to be acceptable were not expanded on, the only suggestion being that parents liked to see this. However, those taking a negative stance justified it, in three cases, on the grounds that participation was only considered worthwhile by some pupils, and another suggested that parents did not really want to know about this and were far more interested in subject attainment.

Positive and negative stances were justified in the same way in school C, where 18 respondents chose to make positive mention of such inclusion but eight were explicitly against it.

In the situation where such participation is purely voluntary, and where the individual's ability or willingness to participate may well be affected by circumstances outwith his control — such as the need to support the domestic arrangements in a one-parent family — it may be worth asking whether the labelling of a specific space on the report for such comment may be divisive. This is not to suggest that such comment is inappropriate, but rather to raise the issue for the designers of school reports as to whether unlabelled space for comment might equally fulfil the role, yet at the same time avoid the difficult blank space for the non-participant.

The inclusion of personal characteristics proved to be equally, if not more, controversial. In school P, for example, three respondents clearly stated that perseverance should be stated on the profile, and two were against it. Leadership was considered acceptable by one and unacceptable by another. Four respondents made a general statement that personal characteristics of any kind should not be included on the profile.

In school C the doubt about such inclusion was even more marked. On prompting, 17 respondents stated that personal characteristics should not be included in the report, while seven were in favour. The reasons given for these negative stances included an assertion that shyness, confidence or whatever had nothing to do with the work which was done in the class and was not the business of the teacher. It was also suggested that negative reports of this kind can be upsetting to pupils.

In school D, comments on personality appeared to be less controversial, and equally in school A, which was the school chosen because of its association with assessment in the affective domain, there appeared to be less antagonism. Fifty per cent of the pupils were unequivocal in their acceptance of such assessments and only one pupil categorically rejected the assessment of character, claiming that reporting should just be about work, as parents already knew about their children's personality.

Overall, respondents in favour of affective assessment felt that, provided teachers had contact with pupils frequently enough, they could make fair assessments. They felt that it would be 'a good idea' to let parents know, and felt that employers needed this kind of information in order to select appropriate employees.

Those taking a clearly negative stance argued that this kind of assessments was not part of the teacher's job. Teachers who were involved in such assessments were intruding on a pupil's privacy and just being 'nosey'. Pupils behave very differently outwith the classroom, so teachers can give only a narrow picture of a pupil's character:

> 'The section about character is stupid. It's not the teachers' job to judge these, just to teach you their subject. Teachers are too nosey — they are always asking about your family but they won't answer when you ask about theirs.'

> 'Teachers shouldn't talk at all about pupils; that's being two-faced. They might pass on unfavourable things about you. And they treat you according to the way your sister or brother had behaved when they were at school. Teachers shouldn't jump to conclusions about pupils but should make up their own minds. When . . . came to visit my primary school he drew me a terrible look when I told him who I was and who my sisters were. When I got to this school another teacher picked on me and told me that my sister had been a model pupil. But it wasn't my sister he was thinking of at all . . . my older sisters got into trouble and the teachers expect me to act in the same way. I hate school because of the way the teachers treat me.'

Amongst those with less emphatic reservations, there was a feeling that teachers can assess some aspects of character (for example, discipline) but not others (for example, friendliness and leadership).

It is, however, interesting to note that in contrast with the controversy surrounding the assessment of such characteristics, there was greater unanimity about the extent to which it was part of the teachers' job to develop pupils' attitudes and character. In school P, 11 of the 15 respondents held the view that helping to develop these characteristics was an important role for the teacher. It was not only helpful to individual pupils, but it also had a socialising or disciplining function which allowed the class to operate better as a whole. Some pupils said they preferred the teachers who took this kind of interest in them, and assumed that they did so because they were interested in their job. In one case it was suggested that teachers who were not particularly committed to teaching tended not to take this more personal role. The evidence would therefore suggest that it is not the development of such characteristics in the classroom which is at issue, but the reporting of them.

Do Pupils Understand Reports?

Overall the answer to this question was in the affirmative. For the considerable majority of pupils the information contained on the reports, especially with regard to subject attainment, was not seen as news to them as they already knew their achievement from discussion with the class teacher. However, throughout the data there is evidence that although the pupils were broadly aware of the message in the report, the detail of the communication, and the exact meaning of some of its components, was subject to considerable misinterpretation.

In each of the schools, we examined the respondents' understanding of the non-cognitive aspects of the report in use in their school. Thus, in school P, each of the pupils was asked what he thought was meant by 'perseverance'. One of the most obvious features of this questioning was that, of the 14 pupils who made an attempt to define perseverance, only four made a comment suggesting that they understood what it meant. These included, for example:

'Whether you stick at something you have been given, for example a whole lot of questions or whether you chuck it halfway.'

'Whether you stick at it or give up at a problem, even if you can't do it but you try it.'

Two, after reflecting on the question categorically said that they did not know what perseverance meant. Three others clearly had the notion mixed up with subject attainment:

'It should also be about how good you are at a subject.'

'Judging how good you are at your work — whether you are brainy.'

'It's the quality of work that counts in practical subjects and getting the answers right in others.'

Four of the others associated a variety of characteristics such as paying attention, punctuality, bringing books, school uniform, neatness, etc. with perseverance, and one may well have known what it meant, although we cannot be sure:

L

'I see that the profile says that perseverance includes reliability. That means taking a note for the teacher and not looking at what it says.'

As the pupils in school P were on the verge of leaving and seeking permanent employment, and as the report on perseverance was to form part of a profile for employers, it is rather disturbing that many were not clear as to the criteria on which they were being judged. For some this did not appear to matter:

'I don't know what perseverance and enterprise mean but I am sure that teachers can judge them.'

Underlying such thinking may well have been the notion of the teacher as being a legitimate authority able to make decisions about them even when they themselves were not fully aware of their meaning. The lack of understanding, however, may explain part of the reluctance of many of the pupils to have non-cognitive variables included in reports. It may well be, therefore, that a clearer understanding of what is meant by such characteristics could be helpful both to pupils and to teachers. Not only might it increase the likelihood of their being seen by pupils as legitimate inclusions, but a clearer understanding of what is meant would give such assessments far greater utility in a formative context.

Problems of definition also arose in school C, where the reports were divided into sections for 'knowledge' and 'subject skills'. Seventeen pupils were willing to proffer definitions of knowledge, but their understanding varied considerably. For seven it was 'how much you actually know', for another five it was 'the general knowledge which you bring to the subject', two considered it to be a measure of general ability, and three could see no distinction between knowledge and subject skills.

Thirteen pupils chose to define the notion 'subject skill'. Three saw this as a measure of how well the work had been done on the worksheets, two as a measure of attitude to the subject, five defined it as 'how good you are at what the teacher teaches you', two saw it as general ability, and one considered it to relate to the skill of explanation. Once again it was clear that the distinctions which the teachers were trying to make had not got through to the pupils, and one is left wondering whether they were able to make maximum use of a subject breakdown when they were not clear about what the breakdown actually meant.

The data suggested equal uncertainty in relation to the types of description used for the grades or marks. Although in school P most pupils were aware that the assessment of their basic skills resulted from a consensus of all or most of their teachers, there was little understanding of the distribution and meaning of these grades. They assumed that there was no fixed distribution in the allocation of pupils to each level. It was anticipated by most that in a particularly successful group, almost everyone could 'get a tick in the top box'.

What was meant by the 'top box' was equally unclear, however. Only four pupils knew that a '1' represented the highest grades, while seven thought that a '4' represented the highest grade or did not know. Overall, therefore, in the situation where the original profiling instructions suggested that there should be a rectangular distribution of grades, and where the school report stated that all assessment should be judged on all pupils in the year group, there was considerable uncertainty about what was intended.

There was also confusion abroad in school C about the way in which teachers arrived at the 'criterion-referenced' statements which they made in the report. Twenty respondents offered an explanation. The most frequent was clearly a norm-referenced assumption. Six pupils assumed that the teacher compared one's attainment with that of other people in the class usually through a 'class average'. Another five did not mention the term class average but said that the teacher set a standard from the 'other pupils in the class' and then compared you against this. Another four pupils felt that there were some external criteria concerning 'what you are capable of', and the teacher compared one's work during the term with that, in order to arrive at a grade. Another three had a similar idea, but also brought in the notion of comparing attainment in the current term with that in the previous term to arrive at the grade. Single respondents offered explanations based on 'comparison amongst the marks for each aspect of the subject', 'comparison of your work with other pupils' work in the same year' and 'looking at your work and then your test results and seeing whether you are doing as well as you can'.

Although one would not have expected a very clear definition of 'criterion-referenced reporting' amongst pupils of this age group (S2), there was little suggestion that the essential notion of rating one's performance against an absolute standard had got through to the pupils. This is perhaps not surprising. It was notable that in school D the notion of reporting on specific aspects of attainment, which was implicit in the diagnostic approach, was fairly well understood, and indeed in school C there was reference amongst a number of pupils to obtaining help about specific aspects of learning. However, it is not a problem unique to the teachers in these schools that the translation of a detailed attainment profile relating to small-scale domains into a broadly-based statement of overall attainment, is fraught with difficulty. It is clear from this evidence, however, that at least in the case-study schools, the notion of criterion-referenced reporting may need further consideration. It is not sufficient simply to come up with a small number of broad descriptions of attainment within a subject and call it 'criterion-referenced' for the pupils, or for that matter the parents, to understand the meaning of criterion-referenced description.

To try to give more substance to our thinking on what sort of information it might be appropriate to provide, the respondents were asked how they thought attainment should be reported. This made clear a distinction about the way in which subject- and non-subject attainment was wanted. For subject attainment there was no clear preference for any particular approach. Amongst the suggestions put forward were grades alone, marks and grades together, marks and class averages with a comment, grades with a comment, and marks with no class average. The discussion from the pupils tended to centre on very practical issues, but it was clear that the notion of comparing attainment with that of one's peers was broadly acceptable, and for many was seen as a better source of understanding about their marks.

When basic skills and non-cognitive aspects of the reports were considered, however, there was a much greater emphasis on comments. Comments were thought of as giving greater scope to the teacher to explain what was meant by his or her report — which was considered important because of the difficulty both pupils and parents had in understanding its meaning. There was far less support for grades or 'ticked boxes' and very few pupils mentioned marks.

What are Reports for?

The most frequently expected recipients of school reports by far were parents. More than half of the pupils explicitly mentioned these as the sole recipient of reports, although in school P, where the pupils were shortly to leave school, they were also seen by an equal number as being important for employers. There was surprisingly little reference to the notion of the reports being for pupils, although many stated that this was because the pupils already knew what grades to expect because they had been discussed with their teachers. On first receiving reports, more than half of the pupils made a point of comparing their grades with those of their peers. A large minority said that they did this only when they were sure that they had better grades than their peers, or only if they were forced to. Only a small minority stated categorically that they did not compare reports with their peers.

All of the respondents claimed to take the report home and show it to their parents, although about half of them made a point of first taking it to their mother:

> 'I give it to mum first when she's in a good mood because she doesn't crack up as much as dad.'

For most, the outcome of taking the report home was a brief discussion with the parents, or in some cases only with one parent.

'If it's bad, mum won't give it to dad in case he blows his top.'

In the considerable majority of cases, this discussion was not considered to be particularly worthwhile.

'They always say 'try harder' but never give me praise.'

Very few pupils described what appeared to be a systematic discussion and follow-up.

'At home I show it to dad first. Dad is better than Mum for talking about it. Mum and Dad read it together. Then I get a lecture telling me to pick up on this or telling me I'm good at something. That makes me try harder.'

This situation pertained even in schools where a cognitive profile was provided — which, of course, is the information which parents claim to feel appropriate to meaningful discussion with their children on how best to help them with their problems. This raises the question as to whether in fact parents do want such information, or whether the schools are not at the present time providing it in a form which they find usable. It may not be unimportant in this regard that a number of respondents clearly stated that their parents had difficulty understanding the report as presented.

'Mum looks at it and asks what the grades mean as she doesn't understand them.'

'My parents look at it but they don't understand the grades.'

Despite these drawbacks and limitations, it was clear that in all four schools the pupils were broadly in favour of the innovations in reporting offered to them, and all were able to offer advantages over more limited traditional reports. Thus, for example, in school P, most pupils felt that the profile would give them an advantage in job-hunting. There were criticisms about the language used in the basic skills section, which was felt to vary from the complex (for example, visual understanding and expression) to the unnecessarily simple (for example, 'can use a screwdriver'). Overall, however, 10 pupils favoured the profile, two were partly in favour, one was against, and one 'wasnae bothered'.

Conclusions

It was perhaps inevitable that in some cases the depth of argument used to support pupil stances on reporting was not as pronounced as that amongst parents and teachers. Young people in schools are essentially working in a system which does not lend itself to criticisms of its basic values and assumptions. Pupils, especially in their earlier years, are unlikely to question what they see as the expected sequence of their education. They typically lack the experience to be aware of alternatives. And as they typically relate to both the authority of the school and that of their parents, correspondence between these two parties in the form of school reports is likely to be accepted by them.

Perhaps for these reasons it is more important to give serious consideration to the comments and criticisms they are willing to make to the system. It was clear that they were willing to have their cognitive attainment, and the relationship they had with the school, reported to their parents. It was also apparent that some of them had misgivings about all teachers' abilities to make assessments of their basic skills, and that there was uncertainty about the value of cognitive profiles. The solution to the former is to make clear to them that only teachers who have the opportunity to teach and observe the development of these skills will be expected to comment on them. The solution to the latter is to highlight the potential that such profiles have for diagnostic dialogue between teachers and both the pupils themselves and their parents. The evidence in this data clearly indicated that attention to the outcomes of diagnosis is both welcomed and valued.

The controversy surrounding the reporting of extra curricular involvement and personal characteristics is more of a problem. In the case of the former, there may be the simple report design expedient of leaving such comments to unlabelled spaces. Where the reporting of personal characteristics is concerned we are involved in a more fundamental dilemma, and one which raises questions of value throughout the system. We have no solution to this, but simply offer our evidence as yet another addition to the existing tension.

The issues which the research highlighted regarding understanding of reports and their use are, at the same time, more mundane and disturbing. It is clear that, especially where innovative reports are being produced, serious and sustained consideration must be given to explaining the thinking behind them both to pupils and their parents. In many cases — especially, for example, where 'criterion-referenced' reports are being developed — teachers themselves may have to think more deeply about what they are trying to convey. When the opportunity so obviously exists to provide such explanations, however, there can be no justification for misunderstanding being perpetuated.

More fundamentally, it may well be that parents need to be given some indication of how to use such reports. It was clear from the parent interviews that many of them WANTED to help their children. There was little indication that the reports we looked at helped them to do this, or gave them an indication of what they could do. In the present situation, where we are — at least on paper — asking parents to make choices for their children's education, it should not be acceptable to make less than optimum use of the principal medium of communication between the two parties.

To an extent, the data we have reported here has become more relevant as it has 'aged'. It seems almost inevitable that in Scotland, where 'external' assessment has moved towards a criterion-referenced model, school reports are likely to move in the same direction. As profiling and records of achievement have grown in importance in England and Wales, it also seems likely that they will come to have a substantial impact on school reporting. Furthermore, if (as seems possible) the main use of these comes to be for formative rather than certificate purposes, their very survival beyond the innovation stage may depend on their becoming acceptable as part of the school reporting system. But what is abundantly clear from these findings is that the introduction of at least some aspects of the innovations is not without controversy. The principal beneficiaries of these changes should be the young people themselves, and it would seem important to pay more attention to their views and their needs.

SCRE (1977) Pupils in Profile, SCRE, Edinburgh.

RESEARCH AND POLICY-MAKING IN ASSESSMENT: SOME UNANSWERED QUESTIONS

PATRICIA BROADFOOT
School of Education, University of Bristol

In his speech to the 1984 NFER Annual Conference, Sir James Hamilton, former Permanent Secretary at the DES, returned to the well-worn theme of the lack of impact of educational research on policy-making in education. Echoing the arguments of a now substantial literature on this subject (see for example: Husen and Kogan, 1984: Nisbet and Broadfoot, 1980: Nisbet *et al.*, 1985) Sir James laid the blame for this state of affairs on the inability or unwillingness of educational researchers to shape the content of their research to the needs of the consumer. Schooled in the traditions of the positivist physical sciences, he argued, the majority of such consumers have little sympathy for the more 'soft' styles of enquiry now increasingly characteristic of educational research. It is the frequently expressed view of senior civil servants and politicians that such studies, often wordy and jargon-ridden, their conclusions hedged around with caveats, are likely to have little impact on the pressing business of policy-making.

Whilst there is considerable substance in these arguments and a corresponding need for the research community to question its methods and motives, there is arguably a much more profound set of issues inherent in the nature of policy-making itself. It is apparent that a significant number, if not the majority, of policy initiatives are not informed by any systematic enquiry about their potential impact on the educational process itself. Rather, decisions are taken which represent some compromise between prevailing political pressures and available resources. In some cases evaluation then follows, but the terms of this evaluation may also be limited by the political power to determine the questions to be asked.

It is arguments about the role of research in educational policy-making which form the context for this paper. In it, I review some of the more significant developments in assessment policy in England and Wales in recent years and, by making some brief comparisons with other countries such as Scotland and France, suggest the extent to which such initiatives have been dominated by considerations of ideology and political expediency and have paid scant regard to the need for the assumptions on which they are based to be subject to systematic enquiry. In the final part of the paper, I examine some of the implications of this relative neglect.

Rather than attempting to review in its entirety the complex spectrum of the assessment policy initiatives that have taken place in recent years, I shall identify three broad themes that seem to me to be underlying current policy initiatives in this domain. In so doing, I hope to draw out some of the implications of such developments which have yet to be subjected to public scrutiny.

Structural Implications

The first major theme I want to examine concerns the potential impact of contemporary assessment policy developments on educational selection. These 'structural' policy implications may be further sub-divided in terms of

(1) attempts to secure finer discrimination between candidates; and

(2) attempts to provide for the control of frustration and disaffection among pupils.

One of the most marked phenomena in recent assessment policy has been the extension of public certification to the majority, rather than the minority, of pupils. Before 1951, less than 10 per cent of the year group sat for School Certificate; this figure steadily increased during the 1950s after the advent of GCE 'O' level in 1951, leading to the establishment of the Beloe Committee in 1958 and its recommendation for an additional level of 16 + certification in the form of a new examination to be aimed at the middle band of secondary school achievers. But, in appeasing the pressing demands for public certification among the hitherto disenfranchised 'middle 40 per cent' — the top secondary modern pupils — the new Certificate of Secondary Education (CSE) postponed the necessity to face up to the provision of a truly comprehensive certification procedure for at least 20 years. The CSE also presented an administrative and curricular problem for schools in deciding which pupils to enter for GCE 'O' level and which for CSE, given that the latter was an explicitly inferior qualification and also lacked the credibility of tradition. Not surprisingly, therefore, the CSE examinations had hardly begun before attempts were being made to devise a common system of examining at 16 + .

The Schools Council presented its proposals for a new 16 + in 1971 and in 1973 the first feasibility trials were held. By 1974 trial examinations were being taken by nearly 70,000 candidates with a target date for introduction of 1978 (Schools Council Examinations Bulletin 23). It was recognised that a common examination per se was unlikely to be able to discriminate adequately across the ability range concerned, so that a common *system* of examining rather than a single exam per se might be more appropriate. Although reaction to the feasibility studies was mixed, by 1976 the Schools Council nevertheless felt able to recommend a joint 16 + to the

Secretary of State for Education. The reaction of the then Secretary of State, Shirley Williams, was to initiate still further study in the form of yet another committee. In 1978 the Waddell Committee reported that a single system of examining at 16+, based on a seven-point grading scale and tied in to existing GCE and CSE grades, was feasible. Notable in the proposals was the recommendation that the new examination be run by three or four regional consortia combining both GCE and CSE Boards and the proposal that national criteria be formulated which would define the achievements to be sought in each subject.

Despite the endorsement by the Labour Secretary of State of many of the Waddell Committee's proposals in the 1978 White Paper 'A Single System of Examining at 16+', provisional commitment to a new 16+ examination was not forthcoming until February 1980, and the advent of a Conservative Secretary of State, Mark Carlisle. But it was Sir Keith Joseph who in 1984 finally gave the go-ahead for the new GCSE examination to be launched, with the first candidates being examined in 1988.

Sir Keith also proposed that 'distinction' and perhaps also 'merit' certificates should be awarded to candidates who could show outstanding achievement over a wide range of subjects. It was this latter initiative, rather than the GCSE itself, which provoked controversy, since the 16+ exam itself is mainly remarkable for the length of time it has taken in coming. In 1988 when the first pupils sit their GCSE examinations, it will be nearly 20 years since the Schools Council recommended the relatively minor reform of combining the two existing 16+ certification systems into a common system of examining.[1]

The intensity of debate over the details of a procedure that most equivalent countries have already abandoned is indicative both of the 'British disease' of excessive commitment to an external examination-dominated approach to pupil certification and of an Establishment tendency to confine debate to what are essentially technical issues, leaving other assumptions unexamined. Thus repeated calls in major government reports for the abolition of external examinations, such as that by the Norwood Committee in 1943, have had little or no impact (Broadfoot, 1979).

One of the most significant of the assumptions commonly made about examinations is the relationship which is taken to exist between such formal, public exercises in evaluation and

---

[1] The movement for such combination goes back even further to 1966, only a year after the CSE was launched in 1965, when the Joint GCE/CSE Committee of the Schools Council recommended that GCE and CSE Boards, with the help of NFER, should set up a programme of research and development designed to examine the technical means of moving towards a common system of describing the results of O-level and CSE examinations.

educational standards. Attempts to minimise or abolish external examinations tend to provoke a public and political outcry for just this reason. In the same way Sir Keith Joseph's attempted introduction of 'distinction' and 'merit' awards whose rationale is as much the desire to encourage curriculum breadth as it is ostensibly to maintain standards, found support among the traditional, elitist educational lobby, despite much opposition from elsewhere. There is little evidence that the policy-makers behind this initiative seriously considered what the effects of these arrangements were likely to be. As with the 'Advanced Supplementary' level qualifications now being introduced, the ideas seemed to be couched at a commonsense, if not naïve, level of analysis that procedures will work in the way intended.

It is perhaps for this reason that so little research has been initiated into the possible effects of the GCSE itself. Despite the long history of feasibility studies described above, such 'technical' assessment policy research shows no signs of being complemented by an evaluation of the practical implications as the new exam is introduced. Apart from a small implementation study being conducted at NFER, the crucial questions remain unexamined. What, for example, will be the effect of GCE Boards taking responsibility for Grades A-C with CSE Boards taking responsibility for Grades D-G? It is possible to surmise from this arrangement that the real policy concern is for the top grades, with the implicit assumption that grades D-G may in time be replaced with other procedures such as unit credits and profiles, which may better match the curricular objectives for these courses. Although there would be a measure of logic in such a development, its effects would almost certainly be deeply divisive. Certainly the design of the GCSE such that the average grade awarded will be 'F' raises the question whether pupils and their parents will really see GCSE as a record of positive attainment in the way intended.

It may be argued that the GCSE is an initiative of the eighties which uses techniques developed in the seventies based on research carried out in the sixties to meet a need identified in the fifties. If so, it is wildly anachronistic and, as Nuttall (1984) has pointed out, there is 'every danger that the common system now being created will be divisive, bureaucratic, retrogressive and obsolescent'. But such considerations would appear to weigh but lightly in policy terms. If the perceived political climate is still one in which any too radical change would be pejorative to electoral popularity, then research and evaluation into the effects of this new version of the status quo would appear to be unnecessary in the eyes of those charged with implementing it.

Thus current examinations policy seems set on perpetuating expensive, academically limiting, organisationally-disruptive and, for the majority, de-motivating forms of assessment. There is over-whelming research evidence, dating back to the Hargreaves and Lacey polarisation studies of the mid-sixties (Hargreaves, 1967; Lacey, 1969) that the model of external, public examinations as the basis for school certification, a model which originated in the early twentieth century for a small fraction of the population, is inappropriate in an era of mass secondary education. Equally, research evidence is now emerging (e.g. Hustler, 1986) that where relevant and attainable educational goals are provided for *all* pupils, such disaffection can become largely a thing of the past.

It is indicative of the extent of the gulf that exists between the worlds of research and policy-making that the imperatives of one are rarely the concern of the other. Thus despite its curriculum novelty, its pioneering use of assessment criteria, and its emphasis on continuous assessment, the effect of the GCSE may be quite opposite to that intended. Instead of fulfilling its expressed intention of introducing breadth and balance, differentiation and relevance into the secondary curriculum, the GCSE may well prove to be simply the latest mutant in a long line of external examinations the effect of which is to perpetuate the extensive disaffection characteristic of an anachronistic approach to the purpose of statutory secondary schooling.

But while the voice of the research community may go unheard, there is nevertheless a growing and vociferous lobby that argues against the divisiveness of existing public examinations procedures.

The power of this voice is reflected in the fact that a second major strand of recent assessment policy has been the search for complementary, if not yet alternative, forms of certification. Following the lead of its Further Education Unit which has taken up enthusiastically the idea of comprehensive 'profiles' of attainment, first launched in its current form by the Scottish Council for Research in Education in the early seventies (SCRE, 1977; Broadfoot, 1986), the DES has also taken up the cause of promoting more teacher-learner dialogue, more student participation and motivation, more democratic relationships and more vocational relevance which is now associated with such 'records'. Thus in their June 1984 policy statement on Records of Achievement that sets out a commitment to providing all school-leavers with such a certificate, the Government give support not only to the original concern of the profiles movement with detailed, positive, relevant and comprehensive certification, but also to the ideas pioneered in further education of a formative, diagnostic dialogue characterised by, for example, pupil self-assessment and teacher-pupil negotiation of record entries whose purpose is to encourage pupils' ability to be insightful and self-critical.

In educational terms, the aridity of the previous decade's debate over examination reform is marked when compared with that of the profiles movement. Unable to convince by sheer force of argument, the proponents of radical changes of principle in certification procedures have been able to demonstrate, rather than simply talk about, their case in the growing support for Records of Achievement. But, whilst DES support for such Records is now official, the more general impact of this policy on thinking about certification procedures as a whole is still negligible and the traditional public examination machinery remains intact, apart from some minor tinkering. This may well be because as Goldstein and Nuttall (1986) argue, such reforms are still 'all tarred with the same election brush' so that the assumptions about what school assessment is and should be for are scarcely challenged. Reliability and comparability, standards and objectivity retain their prominent place in the discourse of certification, despite changes in the employment and training context post-16 which argue the need for a much greater emphasis on the *validity* of assessments as a basis for suitable training and career choices.

Thus the overt motivation for instituting 'records of achievement' is still cast in this language of selection, though including a novel concern to provide a means of recognising students' diverse talents, qualities and achievement. However, it may be that the actual effects of such recording are again quite different from those envisaged and concerned principally with the second structural dimension of assessment which was identified above. In exposing a much greater part of their personality to a continuous, pervasive and above all irrefutable, since it is a *benign,* assessment process, students may be subject to much greater social control than at present. It is not without significance that such records have been most widely adopted in more vocational courses such as those associated with the Certificate of Pre-Vocational Education (CPVE), the Technical and Vocational Education Initiative (TVEI) and the Youth Training Scheme (YTS). Thus, although profiles are important in providing a goal for all pupils — thereby reducing frustration and promoting social control — they also allow the possibility of a much wider application of norms than hitherto in which it is not just the individual's intellectual activity which is subject to 'hierarchical authority and normalising judgment' (Foucault, 1975), but, as in the elementary schools of the nineteenth century, the whole person. There is a not insignificant danger that the systematic recording of criterion-referenced outcomes in relation to a pre-defined list of competencies which is characteristic of many current profiling approaches, will constitute a twentieth century reincarnation of the nineteenth century 'cul de sac of skills' curriculum offered by the Victorian elementary school (Johnson, 1976).

Ranson (1984)[2] has offered his explanation of the contemporary changes affecting assessment policy in arguing that the 'new tertiary tripartism' is almost an exact replica of the old secondary tripartism and the control that provided. The combined effect of this trend towards educational utilitarianism combined with on-going 'orientation' or 'profiling' is likely to be, Ranson suggests, earlier, rather than later, selection for different curriculum paths, selection every bit as divisive as that provided for under the 1944 Act but now endowed with the new legitimating rhetoric of guidance and personal choice necessary to a much more aspiring society. Whether this does indeed prove to be the effect of contemporary assessment policy depends very much on the kind of curriculum pupils are offered. Where early division into 'academic', 'technical' (TVEI) and 'pre-vocational' curricula occurs, such tripartism is almost inevitable. If, on the other hand, a commitment is made to provide during the compulsory schooling stage a common core curriculum for all pupils, not only will such a tripartism be much less likely, but associated inequalities of race, sex and class should also be less in evidence. Certainly this is the logic espoused by other countries such as New Zealand who are already very familiar with school-based, rather than external examination certification (McNaughton, 1986).

Some Bases for Comparison

The long-term structural effects of contemporary assessment policy are unlikely to be apparent for some years. What is at issue now, however, is the extent to which policy-makers are prepared to widen their deliberations to include some of the more reflective, even theoretical arguments about the possible outcomes of particular courses of action. While it is clearly impossible to anticipate the impact of a policy in advance of its implementation, international comparisons can provide a useful laboratory in which to review developments and question assumptions. The impact of the French 'orientation' procedure, as described in the recent Prost Report for example[3] should sound a powerful warning note about the assumptions underpinning the move towards records of achievement.

'In the first place, the criteria chosen are uniform. Orientation rarely takes into account pupils' centres of

---

[2] Ranson, S. (1984) 'Towards a tertiary tripartism: new codes of social control and the 17+' in Broadfoot, P. (ed.) *Selection, Certification and Control*. Falmer Press.

[3] Prost, A. (1983) *Les Lycées et leur études auseuil du XXIième Siécle* Rapport au Directeur des lycées presenté par le Groupe de Travail National sur les Seconds Cycles. Service d'Information, Paris.

interest and the diversity of their aptitudes. The two major criteria are their results in mathematics and their age (as we have already indicated). In the second place, orientation is frequently transformed into a procedure of practicality. Pupils must be divided up between the sections that exist, according to the space available in different establishments. This bureaucratic procedure, together with the rigidity of the learning programme, engenders in families a feeling of helplessness in the face of a blind technostructure. In the third place, it (orientation) constitutes a vast fragmented distillation which divides up pupils between streams which are strongly bounded and hierarchic as a function of dominant social models: supremacy of training in abstract science, less consideration for technical and professional training. . . .'

That such domination by traditional academic goals is neither desirable nor inevitable is well illustrated by the Norwegian experience where according to Rust (1985), technical and vocational training routes are as hotly competitive as the more traditional academic path. But major efforts currently being made by the French to raise the status of technical and vocational courses at every level of the system (Dundas-Grant, 1986) and even the recent English proposal for 'City Technology Colleges' (DES, 1986) do suggest that a shift in attitudes may now be taking place.

As yet however there is little evidence in England and Wales of any coordination between the various initiatives being undertaken in this respect, although they all involve an element of profiling. Initiatives sponsored by the DES such as those on Records of Achievement and Low Attaining Pupils, run alongside those of the MSC such as TVEI and YTS to be matched by a plethora of new developments being undertaken by The City & Guilds of London Institute, the Royal Society of Arts, The Business and Technical Education Council, the new Joint Council for Vocational Qualifications, and many of which, such as the Certificate of Pre-Vocational Education, are to be found in schools.

Without some more sustained programme of research and reflection it seems more than likely that such initiatives, ostensibly directed towards providing a broader curriculum, more vocationally-oriented courses and an overall increase in the motivation and hence, achievement of secondary pupils, will in practice result at best in confusion and at worst, in even greater polarisation between the successful few and the unsuccessful majority, the latter trapped in assessment procedures which provide well-meaning but irrefutable evidence of nothing but their personal mediocrity. Even the well-intentioned 'unit credit' and modular curricula now being pioneered in some LEAs and Exam

Boards could work in quite the opposite way to that intended by providing more regular and frequent evidence of failure to some pupils (Goldstein and Nuttall, 1986).

Educational Implications

In addition to such structural implications, the possible content of 'records of achievement' is clearly a key issue in their potential impact. It thus constitutes one example of the second major theme in this review which is concerned with the possible *educational* effects of current assessment policies. Two of the most recent developments in the 'profiles' movement — the growing emphasis on profiling as the basis for a formative dialogue and its increasing association with the Examination Boards — do suggest however that the parallel development of public examinations on the one hand and records of achievement on the other, is unlikely to persist indefinitely. As TVEI, the DES Low Achievers project and other such curricular intiatives help to push the new *formative* approach to profiling towards the centre of the educational arena, it is likely that what started as simply a more comprehensive and relevant form of school record will come to pose a major challenge to existing educational arrangements — at least up to the 17+ level. Whilst such a challenge may be welcomed in many quarters, its superficial homogeneity conceals a potentially deep and important value conflict between the kinds of educational priorities such procedures should enshrine. How far, for example, is a student's personal development compatible with vocational training? To what extent will the traditional subject bastions of academic learning be able to withstand the onslaught of the prevailing educational utilitarianism and whose voice should prevail in such arguments?

On the other hand, Macintosh (1986) provides a much more optimistic scenario of the possible outcomes of this challenge in suggesting that as the sacred cows of traditional examination theory such as reliability and comparability are exposed for the insubstantial spectres they really are, teachers will have to be accorded increasing responsibility to carry out the kinds of assessment that will be required in skills-oriented curricula. As course work assessment by accredited teachers and schools proves itself to be both the basis for more valid judgments of attainment and the only practicable approach to the assessment of many curricular objectives, Macintosh foresees the dismantling of the GCSE external examination system in favour of a much more comprehensive 'record of achievement'. Certainly the analysis of both Macintosh and Torrance (1986) suggests that the curriculum development likely to be fermented by the course work assessment requirements of GCSE will render the very distinction between academic subjects and vocational and technical skills anachronistic.

It is too early to say which of these two outcomes — conflict or synthesis — will prevail. The structural context for change is currently evolving at such a rate that it is difficult to see even five years ahead. Meanwhile it is vital that at this relatively early stage in their implementation we should not ignore the process dimensions to these changes. The educational assumptions on which records of achievement are based need to be subjected to systematic scrutiny. Thus for example, we need to ask whether teachers will be able and willing to respond in a non-judgmental way to the whole range of personal interests and aspirations with which their pupils are likely to present them in the process of negotiation. We need to question the impact on a pupil's motivation if he is made aware that certain affiliations, such as the National Front or Rastafarianism, certain affectations of personal style such as 'punk' or 'new romantic', and certain cultural norms for leisure-time activities such as heavy rock are unlikely to endear him to future employers. And is a teacher who does succeed in holding her own values in check and who responds in a non-judgmental way being fair to pupils who will face hard realities when they leave school or college? If records come to be 'massaged' so that they approach as closely as possible an identikit of desirable qualities, this will represent yet one more example of pupils learning to 'play the system' (Wood, 1976) and perhaps in the process subverting its true and initially laudable, educational purpose.

Equally it is important to question whether such recording will favour particular groups. There are already indications that some parents are worried that such comprehensive records may reflect upon them and the experience they provide for youngsters at home as well as differences between schools in the experiences they make available to pupils. Will girls be constrained by stereotypical expectations of appropriate activities and goals? How will different cultural and ethnic styles find expression in this very personal process? Now that several major research projects are being undertaken in this field, including a national evaluation of the government-funded Records of Achievement development schemes,[4] it is vital that this research is not confined to the technical, managerial, problem-solving stance so characteristic of

---

[4] Pilot Records of Achievement in Schools Evaluation (PRAISE) project based at the University of Bristol and the Open University. See also research work being undertaken by the South Western Profile Research Project, the City & Guilds of London Institute, the Northern Partnership for Records of Achievement and the TVEI unit among many others.

much assessment policy research. As the profiles movement
develops out of its early, relatively uncontroversial stage in which it
was concerned with extending and complementing the educational
status quo, into a phase where it has become a prominent part of a
radical challenge to that order, it is no longer adequate to confine
the research questions it poses to issues of practicability and utility
alone.

But whilst the issues surrounding the *formative* implications of
Records of Achievement are profound in themselves, they must
also be seen as part of a much larger set of policy questions
concerning the relationship between the major elements in
certification procedure currently under discussion — records of
achievement, GCSE, unit-credits and 'graded-assessments'. While
some schemes such as the Oxford Certificate of Educational
Achievement and the London Record of Achievement offer a
model for bringing these strands together, there is little sign as yet
of any attempt by government to coordinate the various strands of
the assessment policies it has initiated and to evaluate the combined
impact of these initiatives as well as their several separate effects.

Perhaps because of its relatively small size and much more
centralised administration, the Scottish Education Department has
been able to bring about a rationalisation programme in assessment
policy which makes a mockery of the confused tangle of GCSE,
CPVE, YTS certification, TVEI accreditation, 'AS' levels and
Records of Achievement currently under development in England.
Scotland's equivalent to the English Waddell Report — the 1977
Dunning Committee Report on 14-16 certification 'Assessment for
all' led to the replacement of the Scottish Certificate of Education
'Ordinary Grade' by a new 'Standard Grade' 16 + qualification to
be first awarded in 1986.

> 'Over a five year period, schools will introduce new ways of
> teaching and assessing the traditional subjects, a number of
> new multi-disciplinary courses (such as health studies) and a
> range of short courses. *All* pupils will be eligible to receive
> recognition for their achievements in a new certificate, the
> Standard Grade of the SCE' (SED, 1977).[5]

The term 'Record of Achievement' is not 'au courant' in these
Scottish developments. Instead the aim is to provide through three
different criterion-referenced levels of award — 'foundation',
'general' and 'credit' — a series of learning goals in which *all pupils*
who complete the course will receive some acknowledgement. More

---

[5] 'School and Further Education in Scotland: a single Examining Body.' A
consultative paper issued by the Secretary of State for Scotland, SED 1984, para. 2.2
(my emphasis).

significant still would appear to be the post-16+ developments which, following on the 1983 publication of '16-18s: an Action Plan for Scotland', now propose a single examining body to conduct the whole range of vocational and academic post-Standard Grade assessments. The aim is to integrate in the relatively near future, the university entrance level 'Higher' Scottish Certificate of Education and Certificate of Sixth Year Studies examinations into the comprehensive pattern of 40 hour curriculum modules which is now the basis for a new National Certificate.[6] This initiative would result in a uniform system of post-16 courses and assessment explicitly designed to break down the division between 'academic' and 'vocational' qualifications in favour of young people choosing a combination of modules from over 2,000 on offer, which best fits their particular interests, aspirations and previous achievement. These modules, each with its own clearly specified objectives and associated assessment criteria, incorporate a wide range of learning experiences and an equally wide range of assessment procedures including objective tests, short-answer and essay assessments, student log books, folios, questionnaires, self profiles and teachers' observations of a range of perfomance skills in practical work.

Thus current assessment policy in Scotland suggests that by combining some of the most recent thinking about curriculum provision with that on assessment, Scottish education can look forward to a nationally-orchestrated reform which embraces similar ideas to those inspiring current developments in England but *provides a coherent integration of these diverse elements*. There are even hints that in the longer term, the new Standard Grade courses will also be incorporated into the single accreditation process. Thus these proposals incorporate the separate elements of graded-tests, criterion-referenced 16+ examinations based on grade-related criteria and 'pupil profiles', into one overall curriculum initiative which would appear to offer a much better chance of overcoming the resource and training issues inherent in any major reform in the educational role of assessment than the piecemeal approach characteristic of English initiatives. It is perhaps also because English initiatives to date have been insufficiently radical by comparison that so many Exam Boards have felt the need to try to develop their own provision for credit accumulation schemes in the 14-16 age range.[7]

But, however attractive such new curriculum and assessment initiatives may appear in theory, we have once again little research

---

[6] Ibid.
[7] Mark Jackson, 'Welsh exam. body upstage 16+', *Times Educational Supplement,* 21.2.85.

data as yet on their implications for pupils' learning.[8] Given that typically such modules are constructed around a model of learning outcomes that are

> 'precise, unambiguous, measurable, few in number, content-related, capable of exemplification, indicative of progression, indicative of minimum competence levels and indicative of operating conditions'[9]

it may well be that curricula so rationalised are curricula that have lost the very heart of what should constitute education. That in the urge to identify clear and obtainable objectives, insufficient attention has been given to different individual learning routes, or different educational philosophies. If England and Wales lack the administrative apparatus to bring about rationalisation on the Scottish scale, this could well be to its advantage in allowing wisdom in such matters to accrue incrementally rather than through 'brain storming'. This will only be the case, however, if the fullest possible cognisance of the Scottish experience is taken and compared with the results of and careful evaluation of the combined effects of current English initiatives.

Political Implications

The third and final element of contemporary assessment policy which urgently requires research attention is its potential political effect. I shall deal with this trend rather more briefly than with the two preceding themes, since this is an element in contemporary assessment policy which is now widely remarked. Nevertheless a great deal more attention needs to be given to identifying the likely effects of contemporary initiatives on the part of central government to increase its control of the education system by increasing its directive power over a wide range of assessment procedures.

In a series of policy developments dating back to the mid-70s and the establishment of the Assessment of Performance Unit (APU), the two most obvious themes underpinning assessment policy have been those of cost-conscious accountability and more industrially-relevant curricula. Around these two major trends is a network of interacting and sometimes contradictory pressures in which arguments for educational reform, administrative rationalisation, traditional elitism and new Right utilitarianism figure prominently.

---

[8] Research into some aspects of the new National Certificate is now being undertaken, see Black, H. *et al.* (1986) 'National Certificate Assessment: some early reflections'. Paper given at BERA Conference, Bristol 1986.

[9] '16-18s in Scotland: An Action Plan.' Guidelines on Curriculum and Assessment. SED 1984.

But, whilst an understanding of the pressures underpinning contemporary policy initiatives is an important step towards effective pressure group activity, much more important is a consideration of the longer-term effects of those changes that have already taken place. A key issue in this respect is likely to be the changing responsibilities of teachers.

Whereas formerly teachers exerted considerable indirect power over public assessment procedures through their activities on Examination Board Panels, this role is now less significant as national level policies constrain the form and the criteria of the new qualifications being developed. Teachers and the Examination Boards they serve have had to cede a considerable measure of their autonomy to decide the *level* and *content* of examinatons to central government and its organ — the Secondary Examinations Council. Only a handful of teachers are now involved at national level in developing the criteria. Yet at the same time, teachers have been acquiring increased responsibilities for the *process* of assessment.

Not only does the new GCSE require a substantial measure of internal course assessment (at least 20 per cent, and 100 per cent in some cases) even more potentially significant is the quite new responsibility teachers are likely to have in the production of Records of Achievement. In this context it is probable that the great majority of teachers will be involved in contributing assessment information for summative 'profiles'. Under current development models they will also be responsible collectively for their institution's accreditation and validation to have such 'records' officially recognised. Thus in place of the more familiar forms of moderation which were concerned with establishing equivalence of marking procedures, will be more institutional rather than candidate-focused external controls. In the major developments currently taking place towards the provision of local authority and/or Examination Board-based records of achievement, it is the institutional validation model which predominates.

How significant this trend will prove to be depends upon the degree to which Records of Achievement themselves come to supplant, combine with, or are rendered insignificant by, those external examinations currently developing in parallel. This depends in turn to a considerable extent on whether the newer form of group qualification such as the CPVE, which already contains a strong commitment to profiling, develops at the expense of more traditional subject examinations such as GCSE. Even at the present stage of development, however, it is pertinent to consider how such new responsibilities will impinge on teachers. On the one hand, these initiatives should give them a great deal more freedom than before to build up the worthwhile educational relationships so difficult to achieve within the syllabus constraints of academic examinations. On the other hand, wider and more explicit responsibility for providing both appropriate assessment information and an appropriate environment in which pupils can demonstrate a range of achievements, will expose teachers to a quite new vulnerability to public censure.

Whilst concern over overt initiatives towards the external assessment of teacher competence — as set out for example in the 1983 White Paper on 'Teaching Quality' — is already apparent, such moves towards a latter-day 'payment by results' system may well prove much less significant in the longer run than a new balance of power in assessment procedures, where responsibility for setting educational objectives becomes increasingly centralised and responsibility for their assessment increasingly devolved to the local institution. Whether this emerges as a liberating or a constraining trend, or indeed a significant trend at all, is a question that is of considerable importance.

Conclusion

This paper has briefly evoked some of the significant themes in contemporary assessment policy. Although these have been loosely categorised into structural, educational and political themes, such conceptual distinctions are an essentially arbitrary imposition on the chaos of day to day events which reflect no such neat divisions. Nevertheless, some kind of analytic approach is essential if research into assessment *policy* is to achieve anything like the status and quality already achieved by research into assessment *techniques*. Without such status, we are likely to witness a perpetuation of the current situation in which out-dated assumptions, divisive techniques and uncoordinated attempts at change continue to inhibit the development of assessment procedures which are both educationally desirable, and politically acceptable. It is the responsibility of the research community to ensure that the actual and potential impact of policy initiatives is taken into account by those involved in their formulation. By the same token, policy-makers have a responsibility to themselves, and those whom they serve, to act upon evidence, rather than expediency.

REFERENCES

BROADFOOT, P. (1979) *Assessment, schools and society.* London: Methuen.
BROADFOOT, P. (ed.) *Profiles and records of achievement: a review of issues and practice.* London: Holt.
DEPARTMENT OF EDUCATION AND SCIENCE (1977) 'School examinations: report of the steering committee established to

consider proposals for replacing the GCE 'O' level and CSE examinations by a common system of examining'. London: HMSO.

DEPARTMENT OF EDUCATION AND SCIENCE (1986) *City technology colleges.* London: HMSO.

DUNDAS-GRANT, V. (1985) The organisation of vocational/technical/technological education in France. *Comparative Education,* Vol. 21, no. 2, 1985.

FOUCAULT, M. (1975) *Surveillir et Punir.* Paris: Gallimard.

GOLDSTEIN, H. and NUTTALL, D. (1986) Can graded assessments, records of achievement and modular assessment co-exist with the GCSE? In GIPPS, C. V. (forthcoming) *The GCSE: an uncommon exam.* Bedford Way Papers.

HARGREAVES, D. (1967) *Social relations in the secondary school.* London: Routledge and Kegan Paul.

HUSEN, T. and KOGAN, M. (eds.) (1984) *Educational research and policy: how do they relate?* Oxford: Pergamon.

HUSTLER, D. (1986) 'It's not like school — you don't have to wag lessons any more'. Paper presented to conference on Education and Training 14-18, St Hilda's College, Oxford.

JOHNSTON, R. (1976) Notes on the schooling of the English working class 1780-1850. In DALE, R. *et al.* (eds.) *Schooling and capitalism.* London: Routledge and Kegan Paul.

LACEY, C. (1970) *Hightown grammar.* Manchester: Manchester University Press.

McNAUGHTON, A. (1986) Personal communication.

MACINTOSH, H. (1986) The sacred cows of coursework. In GIPPS, C. V. (ed) op cit.

NISBET, J. and BROADFOOT, P. (1980) *The impact of research on policy and practice in education.* Aberdeen: Aberdeen University Press.

NISBET, J. et al. (1985) Research, policy and practice. *World Yearbook of Education.* London: Kogan Page.

NUTTALL, D. (1984) Doomsday or a new dawn? The prospects for a common system of examining at 16 + . In BROADFOOT, P. (ed.) *Selection, certification and control.* Sussex: Falmer Press.

RUST, V. (1985) Norwegian secondary school reform: reflections on a revolution. *Comparative Education,* Vol. 21, no. 2, 1985.

SCOTTISH COUNCIL FOR RESEARCH IN EDUCATION (1977) *Pupils in Profile.* London: Hodder and Stoughton.

SCOTTISH EDUCATION DEPARTMENT (1977) 'Assessment for all: the report of the Secretary of State's Committee on Assessment and Certification'. Edinburgh: HMSO.

SCOTTISH EDUCATION DEPARTMENT (1984) '16-18s in Scotland: an action plan' *Guidelines on curriculum and assessment.* Edinburgh: HMSO.

TORRANCE, H. (1986) School-based assessment in GCSE: aspirations, problems and possibilities. In GIPPS, C. V. (ed.) op. cit.

WOODS, P. (1980) *Pupil strategies.* London: Croom Helm.

THE IMPACT OF SCOTTISH NATIONAL SURVEYS OF ACHIEVEMENT ON POLICY AND PRACTICE

W. B. DOCKRELL
School of Education, University of Newcastle upon Tyne

Introduction

Like many other countries, Scotland has a system of national surveys which are intended to provide information which would serve as a basis for educational policy and practice. These surveys are carried out in Scotland in the middle years of school. The reasons for this choice are practical. It was thought that it would be difficult to get adequate information economically about younger children, and that information about older children was provided by the system of external examinations. Over 75 per cent of 16 year olds take these examinations in Scotland, so information is believed to be available on achievement at this point (SED, 1985).

The areas of fundamental importance are mathematics, reading, English written and spoken and science. Consideration has been given to extending the testing to cover other areas, but it has not yet been done because these areas are thought to be either too difficult or too controversial.

The programme of testing is designed to provide national information only and not information about individual pupils, schools or local authorities. The scope of the testing is wide, and no individual child takes more than a small part of any test. The numbers of children tested in any school are too small to provide information about that school. Even in large authorities where all parts of the tests will have been administered to some pupils, the composite score would not provide a representative score for that authority. It is only when they are aggregated at national level that the information is representative of the group as a whole. This is a deliberate policy decision, and not an accidental consequence of the sampling procedure.

It has been argued that in an educational system like Scotland's where the approach is organic rather than mechanistic, and we expect change to be incorporated into the system and not imposed upon it, the impact of national surveys of achievement will

---

A version of this paper is to be published in *Educational Evaluation and Policy Analysis*.

necessarily be slow to manifest itself. The present programme of testing dates back only five years; it is too soon to observe any consequences. This paper, therefore, refers back to an early series of national surveys, and looks at their impact on educational policy and practice.

The Background

Scotland has a long tradition of national surveys dating back to 1932. In June of that year an age cohort of some 87,498 children was tested. The results were reported in impressive detail, and with commendable alacrity in the following year (SCRE, 1933). It was intended from the beginning that there should be a series of such surveys. However, by 1942, when it might have been appropriate to repeat the test, British attention was focused on other matters. It was not therefore until 1947 that the next survey was carried out.

These data were carefully gathered and reported in great detail (SCRE, 1949; Maxwell, 1969). They have been used as a basis for secondary analysis on many occasions since, the most recent being 'As Others See Us' (Hope, 1984), a study of schooling and social mobility in Scotland and the United States. These early studies were of ability as measured by intelligence tests. What they provided was experience and expertise in gathering and analysing data from national surveys.

When attention, therefore, shifted to surveys of achievement — scholastic surveys they were then called in Scotland — there was an organisational structure with the required technical competence and experience of the practical difficulties that were likely to be encountered. These surveys provide a good case study of the contribution of national surveys of achievement to policy and practice. The first reason is that they were carried out sufficiently long ago for us to be able to assess their impact and use them as a guide for our own practice. A second reason for choosing them is that these particular surveys were examples of good educational research. They were carefully planned and meticulously carried out, as can be seen from the published reports (SCRE, 1963; SCRE, 1968). A third reason is that the studies did produce valid findings. Much research of all kinds, including educational research, leaves us very little wiser than we were before we began. That is not something to be surprised at or something to be concerned about. It is to recognise the limitations of the human endeavour. In this particular case, however, valid findings were produced. A further reason for choosing these studies is that their findings had relevance at various levels: relevance to policy at national and local level, to teaching and to parents. A fifth reason for selecting them for consideration is that these studies are relevant to general and contemporary issues and not simply to concerns of that particular time and place. Finally, and perhaps most important, these surveys are important because they show the advantages and the limitations of survey work, what can be learned from surveys and what cannot.

The Context

The Scottish system is formally a devolved system, with the local authorities responsible for education in their areas. The Local Education Authorities 'are responsible for the curriculum taught in their schools, headteachers normally exercising that responsibility on their behalf' (SED, 1977). The Scottish Education Department oversees the work of the schools, and takes the initiative in proposing curricula and teaching methods. There is a central inspectorate with responsibility both for judging the efficiency of individual schools and defining the needs of the educational system as a whole. There is no centrally prescribed curriculum, nor list of approved textbooks. This system permits a great deal of diversity and there is substantial variability, particularly among primary schools. In these circumstances it is more difficult to monitor standards of achievement than in more centralised systems, where expectations are more precisely defined. Nonetheless, it was believed in 1953 and there was sufficient consensus for a single set of generally applicable tests to be devised and administered.

The 1953 Scottish Survey

The three main purposes were to provide information about what pupils knew and what they could do in areas of fundamental importance, or in areas of particular relevance to current policy. Second, to provide evidence of comparative standards over time, and finally to investigate ways of using evidence to improve teaching and learning. These early studies were limited to 10 year olds.

The major purpose of the first study was, as with the current series, to obtain information about current standards in the same areas of Arithmetic and English. The Scottish Council for Research in Education took then the position that is now taken: that the results should be published in a form in which it was not possible to compare results of individual schools nor of separate education authorities. No reference was made at this stage to comparisons over time, but there was considerable emphasis on providing information on current policy issues, e.g. acceleration and retardation, the comparative standards in urban/rural schools, the effect of school size and of class organisation — 'on individual as compared with class methods' (SCRE, 1963).

As with the earlier surveys, the results were given in full and informative detail, and a substantial number of conclusions was drawn. These early researchers were pioneers, and were perhaps relieved to find that their hopes had been justified and it was possible to carry out a national survey, though they did recognise there were considerable difficulties. The principal one they believed was 'the diversity of work normally professed by an age group. At the 10 year old level chosen for the survey, this was particularly evident in the subject of arithmetic, where the complicated British tables of money, length and weight were introduced in different ways, at different times, in different areas' (p. 185). The report does go on to say that 'it will be folly to attempt to standardise curricula in this field until it has been shown that one method is superior to others' (p. 185).

This latter quotation highlights two issues which face current surveys. The first is that great variation in test scores which reflect not long term differences in level of attainment, but short term consequences of different teaching methods. The second is the danger of a backwash in the schools. If there are standard assessments administered nationally it may well be assumed that these define a national curriculum. Even in a de-centralised system schools will be under pressure to adopt this putative national curriculum.

The report did try to answer some, at least, of the original questions. There was no association between type of area (city, large town, small town, rural) and level of performance. There were no differences among the 10 regions. The report discreetly passed over the within-group differences which were in the data which indicated, for example, that the scores of children in the Glasgow area were lower than those of pupils in the Edinburgh and Dundee areas. On the question of class size, the report was careful to draw attention to the various factors that might be involved, and rightly concluded that 'it will be apparent that there is no regularity about the results. It does not follow that the size of class has no effect on attainment. The conclusion to be drawn is rather that it will be difficult to obtain definite conclusions on this topic with an experiment which is not specifically designed for the purpose' (p. 162). On the question of school size, an issue which with falling school rolls has obtained even greater prominence in recent years, the conclusion was 'the performance of the pupils in these schools (the smaller ones) was on the whole as good as that of pupils in larger schools. In particular, pupils from one-teacher schools reached the same standard as those attained by pupils in schools where there were more than six teachers' (p. 168).

That early report again anticipated the pattern of later years. Much of the report was focused on curricular matters. The panel dealing with Arithmetic arrived at very specific conclusions 'Division by factors is undesirable in the primary schools . . . more attention should be paid to the lay-out of short division sums . . . there is need for standardising the notation used in recording the time of day by the clock. The panel recommends that for written expression it should be in the form 8.50 a.m. . . . Use of written working in Arithmetic facilitates accuracy. Further, use of working is helpful to a teacher in diagnosing a pupil's difficulties. A standard practice is required for recording remainders in division. . . . The final point . . . is partly a question of the use of English. It was evident that the various aspects of teaching arithmetical problems required further consideration, e.g. the need for accurate reading of the question and for noting units used' (p. 186).

The panel dealing with the English tests arrived at equally definite conclusions. 'The tests in English usage demonstrated the need for persistent oral practice in accepted speech forms and a restrained use of pencil and paper exercises for occasional testing. . . . Reading as a thought-getting process seemed insecure. It is possible that acquaintance with forms of verbal testing and the common use of reading textbooks with exercises make it all too easy to suppose that pupils working through a series of questions have understood what they are reading. The tests in this survey showed unmistakeably that many pupils dealing as well as they could with details have not first grasped the general meaning of what they had read' (p. 187).

A survey which had begun with primarily structural objectives had been used to draw mainly curricular conclusions.

The 1963 Survey

The second survey had objectives which were apparently no more detailed than those of the earlier one. Not surprisingly, the third of the current objectives, i.e. comparison over time, was the major concern, but it was hoped to relate any changes to the effects of new teaching methods which had recently been adopted in some Scottish schools and which were shortly to be endorsed by the Scottish Education Department (SED, 1965) and recommended for general acceptance.

The same tests were used as had been used on the previous occasion. The answer to the basic question about change in levels of attainment was answered in the title of the second report. That book was called 'Rising Standards in Scottish Primary Schools'. There had been an improvement in performance on each of the tests used: 'the sizes of the gains are about one third of a standard deviation or roughly the gains that would be made in six months by an average pupil' (p. 85). These changes were related to ability, sex, types of area, region, sizes of schools, aspects of the tests, and so on. 'The gains have been made by pupils of all levels of ability, by boys and girls to the same extent, in all regions of the country and in all sizes of schools . . . while performances on some items show greater improvement than on others, the gains have been spread over nearly all of the items of the test. They are attributable partly to greater speed and response, and partly to greater accuracy when the responses have been made' (p. 85). The researchers dismiss test sophistication as a possible cause of this change.

They looked first at administrative factors. They concluded that 'areas still using attainment tests (on an area-wide basis) showed gains about twice as large as those in other areas' (p. 85). 'Higher attainments in the English test go with greater provision of school libraries' (p. 85). They point out cautiously 'A cause and effect relationship cannot be assumed' (p. 85) for school libraries, but they had no such reservations about the use of attainment tests. There was then an acute shortage of teachers. They concluded 'no association has been found between attainments and the shortage of teachers' (p. 85) but again caution rules the day, and the report points out 'the sample data provided only scanty information on this point' (p. 85). On administrative matters they generally recognise the risks of drawing conclusions from survey data.

When it came to matters of curriculum or instruction they were willing to make some generalisations. On Arithmetic, for example, 'Computational errors still persist. Fractions are still being treated by some pupils by rote, and long division is still insecure. The concept of zero as a place-holder is unfamiliar to many pupils' (p. 128).

In English, some of the deficiencies noted 10 years earlier were now less conspicuous. 'Pupils were reading with more skill and becoming more independent in their thinking about what they read' (p. 128). They could not, however, resist drawing special attention to a specific point. 'A disappointing feature for Scots was that the Scots poem showed the least gain of any section. Printed Scots is becoming completely unfamiliar to Scottish children' (p. 128). By Scots is meant the language in which Burns wrote. It is also virtually unintelligible to English adults, both in its written and oral forms. The report noted that Scots words were becoming even less familiar than they had been 10 years earlier. 'To the majority, the Scots forms were not intelligible, and from the errors in other words not dialectical it was obvious that a large number did not begin to understand what the lines were about. Neither did they have the benefit of hearing them read or spoken. The 1953 comment is reiterated. 'When one considers the extent to which Scots of some kind is spoken and understood, one can only conclude that Scots in print is completely unfamiliar to three-quarters of the pupils of this age group . . . it would appear desirable to include some printed Scots among the reading material for Scottish children' (p. 100).

The Impact of the Studies

As noted above, the surveys were carefully designed, meticulously carried out, comprehensively reported and many conclusions were drawn which were relevant to policy and to practice. What impact did they have? Many of the findings at national level were primarily of negative value. There were no differences among pupils in different types of areas, so that issue could be dismissed. There was no need, for example, to concentrate the resources on the cities or on the rural areas. Needs were specific and not related to type of area. The same was true of the geographical regions. The survey produced no evidence of regional differences, and therefore no arguments for deploying resources in that respect. There was no argument for more schools, more teachers, or more instructional materials in one part of the country rather than in another. Educational priority areas, such as those that were established shortly after the results of the survey were available, could not simply be defined in terms of general types, or in terms of geographical region. Much more focused intervention than that was necessary, and therefore more specific information.

Another apparently negative piece of information, but one still relevant to policy, both national and regional, was the finding that pupils from smaller schools attained practically the same standards as those in larger schools. Since the publication of the report Scotland has experienced, and is still experiencing, the closing of small one- and two-room rural schools. The evidence of the survey made it perfectly clear that such action was not justifiable on the basis of pupil achievement. The arguments for these changes which proceeded on a massive scale in the 60s and 70s, and which still continue, has to be on the basis of cost or other social values.

There were two more positive pieces of evidence. The first was, that, as quoted above, achievements were greater in those areas where the local authority continued to make use of a battery of attainment tests on the completion of primary schooling. An obvious inference would be that the existence of a formal external assessment of this kind has beneficial effects upon attainment. Also the information about library provision in primary schools has equally important implications. 'Pupils in schools with libraries of various types had made higher scores in the English test than pupils not having these facilities' (p. 80).

The process of policy formation is not one that is easily unravelled, but there is no evidence that even one small school was spared because of the findings of the research. This research has not been cited during the debate that has taken place over the last 10 years and which continues today. The arguments for closing small schools are predominantly economic, though the social development of the children is sometimes mentioned. The protagonists of the small schools usually advance community values and the deleterious effects of travelling on their side.

The impact of the finding on the use of attainment tests at the end of primary school is even clearer. All the authorities have now abolished them, in spite of the evidence that their use was positively related to improvements in attainment. There is no evidence that the provision of school libraries has been based on the findings of the scholastic surveys. In the present period of retrenchment there is no reference to the importance of maintaining the school libraries because of their anticipated effect on achievement in English.

As far as can be seen the recommendations which have had relevance to national policy have been ignored. They have made no contribution to the debate on these issues. In the light of the evidence on the impact of research and public policy-making, this is perhaps not surprising. It is, nonetheless, disappointing and discouraging. If the evidence from surveys is to help to determine national policy then the information provided must apparently speak to immediate concerns.

In any case, the information from survey studies is partial and may therefore be misleading. Perhaps the administrators who abolished attainment testing were right. A notion of what primary education is meant to achieve is not adequately defined by formal tests. Any advantage accruing to schools from use by the authority of attainment tests may well have been outweighed by other more negative effects on the curriculum in the schools.

There are many important issues where the survey evidence is far from conclusive. The authors of the 1953 report said, for example, 'An analysis of the effect of class size has yielded no clear conclusions. It appears that an investigation of this topic would require a specific design in which the accepted principles for organising classes would be altered for the purposes of the experiment' (p. 168). This is a conclusion which might have been applied to other findings also. Were administrators right to ignore conclusions based exclusively on formal tests of Arithmetic and English which could not take into account a full range of contextual variables? More focused studies related to the effects of particular administrative arrangements are necessary to provide a balanced picture for the guidance of policy makers.

Research evidence, if it is to help to define national policy, must speak to immediate issues. It is unlikely that accidental evidence gleaned in the process of a survey and simply recorded in technical reports will have any influence at all. Specific information and explicitly focused studies must be produced at the right time.

Impact on the Curriculum

What contribution did the surveys make to practice in the schools?

There have been no systematic studies which have attempted to relate changes in classroom practice to the findings of the surveys. Shortly after the appearance of the second report the Scottish Education Department published what is known in Scotland as 'The Primary Memorandum' (SED, 1965) advocating major changes in the practice of Scottish primary education. No reference was made in that report to the findings of the surveys. A more recent report, incidentally, has suggested that the changes recommended by the Scottish Education Department have not in fact been adopted in the schools (SED, 1980).

The teaching of Scots as a written, or indeed an oral, language in the primary schools was referred to above. The issue has just become a matter of concern to the media, and there was in 1986 a series of television programmes about it. However, the official survey carried out at the same time ignored the question. No attempt was made to test children's ability to read or speak 'the guid Scots tongue'. There are some school books but they date back to the 1940s and are apparently only used on 'national' occasions like Burns Night. The recommendations seems to have had no impact at all.

Teachers have two interests. The first is in the standards of their own pupils compared with those in other similar schools. As with wages, our reference groups tend to be local and individual rather than national and general. It is a question of each teacher definining for himself what standards are appropriate in his circumstances, finding out whether his pupils are reaching those standards, and taking the appropriate action.

The teacher's other interest is in what he should teach, and how he should teach it. National surveys cannot help any individual teacher to decide what teaching scheme should be used next year, nor how it should be used, and still less the balance of work for individual pupils.

The specific advice to teachers in the surveys illustrates these limitations. Did many schools cease division by factors, or pay more attention to the layout of short division sums, or provide oral practice in accepted speech forms as a result of the publication of these findings? If they did, how many teachers would now think it was good advice? As with other general issues, the specific recommendations relate to a particular perception of the purpose of school which is not now so widely held, and is indeed at variance with the official position.

Even to those who do accept the assumptions of the authors, how should a particular teacher know whether the more attention which it is held should be paid nationally to the layout of a short division sum applies to his class? If he was already providing more attention than the average should he provide not more but perhaps less? Is it not likely that those already giving considerable attention to the layout of short division sums would feel strengthened in their convictions and provide even more? Would not those who were failing to give sufficient attention have overlooked this point in the recommendations of the report?

Findings from national surveys may or may not apply to any particular teacher, and whether any teacher will take account of them will depend very much on their own values and their own perceptions of their current practice. In the case of the standardised notation for the recording of time of day, for example, the survey merely indicated variation in practice. The panel's preference for a particular form arose not from the survey but from their own general experiences.

Information which would be relevant to specific questions cannot, for the most part, be satisfactorily obtained from a national survey.

Similarly, a teacher's decision about the emphasis to be given to layout in teaching Arithmetic is more likely to be based on his own experiences of the situation around him than on any information that the nation as a whole did well or did badly in this respect on a general test. Individual teaching decisions are not made on the basis of general tests, but on the basis of specific information which relates to the teacher's own objectives in the circumstances in which he is operating.

Finally, there is an important issue with national surveys. That is the extent to which they tend, deliberately or not, to lead to the development of a national curriculum. The general trend of the Scottish reports is towards a greater standardisation of curriculum and method. It is difficult to see how it could be otherwise. A few quotations will illustrate the point. 'Examination of the errors demonstrates forcibly the need for persistent oral practice of correct forms and usages. . . . Although pencil and paper must be used for testing this kind of usage, it is not the best medium for teaching' (p. 106). 'The use of subordination is only developing and it is inadvisable to force this development especially by teaching the relative pronouns too early' (p. 100). 'The use of the apostrophe . . . is not taught . . . the correct form should be shown and explained' (p. 107). 'It would appear desirable to include some printed Scots among the reading material for Scottish children' (p. 100). The advice may be good or bad, but the conclusion is clear. Either one has a national curriculum which includes these elements which the authors thought were important, or one maintains the traditional British division of responsibility placing trust in the professionalism of the teachers. The report says that 'it would be folly to attempt to standardise curricula until it has been shown that one method is superior to others . . . if it were possible to determine a standard order for teaching that would be a useful contribution to teaching' (p. 185). The position of the authors of the report is akin to that of St Augustine who is alleged to have prayed 'Lord, make me chaste — but not just yet'.

The authors of the survey wanted their cake and halfpenny as well. They wanted to have in effect a national curriculum but did not recommend so directly, nor did they recommend any mechanism for establishing or enforcing it, perhaps because they anticipated rightly that any such recommendation would meet overwhelming objection from the teachers' organisations.

In the case of the recommendations which were relevant to classroom practice, the authors of the report failed to grasp the nettle and draw the conclusion that was implicit in most of their recommendations, i.e. that there should be a national curriculum. If there was not to be a national curriculum then the recommendations were to individual teachers, but as pointed out above they were not in a form which provided useful guidance to individual teachers.

This issue of curriculum guidance is important, because the proposed new English surveys are intended to shape the curriculum in the classroom.

Information for Parents, Employers and Others

While professionals are concerned with standards, general interest is at best sporadic. There are occasional flurries of interest in national standards with headlines in the national press, but they are usually followed by a period of quiescence. A former Prime Minister, Sir James Callaghan, launched what he called 'a great debate' on standards in education, but for five years little was heard about it. There has been a recurrence of interest in recent months.

The English Secretary of State for Education has chosen to make an issue of 'standards' just in time for the general election and proposes to introduce a national programme to raise them (Baker, 1987).

The call for information about contemporary standards sounds reasonable enough, but it is not at all clear what use this information is. The surveys which were carried out in the 50s and 60s which I am reporting here, and the surveys which we have carried out since in the 70s and 80s, have shown that standards are rising, albeit modestly, in Scottish primary schools, but we don't know why. Recording changes as they occur is less obviously compelling on analysis.

It seems self-evident that we should monitor standards over time as a sort of quality control, but what use can be made of such general information?

When *Rising Standards in Scottish Primary Schools* was published it was not exactly a best seller. No one seemed to want to know. Perhaps the problem lay in the title. Would a book entitled 'What has Happened to Standards in Scottish Primary Schools' have sold better?

There are some circumstances in which national surveys can be useful for national policy-making. These are mainly when the national conscience is agitated by a specific educational issue. If there is concern about standards, then national surveys may play some useful role in providing empirical evidence. Even then the evidence may be ignored or rejected. An article by the Secretary of the Scottish Confederation of British Industry demonstrates that there is a tendency among the protagonists in the debate to question the survey evidence. He said he knew the research evidence, but did not believe it (SED, 1979). More recently 'The Economist' (14th March, 1986) had a lurid cover asserting 'School Failed Them'. Inside, it pointed out that all the evidence we have — and it cited National and International (IEA) surveys — shows that secondary schools are more successful than they have ever been. What will be remembered, the lurid cover or the small print?

It is at least arguable that what parents and employers and others need is not more information of a general kind about standards, but a better understanding of what it is that schools are setting out to achieve and how particular activities fit into these objectives. Employers need to know, as a basis for discussion with educational authorities, what Arithmetic the schools are trying to teach, and what communication skills are being taught. Parents need to know that apparently random play activities in Primary 1, or field studies in Secondary 4, are carefully thought out parts of an overall programme making a specified contribution to children's learning. They also need to be reassured that the schools their own children are attending provide the same opportunities as are available in other schools. Surveys of national standards will not inform them on either of these points.

Conclusions

What can we learn from the Scottish experience? First, if we wish to make an impact on policy we must speak to policymakers about the issues that concern them *when* they concern them. That probably means short-term focused studies rather than a long-term series of national surveys addressed to general issues. Second, what is sought is usually knowledge of specifics which are relevant to particular local circumstances. Studies on the grand scale may be interesting to researchers but utterly uninformative for policy-makers. Third, national tests will inevitably have curriculum back-wash, and will involve pressure towards a centrally determined curriculum, no matter what we may wish.

Finally, research that is to have an impact on classroom practice must be teacher tested, i.e. based upon careful research and development in classrooms, not on generalisations. No matter how well surveys are designed, no matter how carefully the samples are drawn, no matter how thoughtfully the assessments are made, they are unlikely to address the crucial issues of the time, are likely to be forgotten and therefore ignored when the issues they investigated do become matters of concern, and worse, are likely to be misleading to any individual practitioner.

REFERENCES

BAKER, K. (1987) Address to the North of England Education Conference. Unpublished Manuscript.

DOCKRELL, W. B. (1982) 'The Contribution of National Surveys of Achievement to Policy Formation' in KALLEN, D. B. P. *et al., Social Science Research and Public Policy-Making — A Reappraisal,* NFER-Nelson.

HOPE, K. (1984) *As Others See Us.* Cambridge University Press.

MAXWELL, J. (1969) *Sixteen Years On.* University of London Press.

SCOTTISH COUNCIL FOR RESEARCH IN EDUCATION (1933) *The Intelligence of Scottish Children.* University of London Press.

SCOTTISH COUNCIL FOR RESEARCH IN EDUCATION (1947) *The Trend of Scottish Intelligence.* University of London Press.

SCOTTISH COUNCIL FOR RESEARCH IN EDUCATION (1963) *The Scottish Scholastic Survey 1953.* University of London Press.

SCOTTISH COUNCIL FOR RESEARCH IN EDUCATION (1968) *Rising Standards in Scottish Primary Schools.* University of London Press.

SCOTTISH EDUCATION DEPARTMENT (1965) *Primary Education in Scotland,* HMSO.

SCOTTISH EDUCATION DEPARTMENT (1977) *The Educational System of Scotland.* Scottish Information Office.

SCOTTISH EDUCATION DEPARTMENT (1979) *Consultative Committee on Curriculum News, no. 2.* Scottish Education Department.

SCOTTISH EDUCATION DEPARTMENT (1980) *Learning and Teaching in Primary 4 and 7.* HMSO.

SCOTTISH EDUCATION DEPARTMENT (1986) *Basic Educational Statistics (Scotland).* Scottish Office Library.